A SALESMAN FOREVER

By

Carson Heady

© 2016, Carson Heady

Copyright notice: All work contained within is the sole copyright of its author, 2016, and may not be reproduced without consent.

Acknowledgements

This book is dedicated to the family and friends who have supported and stood by me through it all (you know who you are!) and to the memory of Erin Nabe.

This book is a work of fiction and any similarities between real groups, corporations or persons living or dead is purely coincidental.

"If you want a happy ending, that depends, of course, on where you stop your story."

Orson Welles

INTRODUCTION

"Sometimes, we think the more information we give a customer – if we just keep throwing facts and minutia and statistics at them – that they'll eventually cave and make an educated decision to buy based on everything we've told them. That is the greatest myth of sales.

"We also occasionally feel that if we're in a slump, the best way to break it is to just get a sale – any sale! – and that we should just start offering low end products solely to get someone to say 'yes.' Like desperation dating, begging someone to go out with you. It's not true. We haven't even overcome the price in our own mind, so we underestimate our customers' intelligence and we totally break from any behaviors that have made us successful previously. Congratulations: you've decided to settle.

"When you meet with me or with your sales manager, we talk and talk about all of these great new ideas to try on our calls – we see the merit in these ideas and agree to go out there with this new method. Yet, when we face a couple of setbacks – which is normal in this racket where we've got a small percentage chance of even getting a decision maker on the phone, let alone getting one to listen – we just go back to old, comfortable ways of failing. We get so excited to even get somebody to listen to us that we turn back into amateurs. We try something on one or two calls and we stutter a little because it's foreign to us... and instead of staying the course, and seeing out this new way of potential success that we already agreed was better than our old way, we give up and go back to the same old thing we've done to get us to mediocrity or less than expectation.

"Let me ask you something – how many of you are truly happy with where you are on the sales report right now? And, Alan, it's OK if you are."

The room was filled with laughter and Alan Banks – currently the top rep in the department – smiled and acknowledged the statement with a point and wave.

"There's not really any hands up in here, which indicates to me you'd all love to be doing better. And to do better, to do more we have to make a change. A permanent, positive change. Because if we change and then fall back on old habits, we've been counterproductive. And we have to stick with that permanent, positive change through whatever setbacks present themselves. Obstacles are imminent, but your choice to let them stop you or to steamroll through them determines your destiny.

"Closing sales is sexy. It's probably one of the five best natural, legal highs in the world."

This statement also elicited laughter from the crowd.

"So why don't we do it more? The biggest way to figure out why you're not closing is to realize that 99% of their excuses are bullshit and that you're not setting yourself up to win from the get-go. Every single thing you do, from the way you announce your name and purpose with confidence to the questions you ask and what you do with the information they load you up with determines your success.

"Do you think every time I pick up a phone and dial I know every single thing I'm going to say to that customer? Of course not! The problem is we over-think it so much; we try to arm ourselves with every little tidbit about the customer and morsel about the industry – and then we get a voice mail. Come on! Turn your brain off, pick up the phone and dial. When you get a gatekeeper, you have a process: confidently state who you need. If you're questioned, confidently say you manage the account and need to speak to the decision maker regarding the account. Don't flinch. 'Is he expecting you?' 'He very well may be!' And when that decision maker comes on the phone, it's the same thing: confidently state your purpose and roll right into the questions whose answers will help you build your case. It's against their objections and you've got a very brief window. Tom Cruise in *Mission: Impossible* has nothing on you.

"I love you guys. I *love* that you know so much about this product. Knowledge is power, but power is nothing if you don't know how and when to strategically use it. Throwing out random statistics that have nothing to do with showing them how and why they'll make a return on investment do nothing to build your case. Expecting them to buy without following the right process does not have a happy ending.

"It's like you're doctors, getting ready to perform some medical procedure, but you're heading in with your scalpel without knowing anything about the patient! Step back for a minute. Get in your customers' shoes. What do they need to hear before they make a buying decision? That they're gonna make money! That the failures they've had with our competitors are not something they are going to face here. That trusting us to do their marketing is better than having them sacrifice their own time and effort or having their brother or sister or cousin's co-worker do it. That they are going to get more back than they put in. That you're going to be there for them every step of the way. That's what they got into business for.

"I get it, it's like a relationship. When you're in the heat of battle, you'll say just about anything to get what you want and sometimes you get desperate. But they can smell that desperation and it's a turnoff. The words you choose to use and how and when you say them will make or break you. Telling them the history of the product without them asking or telling them you're going to get them guaranteed Internet searches or their contract is extended for free just muddies the water; it confuses them. They didn't ask. Stop the gimmicks.

"Sure, it's great you know the details and fine print but these customers care about a return on their investment and the chances of that happening.

That's it. They've all advertised before – they've had some bad investments and that makes them a little skittish around you. They don't know you and they don't trust you. Until you have established yourself as different than every other salesperson who's called them since the dawn of their business and you've shown your product is better than everything else they've seen, you're not worth their time. And with all of the potential customers we are putting them in front of in our online and paper directories and our fliers and our materials, how in the world can they not make a huge profit?

"Do you believe in our product? More importantly, do you believe in yourself? Every call and day has its ups and downs, but it begins and ends with your decision to excel.

"And I get it – we do the same thing day in, day out, every day. Cold calling two-to-three hundred times in a day sucks and it's easy to get caught up in that. But do you want to be doing this for the rest of your lives? Is this your end game? If you're happy doing this forever, that's fine and good, but a lot of you want to use this as a stepping stone to something better. As well you should! But once you've paid your dues and you've learned how to master the cold call or sell huge programs over the phone to these CEO's and business owners, you can write your own ticket.

"But it isn't going to happen overnight. You can't have a good month or two or even six and just magically expect a promotion and shut down when you don't get it or get an attitude or walk around like you're better than this place. This game it's about bringing your 'A' game every single day no matter what – no matter how many changes occur or things you think are unfair happen.

"It's a marathon race, and you can't let up for a second because somebody will pass you up. Look around – there's 220 people standing with you. Are you the top half-of-a-percent in this group? Because that's what it's going to take to get promoted in this bunch. If not, what are you going to do to get there? Because it does you no good to whine and complain about getting passed up after the fact, after you've already let it happen.

"You just told me you're not satisfied with where you are on the sales report, so what are you going to do about it?

"And here's the thing, ladies and gentlemen: I'm not asking for major, drastic changes. It's just small tweaks to your presentation that make all the difference in the world. Tired of being hung up on? Figure out where you're losing them and fix it. Tired of being told 'no?' Figure out where you're losing them and fix it!

"Tired of being treated like a telemarketer? Don't act like one!

"From the moment they answer the phone, you've got to act as if this is the most important call they'll ever take – you're calling to save their business with an ingenious idea."

The crowd laughed, smiled and clapped, clearly agreeing with these sentiments given to them by their leader at the onset of their selling day.

"There's no reason why you can't do anything I've done. My job is here for the taking. In fact, aim higher. Be fearless. The only thing to fear is continuing to have results you're not happy with. Don't let your name be on a report next to a number that's not indicative of who you are and what you want to become. Don't get off a sales call without either closing the sale or knowing exactly why your customer didn't buy. The truth is, every objection is a load of jive. If they believe in what you have – if their fear of missing out on something outweighs their fear of change – they'll put their partner on the phone… they'll understand that they will make a return on investment… and they'll make the time. There is only one real sales objection. Do you know what it is?"

The audience clamored, but not with answers. They were teeming with excitement over what had been said and what was to come next.

"It's lack of belief. Think about it. If I told you today that you could donate $1 toward the Vincent Scott Aston Martin fund, you'd laugh at me – and rightfully so. Because I didn't show you any value. Maybe if I gave you a ride in it, you would, but that's neither here nor there. However, if I told you that I could turn a $100 investment you make today into $1,000 tomorrow, you'd rush to the ATM. Right? And why? Because I showed you a return.

"Show your customer a return on investment, and they will make the decision to buy. And I want you to think about those words: *they* will make the decision to buy. You don't sell anything, and you can't say anything that will force them to open their wallets. However, when you overcome that one sales objection – their lack of belief – they will make the decision to invest in you and what you're pitching. When they fear missing out, they will make the decision to change what they're doing in favor of what you propose. When they understand that this is a strategic risk instead of just the same old, useless advertising they've wasted money on before, they will follow you and they will sign the contract."

"Yeah! That's right!" the shouts came from the crowd. This team was pumped and ready to dial.

"In closing, team, I get asked all the time what my greatest accomplishment in my career is. And it's being right here, right now, around the greatest sales professionals I've ever been blessed to be around. When I hired each and every one of you, there was this conviction and passion and fire in your eyes. Sometimes, it dwindles and flickers in even the best of us. But I'm telling you right now – every single day, we have to make the conscious decision to re-light the fire. Accomplishments look great on a wall or desk, but the experiences we create today for ourselves and the business owners we save last a lifetime."

More cheers erupted from the crowd.

"Let's finish this month out like the champions we are!"

In Present Day, Vincent Thomas Scott, the Third finished watching the tape of a speech he had given nearly a decade prior during what was now undoubtedly what he considered his peak professionally and personally. His former self pointed to the back corner of the office, behind the gathered crowds that encircled him in the midst of the sales floor of a call center, where sales manager Jimmy Sander activated his computer speakers at full force filling the office quadrant with the strains of Queen's "We are the Champions."

The video version of Vincent waded through a crowd of sales managers and reps that high-fived him and marveled at his presence, his bravado, his swagger. Today's Vincent watched his former self genuinely smile and bask in the praise and accolades while making his way past cheering people he had hired and coached. Ironically, there were also a handful of female sales reps in the audience he had foolishly succumbed to at various points because the workaholic married to his career never made time for anything outside the office pool.

This experience of reviewing documented evidence of such a climactic moment in what felt like a past life was wholly bittersweet.

The longing for those days occasionally crept into his consciousness. He missed the ovations, the responsibilities, the coaching, the feeling of accomplishment and accolades from those days that seemed so far away.

Why he still had the tape, he had no idea; the thought had crossed his mind numerous times to do away with it and any other relic from that seemingly other lifetime ago. However, they remained in a box that seldom saw the light of day. A box that was stuffed with awards, old sales reports and a stack of thousands of pages of documents pertinent to the sum of his career's parts.

He put the tape in the box, glanced at its contents and closed it yet again. Contemplative, he sipped from a scotch at his side.

Asleep in her room midway down the hall was his precious, smart, beautiful 8-year old daughter, Elizabeth Scott. They had spent an evening playing games and watching a movie prior to Vincent's departure the coming morning. When with his daughter, even workaholic Vincent dropped everything.

The 8-year old love of his life had been the shining spot of the last several years of his tumultuous personal and professional existence. That innocent face that Vincent had fought and sacrificed so much for – those cheeks he kissed incessantly both while she was awake or asleep – was what kept him going.

She was the spitting image of Vincent at the same age, albeit in female form and exhibited many of his other qualities in her advanced intelligence, articulation, vocabulary and gifted abilities. She was also occasionally – like Vincent – a little too smart and sassy for her own good.

Now older and significantly hardened emotionally and psychologically, greying at the temples with longer brownish, reddish-blond hair to mask any thinning that had come with age, with the scruff of several days' worth of facial hair and significantly less twinkle in his greyish blue eyes, Vincent sipped from his scotch while he contemplated the past, current state of affairs and potential outcomes.

What seemed a lifetime ago, he had enjoyed a meteoric, tremendous rise eventually followed by a crushing and undeserved fall. In the years since, he had been obsessed with scratching and clawing his way back all by himself.

Tomorrow was a very important day and this stroll down memory lane – while partly necessary – could wait.

The alarm from Vincent's phone erupted to the tune of Huey Lewis classic "The Power of Love" from *Back to the Future* to signify that it was 4 AM. Reluctantly, Vincent reached for his phone, fumbled for it and managed to activate the snooze mechanism. He would utilize it three times totaling thirty minutes on this day, rising at 4:30 to put on socks, tennis shoes and some shorts.

He would hit the treadmill for a run of a few miles, slow to a fast walk intermittently while he could read a novel or watch Netflix or blare tunes and take a break to lift weights. It was the only time of day he could control and only time he could completely block out everything – as his feet pounded against the tread, the music and the motion drowned out any preoccupation with the day ahead or present circumstances.

At precisely 5:50 AM, Vincent would kiss his princess on the cheek, hoist her from her bed into his arms and carry her to the living room couch. Lying in wait for her would be a Netflix selection of kids' shows, a bowl of cereal and her clothes for that day.

Vincent showered while his daughter ate; then dressed.

"Elizabeth, it's time to brush and brush," he said, switching off the television. "Please hurry – we need to go soon."

"Are we late?"

"Are we ever?"

"No."

After the routines of brushing teeth and fixing hair and dressing, Vincent helped Elizabeth put on her coat. He grabbed his black leather jacket, diamond-crusted Bulova watch, his fitness band, a baby blue wristband on which was inscribed "Blue Skies" and a gold ring etched with the emblem of his most prominent former employer that bore a diamond.

"Please grab your bag," Vincent instructed.

Elizabeth picked up her book bag and Vincent retrieved the two bags of luggage sitting by the door.

"I'm going to miss you on your trip, Daddy."

"I'll miss you too, baby."

"When will you be back?"

"I'll be gone for three days, so I'll be back in time for the weekend."

Vincent knelt down and hugged his precious daughter.

Walking outside into the crisp, cool fall air of Minneapolis, Minnesota, Vincent Scott and his daughter Elizabeth walked to the garage. Vincent unlocked and lifted the door, revealing his black Aston Martin DB7 Volante convertible. While ten years ago, he could joke about his aspiration to own one, he had finally made the acquisition.

With the flick of a key switch, the boot opened and Vincent placed his luggage inside. He opened the driver's side door and Elizabeth made her way into the backseat's child seat. It would be mere months and she would not require it anymore; she was getting so big, so fast.

Vincent checked his mirrors, backed out of their garage and headed toward Elizabeth's school which was less than a mile away. He dropped her off at the before-school care he provided for her, hugged her multiple times and relished those last few seconds of happiness with her. She would wave and say, "Goodbye, Daddy!" and blow him a kiss that he caught with his left hand and rubbed all over his face to her delight.

Once he hit the door and walked back into the frosty morning, Vincent's demeanor shifted to mirror his surroundings. He had learned long ago to acknowledge the existence of any feelings of sorrow or doubt and dismiss them into the same oblivion to which he had banished many painful memories of his past. He had to consciously switch from loving Daddy mode to his ice cold, no mistakes persona. He wouldn't see his daughter for three days and had to shut off the part of himself that would allow that emotion to exist.

Today was a very important day and he had no time to let these ghosts of sales lives past stand in his way.

Vincent left his Aston Martin in the garage adjoining Minneapolis-St. Paul Airport and retrieved his bags. A brief stint awaiting his turn in the security line followed by the walk to his gate ensued. He boarded the flight to Washington, D.C., and took the Sherlock Holmes novel from his bag. In a few hours, he would be in the spotlight, and while Vincent Scott didn't allow his nerves to bother him, today they carried with them a slight twinge.

The Vocational Viewpoint, via Vincent Scott
(Republished with permission)
"How do I 'sell myself'?"
Answer: "You're already in sales, and you don't even know it!"

From today's mailbag: "I've been told that sometimes I need to 'sell myself' like when attempting to get a job or to be considered for other projects or roles at work. How do you suggest I do that?"

It's been said everything comes down to the psychology that lies behind selling, whether we're trying to convince our kids to get themselves ready on time in the morning or eat their vegetables or we're selling a dinner companion on going where we want to go or what we want to do. All methods of convincing, from business to politics to personal relationships require utilization of the same principles used when we successfully negotiate a deal - large or small. These interactions require a knowledge of our target audience that can be ascertained through experience or inquiries, of the scenario and of the factors required that could lead to the outcome we desire.

We are constantly utilizing a process of some sort to obtain desired results, for a variety of reasons in a number of circumstances. It is up to us to determine the goal we have in each individual situation, figure out how we will uniquely and exceptionally approach the scenario, what steps we will take to uncover any opportunities or challenges, and ultimately how we will persuade the recipient of our words and actions to choose our proposed course of action.

Look at all of the similarities between the sales cycle and sales food chain (my terminology for the ties that link leadership to sales professionals to customers).

When you seek an additional project or new role for yourself, you have a clearly defined goal in mind.

Similar to when you are selling a product or service, there is competition - other people are also being considered for these potential roles and projects.

Similar to a sales process, it falls on you to show a potential customer/end user - in this case, an interviewer or person in charge of the project you seek - why you are the one and only.

Similar to selling, you have to uniquely stand out, show that your relevant experience is superior to anything else out there, and you must present specific examples of times in the past when you successfully fulfilled tasks that will be required of you in the new position. An interviewer wants to visualize you achieving these things for them; it's far easier to do this if you have done these items before to great acclaim and have the numbers to back up the success you claim.

1. What is your goal? Look at what you are attempting to achieve and contemplate fully why you are the perfect choice. It really comes down to you convincing the interviewer or manager that you are the right choice.

2. Foresee challenges and areas of opportunity, and be prepared to answer for them. Do you lack necessary experience that you can make up for with supreme excellence in another area? For example, you do not have any experience on a certain component they are looking for but you have adapted well in previous situations and have a plethora of experiences in a certain component of sales? Closely examine a job requisition or project description so you know exactly what is expected of you. Prepare your approach and how you plan to correlate your relevant experience to the task at hand. Be sure, however, not to brush off the significance of what you do not know, or attempt to undermine its importance to the role; acknowledge the challenge you see before you in making that skill a part of your toolbox and have a plan to do so.

3. Stand out! It's so easy for anyone to have a resume, wear a suit, and show up. What did you do to make yourself memorable? Do you have a video resume, showcasing your speaking and presentation skills? Do you have a brag book compilation of awards and recognition and achievements and letters of recommendation from your career? Have you arrived at the conclusion of why you are a better candidate than anyone else out there? If 100 or even 5 people are up for the same role as you, it's vital to stand out as the obvious choice because the odds are against you unless your distinctive vitality stacks the deck. In most of these cases, unless you are seeking a role that is hiring a massive group at once, there are no points for second place.

4. Learn. No great salesperson was flawless on their very first sales call. Like any situation, you follow a process and make a presentation and you make tweaks here and there as necessary as you learn what works and what does not. You may stumble through a job interview. You may not have a perfect answer to an out-of-left-field question. But the more you seek out and experience these scenarios and the more you put yourself in the situation to be in these discussions, the better you will be at them.

5. Seek feedback. Even if you are not qualified and the final decision is to go with someone else, ask for constructive feedback during and after the process. Find out who other people you should connect with might be. Figure out where your skill set may even be a better match in their department or organization. Following up with these people who took time to consider you for a role makes an imprint!

When in doubt, think about what the average candidate for any of these things would do, and take it upon yourself to do more, do bigger, do better! Remember that when you are selling yourself, you are showing why you are the clear choice; you are rising above the pack of status quo and you are ensuring your target audience sees in you something that they want for their team.

Lack of experience can actually be made up for with passion and enthusiasm; they can train you on what you don't know, but cannot train personality. Lack of sales experience can be made up for with the right attitude and work ethic; you can gain necessary experience on the job, but you cannot be successful in sales without hard work and perseverance. Lack of knowledge of a certain component of their business can be made up with by a track record of adaptability and success – we all have a knowledge gap when we start a new role; if you've shortened that up in previous roles, it can bode well in a new one.

Just like sales, you will not win every time out, so you want to prepare yourself for that and be realistic with your expectations; you also want to take each experience and learn from it, expound upon it and master that process until it becomes second nature. You will take the losses as lessons and the wins will become more frequent.

Selling yourself is like selling a product, only when you sell yourself, you must believe you are selling the greatest service of all!

From the moment you were born until the second your soul vacates your body, you are convincing people to do things: feed you, hire you, assist you and that they need what you have. A certain degree of these survival skills are innate; we cry out when it is our only form of communication to indicate hunger. Many of us find ways to persevere through bad news, dark days and loneliness. But, in the case of using these skills as your occupation of choice, there are those who come with only the weapons life handed them and those who spend their lives improving their craft and sharpening their sword.

Selling ourselves is the most important sale we make. In this life, outside of those who genuinely care about you and are in your corner, few are going to give you "a shot," much less the time of day, unless they see value to themselves in doing so. In a world where many are obsessed with finances and careers and superficialities, if you are going to get ahead you will very much have to learn how to make yourself a product other people cannot live without. You've got to create the demand to provide the supply.

Irrelevant to your current circumstances, everyone has a talent, the fortunate have several and the smart work to improve in numerous areas; there is no better life than the one where you can use yours to make the world just a little bit better for others. Making a difference is not always going to consist of being elected to high-ranking public office or rescuing those in distress. For the vast majority of us, it will come down to being able to leave your mark by giving to others with what you have. It will revolve around finding people and influences and inspirations that make us better and enable us to fluently express the best versions of ourselves and our gifts. It is about being the best we can be in all facets and with everyone we are fortunate enough to come into contact with.

When the word "sales" is uttered, our minds leap to a variety of connotations – often negative. Any moniker can be sullied by dishonorable inhabitants of the species; not all lawyers or politicians are beloved either despite the necessity for their kind and the hard-working, valiant among them. Salespeople are integral to the economies of our society; they keep the mechanics behind supply and demand flowing by increasing the demand and moving the supply. Many of them are hard-working, bread-winning, example-setting mothers and fathers who take up this noble trade to provide. Others are schooled professionals making their splash in the working world. And a multitude are those who entered the workforce early so they could support themselves. Considering the rewards for ruling this terrain, the population of the salesforce will never waiver and the incentives to master the craft will never dry up.

Your connotation of sales could quite easily be one of avoidance; you elude the sales call, have zero desire to be a part of the selling culture and you lump salespeople all into the same stereotype: over-aggressive, egotistical, unethical pigs who prey on anyone they can to make a buck (and there are plenty of those out there). Nevertheless, unless you never intend on supporting an initiative, landing a job, getting a raise, entering into any kind of relationship or getting your way in any aspect of life, you will require these selling skills in order to effectively forge your path on the road of life.

Figuring out your desired or chosen journey in the workforce is something that takes shape over many years of your existence. While you may be one of the lucky ones who plots your course early and sticks to it for the duration of your career, many are not so fortunate. It can take years to determine a career path, a career can be derailed or an industry can change so much that you must decide to change with it or move on to something different.

Once you have established how you wish to impart your gifts on the world in a chosen field (if you are lucky enough to get to do that), you must determine how you will earn the credentials necessary to start on the ground floor of said industry. You must ascertain how you will utilize or construct a network of people able to aid you in this endeavor. You must compile your qualifications and accomplishments into a piece of paper and a process that will get you noticed by the right people, face a plethora of potential opportunities and likely rejections and weave your way through the idiosyncrasies of the interview and hiring framework required just to participate.

Each step along the way necessitates selling yourself: why are you qualified above all other applicants? Why should a hiring body recruit you over someone with more education and more experience (because there will undoubtedly be someone to rival you)? Why will you keep the promises you make on interview day?

Those looking for rhyme and reason to each and every occurrence in the application and interview process will often come up quite befuddled; these are processes – like games of chance – that are designed for a particular outcome and the House can very well win. The odds are stacked heavily against you even if you are quite capable and qualified; in any particular role you could be up against hundreds – if not thousands – of other applicants.

The automated resume reading tools are designed to eliminate your resume if they do not feature minimum thresholds of required experience and education and keywords that can change as rapidly as the search engine algorithms or politicians' stances on the issues. Getting the interviewer who will mesh with your canned responses can be like getting the right judge in a court case. Being able to recall and recite the right responses at the most opportune times, keeping your interviewer captivated and following all the unwritten rules like following up with a note and showing the right amount of interest and responding to questions about money properly are like Han Solo navigating the Millennium Falcon through the asteroid belt in *The Empire Strikes Back*. "Never tell me the odds!"

In short, you are in the highest stakes situation of your life and you must maintain your calm and cool like James Bond swilling martinis staring death in the face at the baccarat table.

Whether you have it in your job title or not, you are going to have to sell concepts, philosophies, your will and yourself every day of your natural life. You might as well be great at it.

The Principal's Story

Vincent Scott was the smartest kid I ever knew. I came across him for the first time during the summer of 1983 when he took swimming lessons from my wife in the pool at our house.

Don't get me wrong – he always had to be the center of attention. He was a little redheaded boy with freckles and an adorable smile – you couldn't help but like him. And other kids did – they followed him everywhere. He was always the one they sought approval from.

In swimming class, he had to be the best. Sure, he made mistakes, didn't listen and occasionally pissed off my wife but we couldn't help but remark that he was quite a wonder. He talked a lot but he knew a lot. He didn't want to hold back and just do what the class was doing – he wanted to show what he could do. He was 4 years old and talking up a storm with the vocabulary of a kid twice his age.

He came into my life again when I oversaw a summer camp for exceptional students a couple of years later. Vincent had just finished first grade and he was grouped with third- and fourth-graders for a set of classes featuring the various topics of mythology, astronomy, art and literature. We acted out plays and he was the star of each one, his age notwithstanding. A news crew visited our camp and he was the one they wanted to talk to. I never saw anything like it.

In 1979, I had accepted the role of principal at St. Thomas School in Mankato, Minnesota. Vincent had graced our halls in the fall of 1984 as a kindergartener and this was the first time I was on a semi-regular basis of hearing his name mentioned. He could add multiple digit addends together in his head in seconds flat. He was a chatterbox, but he always had something interesting to say. He was bored with the cutting and pasting and drawing and picture stories of kindergarten and then of first grade. It was in September 1986 I met with his parents, Vincent, Jr., and Kay. Wonderful, wonderful people.

"Let's cut right to it: your son is extraordinary," I admitted, as we met in my office. "Might I offer you a cup of coffee?"

"No, thank you," Vince, Jr., responded, answering on the behalf of both. "We don't drink it."

I generously helped myself to my third cup of the morning and turned back to the prodigy's parents.

"I'm not one to beat around the bush," I began. "Your son – as you likely well know – is breezing through his lessons. He's lightyears beyond what his classmates comprehend, achieve and perform in the classroom. It's not been done in the history of our school, however I feel it is in his best interests if he skips the remainder of second grade and advances into third."

The look on their faces was priceless: stifled joy mixed with some apprehension and wonder.

"It's OK," I continued. "I understand this may seem like quite a bit to take in. Mary and I actually talked about this; how we would feel if faced with the same decision for one of our kids. On the one hand, it takes Vincent from his friends he's made thus far. He will have to adjust and make new ones and be thrust into some subjects that are a month in. On the other hand, if he stays in this class, I feel strongly that it can disenchant him with school at an age when engagement is critical. Your son is special. He mingles easily with third- and fourth-graders already – you know this. I know he'll adapt quickly."

There was a brief pause before I continued. "What do you think?"

Kay Scott was the one who spoke. "Well," she said, glancing at her husband, "of course we know that Vincent is…very talented for his age. My fear is that he misses out on something. That he will regret or begrudge us having to make this change."

"I completely understand," I proffered. "Vincent is going to be in a different group and will be treated differently than other kids. His new class will likely wonder about this and about him. But that's going to be temporary. Facts are facts: your son is different than other kids. And this needs to be celebrated."

After a sip from my coffee, I continued, "Of course, it is entirely your choice. I felt it was certainly beyond time to have this conversation."

"What do you think?" Kay inquired of Vince.

"He's a brilliant boy," the proud father returned. "He's reading books for kids twice his age. He's writing elaborate stories about all of his friends going to outer space or time traveling. While I wouldn't want to displace him, I don't want to hold him back."

"Precisely," I responded. "It's my responsibility as principal to always do what's right for each kid and for the school. In your son's case, it is in his best interests to at the very least move into a class where he isn't bored. Hell, I'd damn near consider moving him up two grades if that wasn't the most unorthodox thing in the world." I chuckled. They smiled.

"Mr. Spengler, thank you so much," Kay said. "You've made this very difficult decision a much more comfortable one. What is the timeline?"

"As soon as you decide, he can start in the third grade," I answered. "I've already talked about this with Valerie Martin, who would be his new teacher. She is fully aware of the situation and we will take great care of your son."

"Thank you," Kay stated.

On September 29, 1986, young Vincent Thomas Scott III skipped the remainder of second grade and began third. Obviously, I kept an eye on him over the years; it's plain to see that my decision led to events that forever altered his destiny. Sure, it was an easy decision. I'm sure he wondered about what his life would have been like had it not happened that way. But like I told his parents then, it was my responsibility to make decisions in the best interests of every kid who became part of our school family.

Vincent was a prodigy and I knew he was destined to do great things.

The Vocational Viewpoint, via Vincent Scott
(Republished with permission)
"Perfectionism in Business: Blessing or Curse?"

"Perfection is not attainable, but if we chase perfection we can catch excellence." - Vince Lombardi.

Do we fret so much about making mistakes that we hamper our own job performance? And, if you are an employer, do you allow your employees to make non-fatal mistakes as part of their growth?

At the summit of organizations, at the top of each level of leadership and at the front of every sales pack, you'll find a handful of these folks. Nothing is ever good enough. They are Type A, go-go-go, and even when they're off, they are working, plotting their next move and strategizing on how to conquer the world. They are perfectionists.

Their work is seemingly immaculate and work ethic unparalleled. But the reality is that there is no such thing as perfection: we all know this, and our knowledge of said fact has a variety of impacts on us depending on our personality.

For the most confident among us, we believe beyond our goals. Because nothing is ever good enough, even the accolades and praise and awards and bonuses leave us feeling unfulfilled. We believe we will reach a plateau where each of the aforementioned results equate to happiness but that day never comes.

Others of us approach work not needing or desiring to stand out for the fact that those who do have expectations that always soar one step ahead of them. Some of us merely want to blend in, stay ahead of the bills and it's acceptable to get the occasional pat on the back.

There are other subtle levels of will, skill and thrills, however, at each stage there are decisions we are forced to make about risk and the levels thereof we are willing to take. Some of us have the devil may care approach; we throw ourselves mercilessly forward, haphazardly taking the flying cannonball leap into the deep end of the pool with little - if any - regard to repercussion. Others are so cautious and meticulous that they fear any misstep or misunderstanding that could wind up being construed as an out of compliance mishap - and this mindset prevents them from ever reaching their potential.

Like so many things, balance is the key. True perfection is completely impossible, yet if you set stretch goals and treat budgets like they are literally a minimum expectation, if you go out expecting the best and your potential and you coach to that in others rather than just getting by, and if you conduct yourself and others managing to process instead of results, your likelihood of reaching the "perfection" increases exponentially. Even when you fall a little short, you're still better than expected, than usual, and than goal.

Preoccupation with the prospect of making mistakes makes us second guess ourselves - it makes us second guess process! When we deviate from process, the results suffer and our decision-making process can become even more foolish and misguided in the murk. We become our own worst enemy. Even a short cut that can bring a short-term solution can derail the long-term success that comes from consistency and big picture mindset.

Let's go a step farther: as supervisors, if we are overbearing in our methods and demanding of results – and results alone – we will be the culprits in causing this shoddy behavior. We do ourselves and our teams no service if we divert them from following the right processes.

Rather than harp about or mandate a number result, examine their credence to the various components of the business that will yield success. Are they following the right steps? Are they diversifying the portfolio of their pipelines? Are they managing the mechanics of their role? They have earned the role they are in and we must allow them to perform it in the manner with which they see fit provided it is not a detriment to the business and they are not overtly abusing their freedom to do so. Give them time to employ their process; offer feedback and suggestions and coaching and advice, and examine their execution, but never make them so terrified to do everything a certain way - or your way - that they falter completely. You have them on your team for a reason - let them utilize their unique talents in combination with your tutelage and sage counsel and see where it goes.

Excellence is defined in many ways, is achieved in many more, and everything comes down to odds and probabilities and chance; when you apply as near-perfect a process as possible with a near-perfect will to win, your probability of excellence is at its greatest height.

The Vocational Viewpoint, via Vincent Scott
(Republished with permission)
"Do What You Love and the Money Will Follow: Fact or Fiction?"

Don't just work a job. Do what you love and the money will follow. Fact or fiction?

When we are raised in our Disney-saturated, pipe dream culture, we grow up with innocence and uninhibited faith. We are asked as early as we can speak what we want to do as a career and I'm quite certain there were a multitude of aspiring astronauts and police officers and heroes of various forms in the futuristic view of our 5-year old selves. Upon graduation or entry into the workforce, there are a myriad of lessons and realities we come across - and the learning will not cease until the day our breath does.

It has been said that we follow our dreams and everything will fall into place. Fortunately for us, we are all blessed with unique talents that make us qualified for various walks of life. Sometimes these are what we aspire to do; other times, and quite often, we find we are quite efficient at something we have no desire to be good at. We are all faced with the decisions of chasing money or chasing our passions. Sometimes they coincide, sometimes not.

So many variables factor into this equation: do we go to college? What do we select as area of study? What types of sacrifices are required for following our desired course of action? What type of commitment does it take to get the career we think we want? Do we really want a particular career, or have we been influenced to select that occupation by another source? Does our current financial predicament promote or preclude us from chasing that career path? What types of competition and obstacles will we face getting into this chosen field?

The reality is YES, you can target specific desirable goals, plant proper seeds, lay necessary foundation and work toward your dream role. Your "dream role" may change in time or you may find solace and satisfaction in what you wind up doing instead. Furthermore, you may have to spend a considerable amount of time accruing the finances and skills and network necessary to launch into your ultimate ambition. Rome was not built in a day, nor are your reputation and results.

Often, we must invest a considerable amount of our time and energy into roles that allow us the eventual freedom to branch out and do what we want. For others of us, we have the freedom to choose what we want to do and do not fret about the factors involved. In the end, you most definitely can pursue and realize your proposed purpose but the truth may be that you find ways to incorporate parts of it into what you wind up doing through the natural course of your navigation through reality.

How you choose to apply your talents and skills, what you choose to learn and whom you interact and network with will have a massive impact on your experience. Many of us may find ourselves doing something we never envisioned, but by assessing the situation and matching our skills to roles we have or have within our sights it is extremely viable that we can find enjoyment in jobs that align with our greater goals.

It's unrealistic to believe that every 5 year old who dreams of going into a certain profession will wind up in it, because they have only begun to unearth their skills and talents and aptitudes. But whether we're 5 or 50, dream away. Your career, like your life, will take unexpected twists and turns, be endowed with wonder and may take you to a greater realization of your fulfillment needs and wants than you ever imagined.

Certainly, showing a strong level of aptitude in your chosen field (or the field that chooses you, it sometimes seems) will tend to eventually propel you to new levels – in the company or the industry. It's quite common to become quite adept at what you love doing and to garner notice for it; unfortunately it is not always as common to have your favorite skill be the one that pays the bills. There are a lot of waiters who are aspiring actors, service industry professionals who are artists and salespeople who dream to be writers.

If you choose not to pursue your real dream, there is no chance at finding success in it. If you realistically approach your dream and it does not yield the means to surround yourself with food and shelter, it may have to be a hobby while your occupation keeps the lights on. Of course, there are also those who, with tireless devotion and endless energy for investing in their passion, are rewarded. There's no way of knowing which you'll be until you make those choices for yourself.

There are many who do what they love and the money follows. There are many who do what they need to do to get the money so they can afford to follow what they love. And there's plenty of room and appreciation for both.

The Vocational Viewpoint, via Vincent Scott
(Republished with permission)
"The 5 Ways to Erase Fear of Rejection"

Those moments prior to dialing, pulling that door or entering the board room are like stepping in the batter's box or breaking the huddle.

You formulated a semblance of a strategy, thought (or over-thought!) and now you have to execute the play. But what if I whiff? What if the pass is intercepted? What if they say no?

So, how does one eradicate the trepidation surrounding rejection?

Overcoming "No"

1. Be Prepared.

The more ready you are to confidently present your product, service and yourself, the less likely you can be deterred from that path. Knowledge and the ability to delicately drive through the selling process are what lay the foundation for the successful sale. Preparation builds confidence because it's one less thing to worry or think about. Arm yourself with as much as you can in the situation. Go in with your intended qualifying questions, plans for rebuttals and confidence to close. The more prepared you are with the tools available and your wits about you, the more likely you are to be prepared for the things you cannot control.

2. **Name the fear.**

Recognize the fear and work to dismantle or dismiss it. You have more control over it than you think. If you have a fear of rejection, acknowledge its presence and contemplate why it exists. Are you afraid of not selling because you fear repercussion? Do you feel unsure of yourself or your pitch? Similar to the "release the mechanism" scenes from the Kevin Costner baseball flick *For Love of the Game*, you hone in on your directive and drown out everything else. If you allow yourself to deviate from the game plan because of desperation or fear, you certainly will hear "no;" so it's all the more reason to ensure you remain undeterred. Naming your fear gives you a defined obstacle you can employ a direct strategy to overcome.

3. **Focus on process.**

The real "fear" you should have, if any, is that you leave out a crucial step or do not give customers a clear picture of why they need what you have. Replace the fear you have of being told "no" with a focus on simply sticking to steps. You cannot control what your contact will do, but you certainly can control what and how you deliver. When you leave the conversation, your goal is to have a signature or a clear-cut reason as to why the customer decided against buying with a specific plan to follow up or move on. In essence, your real mission is to progress as far as you can in your process – prepared for potential roadblocks and able to advance the conversation step by step.

4. **Learn from the rejection.**

Customers may decide against buying for reasons completely out of your control. That said, what worked during your presentation? What did you say that you may want to omit next time? Are there ways to tweak your product offerings or strategy based on the reason for opting out? It is very possible to lose the business today only to regroup, retool and revisit with a better solution that your customer will choose to use. It is not a misstep if you learn something on the altered path.

5. **No isn't forever.**

The customer who decides against change today may feel differently given some time or evolution of circumstances. Leave a solid, lasting impression: Stand apart from those simply trying to get a sale at any cost. Earn the relationship. Stay in touch. Offer to help in any way you can. Find a way to be valuable, even if it brings no immediate monetary gain. When they have a need you can fill, you'll get the call. By finding ways to stay top of mind, sending relevant articles or information, being the trusted advisor, showing your expertise and being available and responsive, you can certainly earn the business when the timing is right. The greatest achievements can take significant investment and time; earning a customer's business is no different.

Bottom line

Never even think about the "no." Your focus should be to control what you can in the selling process. We spend too much time worrying about what never comes to fruition. You control truly learning your customer's needs, formulating a plan to address those needs, and addressing any concerns. You won't win them all, but if you leave each conversation knowing the specific reasons your customer did not purchase, you did your job and can learn, grow and get ready for the next "yes."

Fear of rejection exists because we allow it; it's a misdirection from what should be the chief concern: focus on process every conversation, each step and customer at a time.

The Vocational Viewpoint, via Vincent Scott
(Republished with permission)
"These 2 Elements are Essential to Successful Sales Management"

People and Process: The Axes on Which Sales Management Revolves

So, you have earned the promotion to sales management. Congratulations! Now the real challenge begins.

It is one thing to carry the title of manager, but another entirely to be an effective sales leader. Being their buddy, patting them on the back a few times and just inspecting their work and hoping they do better will not get the job done or gain you the respect you must command to truly master sales leadership.

Picture this: you just had a breakthrough conversation with your sales rep and feel like you really got through to them about changing their behavior. They left and immediately reverted back to the exact same old comfortable ways of failing. Sound familiar? You are not alone.

It sounds too simple, but mastery of sales leadership really comes down to just two things: people and process. Where we get into trouble is when we over-complicate the equation and take our eyes off those balls.

You must have the best people in place and they have to follow the most effective process to achieve optimum results.

The best athletes in the world cannot play a game if they are taking shortcuts in their swing or follow-through. You also cannot put wild mammals from the jungle in a call center to read your "perfect" sales script.

Once you learn and implement these two jewels, you are way ahead of the curve – because most managers never figure this out. They spend countless hours telling people to get numbers or trying to find ways to fire people who don't automatically produce rather than investing in training and selling change to their chosen team and ensuring the proper strategy is being executed.

You cannot do the job for them every time. You cannot go on every sales call or assert your will on their every move. Your big picture job as sales leader is positively impacting as many futuristic transactions your employees partake in as humanly possible; that is why you devote time to ensuring they (1) know the proper process, (2) are following the proper process, (3) are improving on areas of opportunity in their arsenal and (4) are being disciplined for failure to do so.

This process – whether it was created by higher-up's or just agreed upon by you and your employee – exists for a multitude of reasons and, while there likely can be variations on how it is executed, the basics of any sales steps must always exist: quality introduction, transition to fact-finding, presentation with benefits addressing needs/weaknesses, closing and overcoming objections using the customers' own words and progression from one step to the next. Many managers fail because they get caught up in day-to-day minutiae or take their eyes off the sales process ball when fires pop up. The fires must be tended to, but prioritization will make or break you and your team.

That said, the process can be trained, monitored and followed up upon, but if you have people just clinging to a paycheck, letting their personal lives wreck them or who lack work ethic and ambition reporting to you, the battle is lost before it is even fought.

Putting together a sales team is challenging because you will make mistakes in judgment, but, at the core, you are looking for a nucleus of talent that completes one another: works in relative harmony and exhibits different strengths and skills that complement one another. Like the Avengers.

It is imperative you find people with a thirst for knowledge, success and growth, and people you truly believe will be the same person you met on interview day for the duration of their time there. It is a gamble, which is why your best interview questions are situational to determine what they have already done under certain circumstances, but you must surround yourself with people who will not give up. They have to adapt, be able to weather the storm and take the right steps to lead to the success of the unit.

The bulk of your coaching sessions with your team will be spent selling them on why they should risk lackluster results they are getting with faulty process to do things your way and achieve respectable results. Once achieved, the bulk of your follow-up is to ensure they then do not revert to their shortcut-laden, poorly producing method that got them there to begin with. Having the right people in place ensures you will have a better chance at actually seeing this transition to completion.

Earning their respect and buy-in to your process comes from elimination of any legitimate obstacles to their success; listening to and observing their true needs and doing something about it. Sure, you will have to discern and effectively dismiss the excuses piled in there, but if your team sees you rolling up your sleeves, getting in the trenches and positively affecting policy, they will follow you anywhere. You will not be able to remove every roadblock nor will you be able to get everything changed that they request, but if they see and believe you have listened and tried (1) they'll see some of the changes they requested occur and (2) they'll know you support them. In turn, they will support you.

Ideally, once you have the right team and technique working for you, much of your work will be checks and balances; making sure the engine is running smoothly. Consistency wins the race, but your "perfect team" and "perfect process" can sometimes not be giving you "perfect results." An athlete in a slump should never drastically change his swing or shooting style. Stick with the tried and true process, do not lose hope or faith and stick with the fundamentals.

Doing the right things by your team, surrounding yourself with the right people practicing the right process and inspecting what you expect in a consistent fashion will achieve the consistently optimal results.

The Neighbor's Story

The first time I met Vincent Scott was in 1986. Our mothers were teachers together for many years at public school in Mankato, Minnesota, and I was in fifth grade when we moved to the same subdivision at the Scotts.

Vincent's family had moved there in 1984 and we were separated by two houses on a side street; my mom found out about the house from Kay Scott and my parents were enamored right away. It was a great neighborhood, long before a ton of development was done in it and several streets in the subdivision had no outlet and plenty of open field for us to play and ride bikes. I was 10 and Vincent was about to turn 8.

It was a fast friendship. We were brought up with similar morals and both in the same private school. While we did not interact as much through our schooling, we spent nearly every bit of down time in the neighborhood together and with the other neighbors. We had mutual interests in the way of sports and video games and got along quite well.

But there was always something different about Vincent. Even then, he was a natural leader. He was charismatic, he was someone people gravitated toward. Sure, he could be stubborn and a little overbearing at times, but can't we all in our youth? He may have been a couple of years my junior but he was just as competent in conversation and socializing as my own classmates.

It was likely our mutual love of basketball and sports in general that helped catapult our friendship. Both of us had basketball goals in our driveway and we spent thousands of hours shooting and playing HORSE or pretending we were NBA Stars – making up our own games and giving play by play to no one but each other. As we got older, Vincent's dad would take us to play with college players from the University of Minnesota-Mankato. Basketball was certainly a consistent theme through our years of friendship and we both played throughout grade school and high school.

We would ride our bikes around the neighborhood back in the days when that was just considered the safest thing in the world – creating trails and routes we'd dub the "Tour de Mankato." Now, I have a hard time letting my kids out of my sight.

On Vincent's street lived Randy, on the one joining Vincent's street with mine lived Justin, Kelly and Natalie, and on the street one past mine leaving the subdivision lived Gary and Michael. Literally we would house-hop from one to the next depending on what was going on. There was an empty lot nearby where we could play baseball, kickball, volleyball. Vincent and I both had ping pong tables. And, with it being the mid-80's, Nintendo became all the rage and as games would come out and one of us would get them, we would have endless sessions of Super Mario, Contra and competitions on the sports games.

Where my friendship with Vincent differed from that with the other kids was likely because I was the oldest and because he was the most advanced. He was the one I felt more like an equal to, and he looked up to me which made me feel good.

We spent a lot of time with the other kids of the neighborhood, but he and I would take it a step farther: we would use baseball card games like Strat-O-Matic and simulate baseball seasons by ourselves – then come together for championship series. We would narrate our own play-by-play to baseball video games starring as our favorite players and teams – his were always Nolan Ryan, Bo Jackson, and – of course – like everyone from Minnesota, Kirby Puckett.

Literally right behind Vincent's house was the 15th green of the golf course we played on. In our teen years, we had season passes and played relatively often; we could walk on the course in the evening when it was not congested and play the 16th, cut to the 12th, then play 13, 14 and 15. They allowed us to fish in the pond that was adjacent to the 16th tee box provided we threw them all back. It's these carefree, responsibility-less days and nights I fondly recall when I think of Vincent Scott.

I think about his basketball shot – he was a phenomenal three-point shooter. I recall his biggest game was against New McKinley when he scored 32 points. He actually had to fish a piece of gum from someone in the crowd because he had forgotten one; as one would never see Michael Jordan playing without chomping away, Vincent insisted on chewing gum during every game. I remember when his teammates complained once that he shot too much; he spent a whole game without shooting and garnered 23 assists even while they were barking at him to shoot.

I laugh, because that's just what Vincent always was: a crowd-pleaser – but a stubborn one at that. He may have been bossy and he may have always wanted to be in control, but at the end of the day he wanted everyone to love him, to be happy with him, to think he was the best. It's quite a feat to achieve all three.

When we would play golf, he was such a perfectionist that he would take multiple attempts at shots just to make them – even if he wasn't going to fluff his score on the scorecard. But he would rush due to his impatience; I don't think he ever reached his potential in golf because he tried so hard to play quickly and efficiently and in a game of leisure that's just not done. I did play with him the day he shot a 68 but when we got older and he wasn't playing as much, he didn't even want to play for fear of being a shadow of his former playing self. I saw him drain 30-foot putts, chip in for eagles and he still holds the record for best round on our old high school golf team. But he didn't want to play if he couldn't be that player.

Vincent liked to have fun, but I don't think he had fun unless he won. And he usually did win, specifically in the things he would agree to do.

Inevitably, we got older. In high school, I was transported into another world of having to fit in and be cool and talk to girls and with Vincent two grades behind me and not in the school until I was a junior we didn't have as much contact. Of course, when he launched on the scene, specifically with that three-point shot that grabbed the attention of even my ball-playing classmates and basketball coach, he was back in the mix.

Things changed dramatically from there: I went away to college at Southwest Minnesota State in Marshall and – while it was just a few hours away – I lived on campus and got into sports journalism. Because of that, I was traveling with the sports teams frequently and was rarely home. It makes me feel old to say it, but this was about the time e-mail emerged as a way of keeping in contact, so Vincent and I would exchange the occasional note to touch base. But once you go away to college, discover girls on that scale and start exploring your career, your ties to your home can diminish.

Chasing my aspirations took me to Portland, Oregon for several years before I eventually relocated to Minneapolis. Vincent moved to Minneapolis in 2001 and I did in 2010 when I married Jamie. Marriage and having two children certainly has not equated to more time with childhood friends, but Vincent and I made time about once a year to go to a museum with the kids or to Twins games.

I have noticed the dramatic changes. I know the details he allows me to know about the ringer he's gone through personally and professionally. But I also know that he loves his daughter, Elizabeth, more than life itself. I know that while sales was never his first choice – he loved writing, journalism, sports – he is great enough at it that it cannot be ignored. When Vincent Scott is good at something, he has to be the best at it. Sometimes he's the best at it without even trying.

"Donnie," he told me the last time I saw him. We had just finished eating with our families and the kids were running around, playing nearby. "I'm exhausted. I mean, my God – we had no idea, did we?"

"What do you mean?"

"When we were growing up. When we were riding bikes around our neighborhood. Shooting hoops. We had no idea what we had in store for us. And now there's no going back. We've got kids, careers. And it doesn't let up. I mean, I can't take my foot off the gas pedal for even a second. I spend every second I can with Elizabeth and every second I'm not working for fear that I'll hit the pause button and somebody will pass me up. I'm not in my 20's anymore – I'm a hell of a lot closer to 40 and every place I've been is the same. The demands are the same. The politics are the same. The only thing that's changed is me."

And he's right. Don't get me wrong – I would never have any desire to be in sales or to climb corporate ladders like my good friend Vincent Scott. But I think we all are faced with a choice at some point – do we want to take over the world, or do we want to be happy in our lives? For Vincent, I think the two were tangled. I think for him, he'd see something he had to achieve and he'd achieve it but it was still not enough because now there was something else to chase. I know most of the people he's trusted and called friends burned and abandoned and used him. Frankly, I'm just happy to say that that never happened between us.

    I found happiness in being in the sports industry like I always envisioned and having a family and leading a quiet life. As for Vincent, there is no quiet; there is no rest. He's always had unlimited potential but difficulty committing to one course of action or outcome because he fears missing out on another. We're talking about a guy who has given sales speeches to hundreds, been promoted a half dozen times, writes books, gives interviews, drives his dream car, has an awesome family but is still desperately searching for the next winning thrill.

    In my best sports analogy, I'd call him a big game player who always goes the distance through all the wins and losses and is destined for the Hall of Fame.

The Vocational Viewpoint, via Vincent Scott
(Republished with permission)
"Advice for a graduate entering the workforce?"

From today's mailbag: "I'm graduating college. What advice do you have as I enter the workforce?"

What an excellent question, as I'm sure many of us had no idea what we were getting into when we faced this moment of truth. (Myself absolutely included.)

Ideally, you've spent time in an academic institution that has truly prepared you for what's to come, but no matter how accredited the school very few will accurately delve into many of the topics you'll run into - many of which have been tackled as topics in my columns.

1. **Develop a network.**

I can't tell you how vital this one is at every stage in your career and it is one whose importance will only increase with time. Yours may be limited at this juncture for, before you start a professional network, much of your existing network is limited to friends and family. Nevertheless, these connections may be quite strong.

Know that each seed you plant in the various segments of your career garden will spring forth in their due course; you undoubtedly have family, friends and perhaps other colleagues with whom you have worked during college, etc., who may be able to help you.

We exit college stage left and many of us believe with all our hearts that our degree will magically transport us into our field of choice - and those hopes are often quickly dashed. We also believe we can drop 10, 15, 20 resumes onto online search engines and strike oil. That myth, too, will be debunked soon enough.

Looking back over my own career, I certainly notice the symmetry in the connections I made in each role by various means and how they yielded fruit. However, there is no silver bullet; you'll never know which networking event or which LinkedIn connection or which acquaintance or prominent past or present co-worker will lead you to the next big opportunity. Just be open to where each relationship could potentially lead - a contact could generate an opportunity for you now or even several years down the road. That's why you'll be warned not to burn bridges – you may one day need access to where they lead.

2. Establish your brand.

Standing out as you set foot into the workforce and evolve your skill sets and experience is very important to ensure that you emerge as uniquely qualified for roles you seek. While this is a different ballgame at the onset of your career than it will be years later, the earlier you embrace this process the better. Your resume and how you put it out there (whether you have a basic one-sheet like the rest of them or you have a video resume and extensive networking attempts online and at events to make connections), your utilization of social media and quality content focused on your career interests, your blogs, your projects and how you tout them - they are all part of your body of work and sum of your parts. Your growing brand is what you want others to buy into - how you package yourself and make yourself known will go quite far in dictating your ability to latch on where you want to be.

3. Have realistic expectations.

We emerge from our collegiate career full of life and ready to take on the world - do not let the inevitable initial setbacks take away this feeling. Many of us spend years in the workforce before making a splash in our true passion - some of us may never reach that point. We all have to start somewhere and this is your entry level role unless you are continuing a journey started while in school. Be fully prepared to pay dues to reach the place you want - and you will never stop paying dues of some sort to gain access to the next phase.

In each role you fill throughout your career, there will be rites of passage to earn access to the next segment of the path you desire; every job has issues, each one will have unique challenges that may go unresolved and it's up to you to fulfill your duties but provide helpful feedback and maintain positivity and persistence in the face of all forms of adversity.

College does not always prepare us for the politics, the swift and regular process changes and how much patience will be necessary to achieve your career goals. It also does not encapsulate what is incumbent upon us to truly do what we think we want to do. Finally, our career may take numerous detours over the years; plot a plan and chart a course, but be prepared for anything.

Certainly visualize what your long-term career goals are and put them to paper. Chart what you feel are your realistic career destinations in 2, 5 and 10 year increments. Decide upon the steps you know you will need to take to reach each target and continue to modify the list as new steps become apparent. Develop a rapport with your supervisor to ensure they are on board with what you want to achieve and garner from them the steps they and the company expect you to take to reach desired goals.

Congratulations on a milestone in your life and career! You have graduated college and have your whole wondrous career in front of you with unlimited possibilities. Be very open to what is ahead, ensure that you are always seeking knowledge and experience and be mindful of the people, places and things that will aid you in your journey. You never know where you will find value, so create your own value and always seek ways to provide value to everyone you come into contact with wherever you go. The rest will truly fall into place in wondrous ways you may not currently be able to imagine.

And enjoy the ride!

The Vocational Viewpoint, via Vincent Scott
(Republished with permission)
"Our Love-Hate Relationship with Sales"

The phrase "Everything is selling" is right on the money – we spend a large amount of our time trying to convince others of our ways of thinking, to perform tasks the way we want them done or to go along with our program. Sometimes it works and sometimes it does not. Either way, no one can undervalue or understate the role "sales" plays in our daily lives.

When I first landed in a sales job, I had no idea what to expect nor did I know if I would be any good at it. However, sales is really just about human psychology and relationships and communication. Focusing on investing yourself and your time in your customers and your company pays dividends. Like anything, sales has good traits and some negative connotations when its very noble cause falls into the wrong hands. For the latter reason, many view sales as a curse word and condemn its place in mainstream society.

Love or loathe it, capitalism makes much of the world go around. In its pure, utopian form, capitalism is literally essential. Supply and demand are the fundamentals that drive business and economy and way of life. However, when unethical, unscrupulous people wanting to manipulate others get involved, it takes a turn for the worst.

There are many philosophical questions and conversations to be had about selling and its place in Corporate America. Let's face it, if every product or service was "the best" or as great as each company or person touts it to be, that would be quite astronomical, not to mention statistically impossible. However, again like politics, the job of the salesperson is often to cater to needs and weaknesses based on benefits of their product or service – regardless if it is the best fit – because that is what their company pays them to do. When a compensation structure or even employment status hangs in the balance, some salespeople will react accordingly and do what they must to survive.

Sales can be the bane and beacon of your very existence, in the same breath. Some employers will tell you to steal, cheat, lie and lead without morals or principles. When the best interests of the people they are paid to support requires work on their part, they look the other way. When the interests of the people and the needs of the many are outweighed by the greed and politics of the few, that is where we as society and as sales entities get into trouble.

Many employees choose sales because customer-facing roles have enhanced job security and financial benefits. The toll the long hours, occasional micromanagement and stress take on you can sometimes tip the scales.

Who wins in sales? Answer: the person who can find a career in something they genuinely enjoy doing. Sales is in the air we breathe, the water we drink and the food we eat. There are roles in existence where you can sell a quality product and be rewarded handsomely - sometimes, you may just have to look around a bit. And it is when we master the selling game - the relationships, the networking, the presentation and the follow up - that we can take our career and our finances by the reins and reign supreme.

The Vocational Viewpoint, via Vincent Scott
(Republished with permission)
"If You Have a Gift, It Is a Crime Not To Let Others See It"

As a parent, one of my primary goals is to instill the principle and concept of putting others ahead of ourselves. While it is not always easy or desirable to do, the outcome pays dividends. This very mantra leads us to invest in others and our relationships with others which will always bear fruit. It is imperative that this approach should be applied in your daily life – be it in career or pursuit of your dreams.

We were all born into this world with something to give. Every one of us. Trouble is, we often get caught up on what we do not have or what is holding us back rather than making the choice to shine. For, after all, it is a choice.

We all need affirmation of some kind – someone to tell us that we are good. This is the very reason many people seek this in significant others and become dependent on their "love" – they have to have this confirmation to keep themselves going. Others of us find that drive and the necessary mechanics internally. Some cower in the corner, afraid of rejection or ridicule. And others of us put on a show to the world while we hide our insecurities and trepidation.

But if you have a gift – which I am quite certain you do – it is your duty to share it with the world.

We all have talents. We all have shortcomings. One of the delicate tricks to life is to keep balance in our focus and not let those shortcomings define us or overtake what we are passionate about or good at. It is our charge to find the ways we can integrate our passions into our priorities.

You may be the best at something or you may be 10th best. The Olympics are not open to just one participant. There is not just one sport, one team, one destination. There is not just one politician, one book, one television station out there. Finding our niche is not always easy but it should always involve responsibly following your heart, your dream and goal of living a life without regret.

Someone once told me that my occupation should be involved with what I would do if I won a lottery. If money was no object and failure was impossible, what would you do differently in your life? Don't completely throw caution to the wind, but incorporate some risk strategically so you can reap reward - reward for others and reward for you.

Life is too short not to find something you truly love. Hone in on your passions, decide how you are going to express those gifts and enjoy the dividends that you receive by giving back to the world.

The gift of existing is accompanied by the numerous talents we possess and it is incumbent upon us to leave our mark and legacy in positive ways for others to benefit and learn and grow and share their talents as freely.

The Vocational Viewpoint, via Vincent Scott
(Republished with permission)
"How to Enter the Sales Arena Like a Gladiator"

Upon entrance of the sales arena, like a gladiator entering the coliseum, one must be ready for battle. You will face unforeseen forces and combat objections that are positioned to defeat you and – in the end – must emerge victorious.

Many of those embarking on the journey of the selling game learn very quickly that it can be quite a different type of beast. Sales is a personality, an attitude and a strategy requiring a unique skill set to equate to success. Presumably, it is these traits that scare a lot of people off.

Thick skin must be developed quickly; the fears you encounter must be overlooked and you have to be willing to take tactical risks. The landscape is what it is: like life, you'll encounter highs and lows and will not have as much control as you desire. Accepting that is key. Realize that your preparation and responses and reactions in both transactional situations and your career can enhance your chance of success. Don't let anything gain enough control over you to inhibit your progress or process.

A vital part of success in sales is **keeping your eyes on the prize and big picture**. What many people consider success typically transpires after tirelessly toiling through the losses to find the wins. Your big picture goal may be 2-to-5 years away, which means you cannot let your frustrations after 6 months deter you or shake you from your dream. Sure, you may adapt and recalibrate your approach numerous times, but you have to keep ascending to the summit of your personal mountain.

Mark my words: No one is going to hand you success. In fact, it's quite the opposite – when you start to get a taste of the new station in life or benefits that come from excellence you will practically always face detractors and haters that wish to diminish your achievement. Everyone else is also trying to scale the mountain to varying degrees; on your journey, you will come across the folks who aren't going to try very hard that want to take shortcuts or that will make excuses as to why you are successful where they are not.

Success requires a gladiator because you will often have to dig and claw through the trials and tribulations and tears to stay on course and achieve your desires. It's one thing to obtain what you need; it's quite another to become the elite gladiator. Fighting is not always with weapons or fists – we can have a fight for our lives just navigating the turbulence that accompanies trying to make it in this world.

In any fight, finding a superior, elevated strategy, sticking to it despite the hits that throw you off and reaching consistency in offensive and defensive maneuvers will propel you through.

Set your goals higher than you initially believe you can reach. That way if you barely fall short, you're still better than anticipated.

If that last line looks somewhat familiar, I wrote a different version of it 7 years ago and reading the difference now shows me that maybe I'm on to something. It isn't always about being the best at everything, but it is about challenging yourself and taking each challenge head on as it comes. Efficient preparation for the battle is key, putting forth your best effort more so and having the outlets to recuperate before the next round is crucial.

Experience and experiencing some success will lead to heightened confidence, but losses at any stage will inevitably invoke some doubt or fear or worry. Any time a negative thought, emotion or feeling enters your consciousness, acknowledge its presence, weigh your control in this equation and either act within your control or dismiss what you cannot control.

At first, this can sound easier said than done but practice makes permanent. In the earlier battles this will keep you focused on the true priorities and you have better odds at a favorable outcome. When you become battle tested it bolsters your confidence and sure-footedness. Even when you become battle-weary and perhaps dwell on doubts more than during your heyday the practice will still serve you: you know what to do even when you don't want to and you can will your body into the necessary action.

Things are not going to always go your way but if you stick to the process and control what you can, your outcomes will be at their optimum level. Don't let the opinions of those who don't matter or the many things you cannot control prohibit you from doing what you know you must do for yourself or for personal and career priorities.

No one but you can make or break you when it comes to meeting your objectives, be it on a daily, weekly, monthly or lifetime timespan.

Like anything – a diet, a workout regimen or a New Year's resolution – you are going to start your new job, new career, new sales encounter with a tenacity. The beginning – how you come out of the gates with a flourish – is usually when you showcase your best. But can you maintain it?

There are strong starts and weak starts; there are slow and steady starts. There are those who have a couple of good months and think they're ready for promotion only to fold when they don't get it – they don't have what it takes. There are those who regularly make the decision to improve – they are in it for the long haul.

The most respectable gladiators are the ones who had to work hard to reach the reputation and level and acumen they are capable of and are reliable and dependable in their excellence and accountability. It's rare to find this discipline, hence its immense value. Flashes in the pan fizzle because they are the ones attempting shortcuts and are not willing to commit to the regimen necessary of a gladiator.

Find the thoughts and visions and solace in routines that keeps you focused and moving forward. It could be that morning workout routine, the escape from work to read or catch up on Netflix, the occasional indulgence or even just surrounding yourself often with those you care for and that care for you. Know also that you'll hit the brick wall: when you tire of the workout or reading or watching the same genre – adapt and expand your horizon. It will only serve to make you the more complete warrior while keeping you fresh and agile. Present yourself with new challenges and create your own new opportunities and learning and growth – don't rely on others or on life to hand you these necessities.

Through it all, never allow yourself to deviate from what you know is the right approach. Be able to look back on every sales visit or call or interaction and either reflect on the sale or the specific reason the customer did not purchase. Every objection boils down to their lack of belief, for whatever reason and if you can answer the question as to why they actually didn't believe – you did your job. Reflect briefly, learn from it and move on without looking back. You did your job – period.

Not every customer will buy, but if you lead as many horses to water as humanly possible some will drink. You can make it more enticing and decide where you lead them. You determine the steps taken before and after each sale or setback. These things are what you have control over – ultimately, control over yourself. The rest will fall in place as it is going to.

The champion gladiator is hungry, assertive, resilient, unwavering and knows the battle isn't complete until they're the only one standing – cuts and bruises notwithstanding. Whether it is the sales day or the objections or the grind that leaves you weathered, see it through until the end and live to fight another day.

The Professor's Story

Vincent Scott. Just the name makes me smile and recall him fondly. For numerous years, literally, it's really just been the pictures and posts of Facebook – specifically of his beautiful daughter – that stand out because I have not actually, physically seen him since 2000 when he graduated from Minnesota State University-Mankato. But of all my students, Vincent is certainly among my favorite.

During his time there, I was his advisor for a brief period, was his professor for several classes and certainly took a particular interest in where he would go in life. It was obvious he would be successful at whatever he did; with Vincent, it wasn't a choice. He was a great writer, though I chided him for not delving into emotion enough. He was a fine student, but I believe he was bored with anything not related to writing and literature and film. And, from the looks of it, he turned into a fine man and father.

Perhaps my favorite story of Vincent is from his junior year. He admitted to me when he jettisoned his advisor after his junior year that he had grown uninterested in the business classes and his real enchantment was in the ones he took in our building of the arts. In fact, one of his business professors lamented his skipping class so often so much that he informed Vincent if he'd at least show up the rest of the semester he'd give him a B. If he skipped again, he'd flunk him. Vincent took the B.

It was the frustration of Vincent Scott; he had never needed to put forth effort for impeccable grades in grade school and high school and when he realized upon college entrance that there was a whole other world out there he chose pursuit of real world knowledge over textbooks. He was not interested in the scholastic pursuit and shared with me years later that even the business classes he took did little to prepare him for the current state of capitalism in the wrong hands.

His junior year, he was really branching out into ladies and liquor. I recall he told me he didn't really dabble in either too much in high school but college was an awakening for both.

In the literature class of mine that he took his junior year, I gave a final where there were bonus points given for every line of prose memorized from a massive collection of poems and songs spanning centuries. Vincent was trying to keep his grade point average above his personal Mendoza line of 3.0 – he had little interest in economics and business statistics (at least to the degree those courses delved into statistics) and his passion was around exploring his creative side. That said, my notes from that time – yes, his file is in front of me as I pen these keystrokes! – indicate he had no idea what he wanted to do. He was a junior and felt pressure to declare a major. It was going into a field in his creative interests with no real guarantees at a future paycheck, or parlaying the business class credits that had been part of necessary curriculum to date into a business major. He chose the latter – his junior year.

One thing I've learned about Vincent – specifically having read some of his later works – is that he knows how to play the system to his advantage. Any great competitor or salesperson would, of course. What Vincent did next certainly made me chuckle.

Vincent scoured the book of poems for something that would strike a chord. Being raised by his father on classic rock 'n roll like Elvis, the Beach Boys, Chicago, Led Zeppelin, the Rolling Stones and the Beatles, Vincent found that one of the works was "Eleanor Rigby" by none other than John Lennon and Paul McCartney. And, yes, the bonus section of my final was all 34 lines of that ballad. Not only did this provide Vincent an A in the class, but it helped raise his semester and year GPA to 3.3.

That summer, Vincent was slated to go to London with a couple of his best friends, who were also attending the University. With his affinity for Ian Fleming's Bond novels and Sir Arthur Conan Doyle's Sherlock Holmes stories, I know he wanted to be entrenched in the history and the essence of those streets. Unfortunately, my predecessor in his guidance counseling misled him on where he stood versus hours toward graduation; he had dropped a couple of classes out of boredom to the point he feared he would not pass them, and had to take a summer class to graduate on time. I'm not sure if he ever fulfilled this goal of making it to London.

Vincent took four of my classes over the years. He wrote a screenplay in my art of film class; it was an almost Kerouac "On the Road" type adventure with a lost soul traveling the country playing pool and finding himself. He told me he would always incorporate his friends in some incarnation in everything he wrote; it helped him speak to the attributes and truly deliver the passion he felt in real life in his writing.

Clearly, business won over his art for many years. The wife of one of my colleagues actually worked for ABM Telecom at the time and assisted in getting Vincent an interview for a call center role. I know he went on to have great success. But the Vincent I know and remember is that full-of-life 20-year old, so passionate about writing and cultivating emotion and inspiration in his readers. He chose business pretty much out of what he deemed obligation, but his spotty attendance in those classes versus his over-achievement in mine paint a pretty defining picture.

Vincent's approach to college translated into his career; he was not interested in what did not interest him. The nuts and bolts of the products or the advertising or the technology meant nothing to him; the ways to infuse his creativity into the go-to-market strategy or the inspiration of his sales teams were everything.

Vincent Scott's creativity, while certainly in a different medium than his chosen profession initially, was likely always channeled and utilized in useful fashion as he climbed the corporate ladder and he penned countless articles and his books. He turned into a Suit, but he's still one of my favorite creative writing students I've encountered. I'll definitely not forget him.

The Girlfriend's Story

When my dad got me a job at Cooke's Grocery Store in January 2001, I had no idea the profound impact it would have on my life for years to come.

Don't get me wrong – it was the least he could do. He was never really much of a father – always choosing his girlfriends over my mom, brother and me, even when they were married. He kept to himself and was a dad only when it suited him, which wasn't often. But every once in a while, I guess he decided to do grand gestures. When I was 18, he put in a good word with Lenny Cooke, the store manager of the most prominent grocery store in Mankato, and I started working in the deli my freshman year of college.

The work was easy and the people were mostly nice. The store was very cliquish but I suppose that is common in the workplace. I've never been one who has to be part of the in-crowd; I gravitate more toward the unique outsider. Enter Vincent Scott.

Vincent was 22, had literally just graduated college and was a clerk in the neighboring meat department. He seemed cocky and confident but I found that in some areas he was quite shy. A week after I started, my dad was introducing me to Ron Hicks, the assistant meat manager and a friend of his. Ron made sure to announce that Vincent was quite enamored with, "the new hottie in the deli." He laughed. I'm not sure what my dad thought. But I definitely started noticing Vincent Scott.

He was pretty aloof in the ways of the interested woman. I tried a few different angles, striking up conversations or making eye contact. Then I had him walk me to my car a few times. Then I had him help me with my calculus homework – and I had an A in calculus! He still didn't seem to get it. He was so cute.

He ran around with several of the employees at Cooke's – but he did it on his terms, much to their chagrin. It's funny, because once I had confided in a few people at the store that I had a crush on him, they tried to warn me off of him. I heard he had been engaged to a girl who used to work there. I heard he had kind of left another of his exes from the store high and dry. In fact, they told me he had been romantically linked to several girls there. But I guess what these people didn't realize about me is that I didn't really care about the rumors. I was interested in finding out more and hearing it from his mouth.

I struck up conversations with Vincent. He was super intelligent, he exuded a boyish charm, seemed genuinely nice in the moments he let his guard down and while he worked hard he also made time for his friends and he was playful.

Finally, one night in February, I just made my move. He was in the back office, adjacent to the meat cooler and the back of the store.

"Hey, whatcha doing?" I asked, attempting to be nonchalant.

Vincent looked up. He was propped back in the meat manager's chair with his feet on the desk looking at a magazine.

"Nothing, really," he said. Sometimes, he showed his slight nervousness but he was always quick to counter with cool. "Just waiting until it's time to go. I finished my work hours ago. What about you?"

"I wanted to ask you a question, but wanted to know if you'll give me an honest answer if I do." I was nervous, too. When I'm nervous, I get flush in the face. Vincent always thought that was cute, too.

"Sure," he answered, noncommittally. "What is it?"

The meat department phone rang.

"Excuse me," he said, taking his feet from the desk, putting the chair on the ground and rising to take the phone call. Of course, right at the moment of truth.

"I'll come back," I said. And, I actually did later. Right when it was time for him to leave.

"So, my question before," I began again.

"Yes?" Vincent said, removing his white apron and retrieving his black leather jacket from the coat rack.

"I was wondering… if I gave you my phone number, would you use it?"

He was definitely surprised by the question. I timidly handed him a small cardboard cutout I had removed from a deli box on which I had scrawled my number. He took it.

"Probably," he said, trying to cover the surprise with indifference. But his slight smirk of a smile gave him away.

"Good," I said, breaking into a smile. "Good night."

"Good night," he responded, putting the cardboard piece in his pocket, smiling fully and then leaving the back room.

It was around that time that Internet chatting and messenger began and we actually chatted until the wee hours that very night.

Things progressed quickly, as just days after our first date, I spent the night with him while we were at his friend Jack's. Nothing before or since really compares to those first few months with Vincent. And while I had been through the business a few times between my dad and some of the jerks I had dated before, it was clear to me that Vincent and I could grow together.

We literally ran into his ex-fiancé Becky on our first date. He told me about his first real girlfriend ditching him while away at school, sleeping with someone else and then trying to get him back when she returned for the summer. There were moments when he was the life of the party and was overly affectionate toward me in front of his friends. There were other moments when he seemed not to want to get too close.

I was a kid. I just wanted to be with him all the time – wanted to hold his hand, hear his voice, kiss him and have sex with him as much as possible. He would pick me up from school and we would spend time at an apartment in Mankato that my mom's boyfriend at the time kept for them.

Vincent was completely into me at times and then others I couldn't penetrate his shell. Sometimes, I would get to spend time with him when he hung out at diners with his friend Jack or drinking at his friend Ted's. He just had this thing about him – everyone wanted a piece of Vincent and they either liked him or were jealous of him or both. It depended on who he was showering his attention to at the time.

Because I fell for him so quickly and it seemed I could walk away and it wouldn't even bother him, I tricked him into a relationship by giving him the impression I was going to go on a date with someone else. It had been a couple of months of just spending time together on his terms and largely acting like we were just acquaintances around mutual friends and I forced the issue. It worked.

When he felt for a moment that he might lose me, that's when he wanted me. And things were so great it seemed – he then wanted to be with me all the time, which is what I was after in the first place.

My school year ended and went into summer, and I was seriously eyeing moving to Minneapolis for a volleyball scholarship for my second year of college. Vincent seemed keen to the idea as he was ready to move out of his parents' home and spread his wings – even though he wasn't sure what he wanted to do.

Vincent always managed to cover any worry he may have had about the future. He was usually pretty silly and joking, but I remember when I had a pregnancy scare and he was the most supportive I've ever seen him. When he needed to, he could take complete control of any situation.

Of course now, considering all current circumstances for both of us, I cannot help but look back and wonder what would have happened if I had been pregnant.

The primary difference when he finally committed to me after months of sneaking under the radar was that he included me in his life. Prior, it was seeing me separate from his friends or us pretending we weren't together to avoid the drama of the Cooke's gang finding out or trying to have their say in our relationship like they did on everything else they had an opinion on. He'd spend time with his friends Ted and Chet and Kurt and they'd go out drinking but I wouldn't hear from him until he was finished. But when we were together, he was – for that period of time – everything I wanted him to be.

He was vulnerable – but only to me. He'd confide that he felt great pressure to do incredible things; he tired of working in the meat department at Cooke's and feeling like an underling. When they did a grand re-opening and all of the bigwigs came from corporate headquarters in Minneapolis, Vincent was consumed with the belief that he had to become what they were or he was a failure. It didn't matter that these were folks who had come into generations of money or were bred in the family business: Vincent Scott certainly didn't operate like most 22 year olds. He had to create his own legacy.

The summer was noteworthy because I mulled moving for college, had to take 11 hours at University of Minnesota-Mankato to be eligible for the volleyball team, Ted and his girlfriend Robin were having their first child, and we enjoyed our final summer together at home – playing softball on the Cooke's team together, going to coffee houses with his friend Jack and going to clubs with my friends. I'll never forget it.

Before the chaos and the elements that come with growing up and the outside forces that would enter our lives, Vincent Scott and I were meant to be.

On August 1, we moved to Minneapolis. I think Vincent liked the fact that circumstances helped make the decision for him. He was able to move with Cooke's at first and had made some connections that helped him get hired shortly thereafter at ABM Telecom. It was great for him and the worst thing that ever could have happened to us.

I won't mince words. I loved Vincent very much and a part of me always will. But I saw this creative, passionate man who enjoyed writing and music and being with friends get a taste of corporate America and more money than he had ever seen previously and with every argument or fight we had he simply threw himself more into his work. He credited me later with helping turn him into this new version of himself, but in reality he simply ran from any type of drama in our relationship and buried himself more in work and what he was trying to become to escape his insecurities and fear of not living up to the expectations he thought everyone had of him. In his mind, the child prodigy now had to make good and nothing was actually good enough.

It didn't help that I trusted him less and less because he was always at work late. I found a note that a girl he worked with wrote him telling him all the things she wanted to do to him. He swore nothing happened between them, but I didn't know. I snooped through his journal and password-guessed my way into his e-mail and discovered while we were having a rough patch before we were a couple that he had hooked up with his ex, Becky. Things were rocky with my dad because he didn't seem like he wanted to be in my life. Then, after being forced to sell his farm and going through a divorce and battling alcoholism, Vincent's grandfather committed suicide. We had just moved and it was all of these barricades in rapid succession.

With some age and wisdom and experience working together to combat these destructive forces, we might have had a chance.

In hindsight, I was a mess. I was a kid, and going through all of this change and pushed Vincent away at times because of my dad. As for Vincent, for whatever reason, nothing has ever been or would ever be good enough for him. He was always discontented with his jobs, specifically after he gave them everything he had and was not appreciated enough. He was discontented with me; I felt good enough for him in Mankato but with the drama we had after moving to Minneapolis I could tell he had being single on the brain often. Apart from his daughter who arrived years later, I don't believe he was ever truly happy with anything in his life. No achievement or accolade scratched the surface of his itch.

Vincent got a taste of a larger world. He was doing well at work – he did well at everything, or he didn't do it. He was in an office of hundreds of people and was the new kid on the block who was leading the place in sales – of course he was getting a lot of attention, and this included girls. It's easy for a young guy to be attracted to the idea of a girl he doesn't know over the one he does with whom he's having issues. We didn't stand a chance.

Miraculously, we did last another year and a half. Much of it was me feeling insecure and not good enough while Vincent kept me at arm's length and was obsessed with his job and getting promoted. We'd pick fights with each other about stupid things. It made me long to move back to Mankato, which I knew he would never do, and I admit I finally checked out near the end. He hated his job and our relationship was no sanctuary for him and that wedge drove a bigger and bigger gap between us until it came to a head in December 2002.

He learned I had made plans to move back to Mankato over Christmas break and live with my cousin – unbeknownst to him. He was furious. He told me one morning that he wanted me gone by the time he came home that day from work. We would briefly "split up" and I'd chase him several times over and over during the prior 2 years but not this time. I wanted to make a stand and statement and branch out from Vincent because I knew I was not myself anymore living in the shadow of our issues.

It's ironic, because in the aftermath, because I stuck to my guns and did not run and chase him this time, Vincent is the one who tried to pursue me. At that moment I was the first thing Vincent Scott ever wanted that he couldn't have. He would send flowers and long e-mails and show up to my work just to see me and asked me to marry him – all the things I had wanted all along.

But I resisted any temptation to get back together, moved back to Mankato, continued school there and after several months and continued second and third thoughts on both sides we both eventually moved on. When I was weakening and ready for reconciliation, he had finally reached the point of acceptance.

I only saw him one more time in the flesh between 2002 and October 2010. We were at the bar we had hung out in so many times in Mankato. I was the closest I had ever been to letting him back in. We kissed and made plans for the following day. But I bailed on them.

Because of social media, we were intermittently connected off and on for years. I'd occasionally check out his profiles on Myspace and then Facebook. It was evident he was having success with work and was never in committed relationships. I saw he got promoted, then promoted again and again. It didn't surprise me at all.

Then I tracked his progress of his first book. When it was available for pre-order, I was his first sale and I called him to tell him how proud of him I was. Part of that conversation was like we never lost touch.

In October 2010, he had a book signing at Cullen's Bar in Greenfield. I had been through a string of non-committal dates and just broken up with someone. Vincent – at this point – was a single dad and had recently been through his devastating termination from ABM. However, he got a book published, which was a lifelong dream, and seeing him was really nice.

We went out a few times after that. I could tell he had changed immensely, but not all for the best. He told me nearly everything – what he had been through with his daughter's mother and with ABM – and I could see how jaded and cynical he had become. I do believe that we had a chance, but it wouldn't work with us because he was unable or unwilling to commit to a real relationship.

And now I'm married. I'm married to the best husband possible – he has always treated me like a lady, we don't fight, we are best friends.

I'll always love Vincent Scott. He was my first true love. But what chance did I really have with a guy whose top priorities didn't include me? It wasn't his fault – that's just not the way he was built. He was interested in things going his way – he chased thrills and ran from drama and sometimes the two were the same thing. He was so preoccupied with reaching what he felt was his potential in life that he felt so pressured to achieve. He was obsessed with career and thought being regarded as great and skyrocketing up the corporate ladder would bring him happiness.

I could tell he was an amazing dad – something I respected all the more because of my frosty relationship with my own. But I don't believe Vincent would allow himself to love anything else because he was afraid to lose it. No matter how or how much he loved me, it would pale in comparison to his flesh and blood and to his direct contributions that he could control. I was an X-factor he couldn't control so the love wasn't absolute.

He was so incredible in his work because it didn't force him to be emotional. He'd come home and feel beaten up, but he went back out there the next day and did his thing – he couldn't stand anyone passing him up in anything even for a day. I always wanted him to feel that I was more important than the dominance in his work, and I know I was important to him. But in the pecking order of his priorities, he was hell bent on taking over the sales world so he could feel validated and I knew I would never be first.

His daughter is a lucky lady, because now she's first – and she always will be.

The Trainer's Story

While I've worn several hats over the years with ABM Telecom, it was in December 2001 as a sales trainer for their consumer division when I met Vincent Scott.

Misty Parsons, my counterpart on the business side, started with a training group in September of 12 in Rockwood, Minnesota, that were hired to be business account managers. Inbound calls from our business customers would be routed to these folks and they would be required to answer account questions, field billing queries, set up services and SELL, SELL, SELL!

Roughly three months into their training, the entire department changed. They shifted the focus of this call center to strictly consumer and the training class was in limbo; in essence, they had to start all over again being trained on the systems for consumer. They had to unlearn what they had learned. That's where I came in.

My area of focus was the sales to consumer, so I came up from Little Rock, Arkansas, to train this group over the three months to come. Training for ABM Telecom was pretty grueling. We'd mix it up with some games of Pictionary after a run-through of typing orders or a role play that tested their knowledge. There were three checkpoints and a final role play, all requirements of successful completion of the training class. Each required a passing score or the person was eliminated from training.

By the time I took helm of this class, the initial 12 had been whittled to 8. The most prominent students in the class were Nina Siegel and Vincent Scott. Nina had done the consumer job previously and had literally only transferred to this office to try her hand at business. Vincent – along with Elise Barnett – were the only two in the class who were from off the street, as in not transferred in from another internal ABM division. That said, others had what were termed "withdrawal rights" whereby they had up to ninety days after graduation from our class where they could return to the job from whence they came.

Vincent stood out right away because even compared to Nina, who had already done the job, he was completing the order typing exercises from start to finish in 3-to-4 minutes while Nina would take a few extra and the remainder of the class took roughly 20. He would blitz through these orders at lightning speed and then he'd sit quietly until the class caught up. Here was this 23-year old kid relatively fresh out of college and new in a big city and he was running circles around the adults all around him.

Much of the class was lackluster when it came to these in-class role plays. I would give them each a scenario and they would be expected to faux field a call from me as the customer that would require them to put their skills to use. I'd say the average trainee would be lucky to pass the majority of the time.

The call flow expectations were very lengthy and nobody hit them all. But this kid Vincent would damn near hit every one every time and the ones he didn't he would give you the specific reason why he didn't and why he felt it inappropriate. I couldn't help but like the kid.

I had fun with him on these things. I'd give him the toughest scenarios and even if we hadn't really covered the topic in training, he'd still dazzle us all. Sure, he was wobbly when we first went out on the sales floor and he took live calls – everybody was. In fact, he wasn't even tops in the class in sales the first week we were out on the floor. But that was all very soon to change.

When I saw it really click in Vincent was when he first faced the fear of potential failure. Up to this point, everything was simple for him. It was classroom learning. The kid was obviously super-bright and used to being the best at everything.

But there are certain coming of age moments for people. When these guys found out that the call center was changing hours – they were going to work six days a week and mandatory overtime every day with 9-to-7 shifts – I lost another three people in that class. The other thing was entering what we called Phase 2 – they had passed their first challenge role plays but they had final role play and their on job incubation period ahead. Vincent got a taste of the extremely high demands and that's where everybody balks – even if it's just a little bit.

Try as he might, the fear and negativity of his co-workers had an effect on the kid. He was impressionable, unmolded and raw.

I had a speech I gave in every class. I remembered delivering it to that class very profoundly because of what he said at the end and what happened in the weeks to come after that.

"Class, how is everybody feeling?" I asked at the end of that Friday after the announcement of the new shift hours and just prior to a week of on job training we would perform after the upcoming weekend.

Their eyes darted to one another. No one really said anything.

"I know. A little deflated," I answered the rhetorical question. "You know, you guys have come a long way in a relatively short amount of time. You've been through more than most training classes already with your mid-training shift from business to consumer, which is a testament to the courage and open-mindedness you bring to the table.

"But there's far more to come. As you know, you have a week of on job next week. You'll be taking more calls each hour of the day than you've taken so far. Sure, we'll huddle up mid-day and at the end of each day, but this is going to be a true test of job fit for both you and us. The sales managers and I will be listening in and scoring your calls. The week will end with your final role play and then you'll start Phase 2 which will see you guys on the phones another week and your unannounced graded calls will determine if you graduate to desk or not."

All eyes were on me. They always were. I had trained dozens of classes already and was already pretty deadened to the emotions that would go on in these rooms. I had to be. I mean, nobody wants to fire anybody or be the reason some employee of theirs is scared shitless. But this job was pretty arduous. I'd be doing them a disservice if I didn't try to scare them off.

"You know, the best rep I've ever seen in this job comes to mind. I like to tell this story to every class. She was incredible – she aced every quiz, she raced through every time trial. She typed orders at blazing speeds. She was incredible in the role plays. Even when she went out on the floor, she did a remarkable job. She led her class in revenue and was putting up numbers in Phase 2 that rivaled what the actual sales floor was doing.

"One day, she came to me at the end of the day – in tears. I couldn't imagine what was wrong. But she was breaking down – she had put so much pressure on herself. But she didn't enjoy what she was doing. She had given up teaching to be here to make a better life for her family but the hours and the commitment and the demands of the call flow were more than she wanted to handle.

"She let it all out. She cried for a bit in silence. I felt bad for her, and I told her that she was amazing at this and she would undoubtedly be a hero to her family. But I couldn't make this the job for her. She had to decide what was most important to her. She decided right then and there that her real passion was elsewhere. She returned to teaching and she resigned on the spot that day – in Phase 2, so close to the end of training."

I paused. Looking around the room, I had their attention. I could also tell which ones would be the next to go. I ended up being right.

"Ladies and gentlemen, this may not be the job for you, either. And there's no shame in that. Each of you came here for a different reason and some of you may go on to be great at this job. But sometimes, even the people who are great at this choose another path because your heart just isn't in it. I'm telling you today, take the opportunity to think over the weekend. If you come to me Monday and decide that you don't want to pursue this path anymore, there's no shame in that whatsoever."

It was definitely pin drop quiet in that classroom after what had been a pretty eye-opening day of fielding real calls and scoring poorly on call flows for the bulk of that group. I'd given that speech many times over the years. I always saw people resign the following Monday. I dismissed the class for the weekend. Vincent Scott stayed behind and approached my desk.

"Darren," he said.

"Yes, Vincent?" I asked, looking up from my laptop where I recorded the notes from the day's session. There was a moment – just a split second – that I wondered if this would be the end of Vincent's sales career. My gut told me otherwise.

"I'm here for very different reasons than anyone here. And I'll be honest

– I never intended to get into sales. I just wanted a customer service job. Unlike most of the class, I have nowhere to go – I'm from off the street and it's either this or back to Cooke's Grocery Store or to looking for jobs on Monster that nobody will interview me for because guys with a college degree in business are a dime a dozen.

"I appreciate the story, if it's even true. I know you have to scare people a little bit so you feel like you did your part in testing us. But from now on, you're going to have to change that story, because I'll be the best rep you've ever seen. I'm not quitting. I'm just getting started."

From there, I saw a switch flip in Vincent. Up until that point, he had been relatively unsure of himself. But the following week, he had his first huge sale. I literally watched him. He actually closed his eyes and recited a script we had developed in class. It worked. And from there, it was more and more.

I watched him get up triumphantly after every sale to march over to the sales white board the next aisle over. I'd watch the other people on his new team physically groan or shake their heads as this kid was kicking their asses in sales. He was single-handedly breathing life into an office of excuses and whiners. Their bullshit reasons for being unsuccessful were being rendered obsolete as a new kid on the block led the entire office in sales his first month on the floor. I even made side $20 bets with some of the guys every day who thought they could beat this kid. I only lost once and came out $420 in the black. Best odds I ever came across.

And from that point on, when I told stories to classes, I told the story about the rep who went back into teaching but I ended with the story of Vincent Scott.

The Vocational Viewpoint, via Vincent Scott
(Republished with permission)
"Why Your Dues are the Most Important Thing You Pay"

Maturity and experience bring with them quite the realization: that the ups and downs, bottoms falling out and murk and muck you've become embattled by have done you quite a service.

It's quite common when you are starting out in your career and the real world to still be touched by naivety; our blinders are on until we take them off - or they are ripped off. We believe right and wrong is black and white; we believe in justice and that hard work always pays off.

Wrongfully and rightfully, we'll find ourselves passed up for promotion, we'll see changes that do not benefit the customers and workforce and we will be asked to do more and more and more. With the ebb and flow of business, it becomes apparent that - to get anywhere - you must stay on target in spite of the constant distractions along the way. There will be good days and bad, but I've seen too many people cry foul, become negative to the point of detriment and jump ship, rather than staying the course and reaching the milestone they claim they want so much.

Realize you are part of a workforce and the puzzle that comprises your business entity; you are a cog in the wheel. Your leadership likely has every intention of rewarding you, making you feel welcome and growing your career; nevertheless, they are also inclined to do this for every other member of their team who shows the same interests. Imagine it as a race; you might pass up others for a time in some areas. You may master several facets of the role. You are not in control of who is selected for a promotion or additional duties but you are certainly in control of your actions, reactions and contributions. That said, when things don't go your way and you decide to stand still or take a detour in the race, do you think you'll still be closer to the finish line the next time the race standings are calculated?

Paying your dues not only gets you where you want to be, but it aids you a great deal in being able to counsel others on doing the same thing - and that's what leaders do. We've all been privy to poor management or questionable decisions and ethics around us - that's nothing new. But it's being able to come out on top in each of these scenarios, willing ourselves to the win and learning from mistakes that truly dictates our value to the overall team. Plain and simple: it's survival of the fittest.

Paying your dues is a deposit you'll be able to recoup later in droves; each day in every way, you make investments in your future and career - in business, in relationships, in life. The more cognizant you are of this and accepting of it, the farther you'll go - because you'll accumulate the wealth of experience and maturity that gets you where you want to be... even if it isn't on the timetable you initially anticipated.

You may pay dues more than once, but with each achievement you will be able to look back and connect the dots to how you got there. It may just not go in the straight line you initially wanted.

The Vocational Viewpoint, via Vincent Scott
(Republished with permission)
"Are these 3 Things Preventing Your Growth and Success?"

We typically have the best of intentions. So how and why do things go awry?

Whether it's re-dedicating ourselves to health and fitness on January 1 or re-focusing in our career, many of us wind up off track relatively quickly. We start making excuses, we tell ourselves it isn't that big of a deal and we remain mired in mediocrity.

But it can be prevented.

Lack of clear focus and priorities - No journey can begin without a destination, lest we wind up wandering around aimlessly and literally lost. Integral to the mission is formulation of a specific, targeted goal for which you can plot a course and consistently charge toward the desired result.

Your goal should revolve around needs and wants, be it in career path, health and wellness or personal relationships. It should lie heavily rooted in something you strongly desire, because that desire must keep burning no matter what comes along to fan its flames. No matter how strong your desire or resolve, it will be challenged many times by unforeseen forces and you must want this badly enough to fend them all off and endure.

Over-thinking and second-guessing - Doubt and self-consciousness and worry and wondering if we can accomplish our goals and are doing the right things will plague us along the way. It's normal, but little can really prepare you for these brick walls you will encounter along the way. Typically, after setting a goal, your sheer will propels you through those first days and potentially weeks unfettered. Nevertheless, after that initial burst, you will start to encounter roadblocks of various natures, and you have to plow through them one by one; your passion, your strength of commitment, your character and your discipline are the only things that can ensure you do.

Thinking too much or wondering if your goals are realistic have no place here; you already set the goal for a reason, right? Did you really want or need it, or not? Once you have committed to a viable, vital goal, you must revisit your commitment in times of doubt and re-commit yourself; sometimes many times over. Settling will lead to regret.

Negative outside forces - Your lack of focus can also be attributed to people who do not understand your drive and determination, who are jealous of it, who do not want to see you successful, who want to keep you on their level of mediocrity or misery. *Don't let them!* Those who really care for you and your journey will emerge just as those who have no place in your life will set themselves apart. When you recognize negativity in thoughts and other people, dismiss and expunge it from your consciousness and life as rapidly as possible.

There is no place for forces and people that will only keep you down.

Setting attainable goals, accomplishing benchmarks along the way and committing to excellence all while enduring the setbacks along the way is the only way to achieve happiness and success. Whatever your brand of those results, you will reach them once you can effectively control these three greatest hindrances.

Success and happiness are there - you just have to go after them and keep going after them until they are yours.

The Vocational Viewpoint, via Vincent Scott
(Republished with permission)
"5 Things Your Job Search Can't Afford to be Missing"

Do any of these sound familiar?
"I applied to a job I'd be perfect for, but I haven't heard back!"
"I've applied to a ton of jobs online, but haven't gotten any interviews!"
"I did great in that interview - why didn't I get a call back?"
If they do, you are not alone.

No matter how hard you try to avoid it, you will likely face the daunting job search at some point in your career - often through no fault of your own. With the new age of ever-changing and evolving company landscapes, the likelihood of staying with one company your entire career is about that of your favorite athlete sticking with one team for theirs. It's possible, however unlikely.

That said, there are steps you can take to boost your likelihood of success.

1.) Realize that many others are applying to the same job you are. Stand out! It's a process of elimination and survival of the fittest, and the folks in human resources simply do not have the chance to call or invite in all 1,000 people who applied. They have a system to weed out resumes that do not feature the exact specifications they are looking for. No offense, but you won't make the cut for every job - not even the ones that sound perfect for you *to you*.

Make a video resume. Make your resume sparkle with actual numbers and results so a potential employer reads it and says, "Hey, I want them working for me!" No resume will get to every decision-maker, but you can increase your odds right out of the gates by being ahead of the curve and doing what others don't. Send "thank you's" every single time. Follow up after a handful of days to reiterate your interest. Be the best one in all areas and you give yourself the best shot.

2.) Rather than leave your fate in the hands of the HR system's shredders, focus on networking with those who actually make the final decisions. Not all jobs are posted, and not all decision-makers see your resume; in this day and age, with mediums like LinkedIn or with referrals in the company you are targeting or with networking events, you can actually connect with the powers that be. Do not leave your destiny up to anyone other than the person calling the shots - that's the one you want to dazzle. And don't go straight for the sale of getting an interview; request a meeting or call whereby you can gain advice on where you could fit in their business. If they like you after this respectful approach, it could very well become the interview you seek.

3.) Play the numbers' game. Far too often, I've heard folks say, "I applied to three jobs but haven't heard anything!" No kidding! Your odds of landing a job - specifically one you applied for online - could be roughly 1 in 1,000 or worse. That isn't meant to sound discouraging; it's meant to convince you to do everything you can to up your prospect of landing one. Apply to as many as you can, with the best resume possible and with the best networking mechanisms at your disposal. If you don't know the decision-makers, use networking with current contacts or current social media tactics to get on their radar.

    4.) Be patient. You will likely get interviews or offers for jobs you do not want. If it isn't what you want to be doing for the foreseeable future and you can afford to be selective, don't commit to it. Taking a massive hit to your income now when you could keep searching and find the right fit will just wind you right back at the beginning. Trust me; I've never compromised in my search and I've always been rewarded for following the right process.

    5.) Do not discriminate against any potential opportunities or methods of applying to jobs. If you restrict your search to strictly one online career board, you are missing out on so many others. A simple online search will yield multiple other ways to search. Furthermore, just because a job does not necessarily pique your interest up front doesn't mean that further investigation of that role or company or the people you can meet will not bear later fruit. Check out everything: if it's not a way to improve yourself, move on. But it very well could be.

    The job search can be a time of reassessing our career and finding something we can really sink into. When we struggle in the search is when we lose sight of the aforementioned process that works - do not let anything deter you from making the right moves so you land in the right place.

The Vocational Viewpoint, via Vincent Scott
(Republished with permission)
"The Charisma and Charm Required of a Sales Champion"

    Whether closing down business, asking someone on a date or taking what you want in life by force, key personality traits are required to reign supreme. Sales is an attitude. It is a psychological tug-of-war, and, to come out on the winning end, you have to have a healthy stockpile of wits, charm and swagger in your bag of tricks.

    People often mistake or misuse aggression for assertiveness, arrogance for confidence or boorish bullying for clever closing. A customer will not be strong-armed into making the decision you want them to make. In fact, it really all begins with realization that the sale itself is the customer's own decision! You can give them all the food for thought in the world, but your prime directive is making their fear of standing pat outweigh their fear of making a change. This is done by making them see the parade passing them by; making them understand that they are missing out on something significant by doing nothing.

All of this said, a customer, a dinner date or anyone else with something to offer you, for that matter, is not looking for status quo. Like a seasoned sales professional, they have seen it, done it, and lived it all - or so they think. This is why constant reinvention of yourself is paramount to survival and success; you have to become a true student of the selling game to master it. While a potential client cannot be steamrolled or taken by force, they are attracted to less-than-subtle gestures or personality traits that you want to exhibit and exude.

Confidence is #1. No one is going to instill any faith in someone with no confidence; be it in the product or in themselves. I have to say, there are many people for whom this comes naturally. If being confident or portraying an aura of greatness does not come naturally - fake it. Learn to turn off your fear. It is a must when it comes to breaking on through to the other side in the sales arena.

In life, we often have to strategically throw ourselves into daunting situations; this somewhat risky, devil may care attitude may not always go as we planned, but the trick is to be able to look back with no regrets and know that you did all you could. Showing confidence in yourself and your product or service is infectious; your high level of belief will rub off on the customer.

Everything your customer says or does must appear to be anticipated. Never let anyone see you bleed or affected by even the slightest unexpected action. This will come predominantly with regular repetition of a heightened sales strategy; once you have done several hundreds or thousands of sales presentations, you get used to the objections and the rejection and you can often anticipate their moves before they make them.

Intertwine your overcome for a common objection before you even hear the objection. Surprise your client by saying, "Perfect!" or "Exactly!" when they try to deal you the death blow of an objection, acknowledge the objection, put it in its place with their own words or phrases you gleaned during the fact finding and move on undeterred. The big thing about sales is guiding (not pushing) customers as far as you can through the selling process. You cannot make them do what you want them to do, but you can influence. You can tell them how darn good the outcome is and work to eliminate their fear of change. If you make that outcome irresistible, chances are at their optimum that things will go your way.

Finally, know that mistakes are not mistakes. They are experiences. Take the good out of literally everything you encounter. Every place and stretch of time has a rainy season, which is a necessary period of cleansing. Sure, the rain may inhibit activity but it nourishes the ground for what is to come. Your rainy season may be a slump where that sales "sun" refuses to shine but you must learn from each and every stumble across the path. Be able to look back on each sales visit or call and recognize the specific reason you fell short or what you could have or would have done differently. Quickly analyze those items, keep the learning material and discard the emotions attached to the defeat. Do not wear the losses (or wins, for that matter) on your sleeve. It is over. Move forward and apply your heightened sales strategy to that next potential customer.

Personality, charm, charisma; these traits go a long way in setting yourself apart from everyone else who has called your customer before. That said, they will dictate if you will succeed or if you will befall the same tragic defeat your lesser skilled peers did.

Is it in you?

The Vocational Viewpoint, via Vincent Scott
(Republished with permission)
"Why do I get rejected for jobs I am perfectly qualified for?"

From today's mailbag: "Why do I keep getting rejected for jobs I am perfectly qualified for? I don't even get a response the majority of the time!"

I believe this has been upgraded to the eighth wonder of the world... though, after years of being on both sides of the coin I don't wonder about it anymore.

Think about it this way. Yes, you applied to a job you are qualified for - heck, maybe overly qualified for. Depending on unemployment rates at any given moment, you are one of 100 to 1,000 people who likely applied to that role. You are up against a human resources automated system that is designed to eliminate candidates based on not having the right buzz words, experience or degrees. Literally, it's like Han Solo navigating through the asteroid field in *Empire Strikes Back*; though, they had a Wookiee so I'd place more money on them.

No hiring manager wants to sift through 1,000 resumes; honestly, they sometimes do not even have time to interview the top 50 of the most quality candidates! This is why it is so important to stand out in every single way possible. This is also why hiring managers often hire referrals or someone they know; it's someone who has been deemed worthy of the job versus the unknown: you. Video resumes, networking to expand your network, truly utilizing your network and staying in touch with them even when you don't need them for something, applying to 1,000 jobs instead of just 10 and wondering why you're not getting a call.... THAT is how you land a job.

For those who have any length to their career, you know that most roles you landed were due to knowing someone – one way or another. Sometimes, the connections are created for us and other times we must create the connection.

For the ones when you did not, something about you stood out. Either way, it's a brutally challenging numbers game that you cannot win without tipping the odds in your favor.

Like anything, it comes down to as effective a process as possible; the best possible approach (resume, cover letter, other attention-grabbers) the most number of times with strong follow up and effective interviewing skills. Don't get attached to ANY job - before, during or even after several interviews - until you get the job offer. Until that moment, you must put a full court press on your turbocharged process.

And..... GOOD LUCK!

The Vocational Viewpoint, via Vincent Scott
(Republished with permission)
"The 5 Musts to Motivating Your Sales Team"

Finding and maintaining the happy medium of motivation is critical to the success of you and your sales team. That said, while we all strive to obtain that balance, few sales managers are consistent in the endeavor.

Like many facets of the selling game, it does not take drastic measures to invoke positive change and results; it merely takes tweaks to the process. Most importantly, the dynamic of a sales team starts in the beginning. The right foundation must be set with mutual respect and partnership. Know your role as sales manager: you are there, like the fire and police departments, to serve and protect.

(1) Know your team. Spend time understanding what makes them tick, why they work here, what they want out of the role, their strengths and areas of opportunity. Know their kids' names. Know what is important to them. While you are not attempting to make friends, it is important to them that they're important to you.

You will utilize your knowledge of their skill set and career aspirations to mold your approach toward managing them and supporting them. How do they like to be coached? Some managers take a blanket approach to their team, yet you must be unique in your approach to each unique personality you train and manage. It will go a long way with your team when you extend them this consideration. Also - how would you personally or did you personally want to be managed if you were once in their shoes?

(2) Show them respect - it's the only way to gain theirs. Many managers come in, make drastic changes because they think they can have positive, immediate impact, and they glean absolutely no feedback from their team on what changes should be made! It's a team, not a dictatorship. Know their opinion on how things should be done; certainly, you will call the final shots, but if they are part of the decision-making process or the go-to-market strategy, they

will have more buy in. Furthermore, they earned their right to be in their role, so until they are jeopardizing their position, do not come in, have knee jerk reactions or tell them how to do things your way.

Ultimately, if you want them to change, you have to know their way of doing things, identify gaps in their process and legitimately sell them on changing, so let them do it their way to a point. Show them the respect of some autonomy but absolutely be there to help eliminate legitimate obstacles to their success and have a good enough rapport to call them on it when they make excuses.

(3) Agree together on strategic, permanent, positive change. You need to meet with them regularly - often for the middle of the pack you can move and make a difference, occasionally for your superstars you want to keep on track, and enough with the bottom quartile to figure out if they can move into the aforementioned groupings and move forward accordingly.

Your observations of their selling methods from prospecting to pitching and overcoming and closing are one thing; how you acknowledge their prior successes and areas of opportunity is critical. Lead through fear or criticizing and they will rightfully shut down - you'll never get their best. Lead with all knowledge of their aspirations and look for ways to guide and help - you have their heart.

Like any interaction on the sales food chain, your role is to sell them on why they should give up on any fear of changing versus sticking with their comfortable ways of mediocrity or - in some cases - failing. Agree on a strategy together; again, this collaboration gives a higher probability of success in execution.

Positive results are a result of strong process - period. No amount of barking orders or telling them to do more of a widget will ever result in anything good.

(4) Follow through on your part of the commitment. It's one thing to get a result and quite another to consistently deliver the result. Like anything, your plan will need tweaks and course correction, but provided you have followed the previous steps and established the relationship, delved into common goals and worked together on the process and its execution, your probability at success will be at its optimum level.

When you hire a salesperson, you enter into a contract. You agree to give them training - initial and ongoing - and support - elimination of their legitimate obstacles, being responsive, being available, and even if you can't get them the answer or the outcome they want, when they see you are always trying to do so they will believe in your leadership. You cannot always control if they live up to their end of the bargain (namely, being the person they promised to be on interview day) but you can control keeping up with your commitment and doing so is certainly more likely to garner a positive response.

(5) Work to get them what they want and where they want to go. Many managers do not wish to proactively support their top producers because they fear the loss of productivity; however, if they actively promote those folks, others will rise to the challenge to take the mantle of top producer because they will believe in your support. On the flip side, even if the job isn't a fit for a member of your team, don't cast them out and fail to live up to your commitments to them; get them the training and answers they need, even if you both ultimately come to the realization they would be better for another internal or external role.

A great deal of managing a sales team is akin to managing a household or a sports team or a business - everyone has their role to play. Yours is responsible for safeguarding people and process, ensuring the right plays are set and called, watching the execution, sharing your notes on how the plays can be run better, being accountable, being transparent, being supportive, and being responsible.

Motivating your sales team comes down to determining what motivates them and using that knowledge as you set the game plan and as you review the game tape; as you discuss what they want to be doing in their career and as you work with them to determine the path that will get them there. It's up to you to keep them on the path. Motivate your team properly and they will do great things for you.

The Boss's Story

I first became aware of Vincent Scott in January 2002. As a line manager for a call center sales team in Montrose, Minnesota, we had a sister office in Rockwood who did the same function. Vincent was in training at the time and was the talk of the town on the conference calls we utilized to stay in touch as a Minneapolis sales department.

Ashley Flowers was his first manager upon graduation of training in Rockwood. In July 2002, Shelly Cheekwood took over our division as the Area Sales Manager.

My ABM Telecom career had started in 1999 – I was a call center sales rep in Montrose and was promoted after 2 years in the position. My team was the top selling one in Minneapolis and Shelly was interested in making some changes to improve our management team a few months into her time in position.

Vincent and I first met in September 2002 – Shelly arranged a day where my peer Lucy Hansen and I swapped offices for a Monday with Ashley and Stacey Worth from Rockwood. While most reps engaged in conversations that were far too long and contained half-hearted mentioning of our products, Vincent was animated, he stood up, he was boisterous and assumed the sale with every customer. I'd never seen anything like it.

Most reps in the office were lucky to get 5 sales in a day while Vincent would turn in sales sheets with 20 or 30. No customer was getting off the phone without making a change that made him money – whether it was a tweak to a service, a new long distance plan, a cordless telephone or a new package. He would swap out features in plans knowing it would make him money; he would spend the time investment getting whatever he could on every single call even if it was a few dollars in revenue. It added up.

Vincent called my attention to him for practically every sale he got that day. I recognized then and certainly later, when I became his manager in October, that he thrived on the praise and recognition. He needed nothing else. No recommendations, no coaching. He just wanted people to marvel at his results. And that I certainly did.

Shelly demoted Ashley for her poor performance as a sales supervisor and transferred her to Montrose, setting the stage for me to get a fresh start in Rockwood. Many reps in Montrose were unhappy with the fact I held them accountable; if they weren't producing results, I would coach them up or out. Period. The union was clamoring to Shelly about me and to keep the peace, she made a few shifts. Moving me to a team that was used to Ashley's incompetence and drama delighted that team and my own.

This kid made me look good so I did everything I could to sing his praises. I knew Shelly was interested in him for management when she was able to make additional changes. I also knew he just needed to be left alone to do his thing, and I was fine with that. My primary interest at this point was to get a change of scenery and to be groomed for a second-line management position.

It was never a priority of mine to get to know my reps on too much of a personal level. However, it was a day in December when Vincent arrived, took three calls and came to me completely defeated. I took him to an observation office and he told me that he had split up with his girlfriend of two years.

Of all the years I've known Vincent, it was the only time I saw him break from character. He told me about their troubles, about how he had kicked her out of their apartment and how she was now being cold as ice to him.

I saw quite a rarity – Vincent Scott cried. Never before or after did I see him allow emotion to that degree into the picture.

As a sales rep, he was a machine – piling up sales numbers that were 2-to-10 times that of anyone else in the office. He set records that stand to this day. Later, when he was a sales manager, he did confide in me about a relationship he had with married Stacey Worth – one of our management peers. She pursued Vincent while having problems with her marriage, told him she'd leave her husband for him and ended up staying married.

While he would tell me about these troubles, he seemed to be becoming less emotional and more able to throw these frustrations into his work. By the time I had my last working experience with him, he was my boss and he was somehow navigating through a rocky time with his daughter's mother while working for our ruthless dictator of a director taking daily verbal abuse. He endured the worst factors of his life and effortlessly turned an initial 10-person project into a $50+ million annual operation with himself a superstar.

My favorite memory of Vincent was when I lobbied for him to go to a town hall meeting with our CEO Wick Eckert in December 2002. Until Vincent's arrival, Bambi Jennings had long been the top rep in the department. With Vincent's presence, she was yesterday's news – and it frustrated her to no end. Despite his relatively brief tenure at that point, Shelly agreed, and he accompanied me to our downtown Minneapolis office.

"Come on," I said, as the meeting had concluded and attendees were making their way out of the auditorium. He could see I was not following the crowd.

"Where are we going?" he asked.

"To meet Wick Eckert," I responded, matter-of-factly.

He looked puzzled at first; I knew that Vincent – while he was dominant and powerful when he was on the sales call – had no desire to step out of the shell of an introvert when he was in the real world of the public. If he was going to stand out and be noticed and be a leader in this world, I was going to have to give him the nudge. He couldn't learn much from me, but he could certainly take a dose of my fearlessness.

What is there to lose? In these corporate environments, everyone's a number. I learned this lesson so long ago. And here was Vincent Scott, this wunderkind 24-year old who was the top sales rep in an office, district and channel competing against people who were mostly 5-to-20 years older than he was. He did not have any business acumen. He was completely raw. Over the years, I got the pleasure of seeing him transform into an influencer and unbelievable leader but right then, he looked at me incredulously with wide eyes.

"Seriously?" he asked.

I halted in the aisle, briefly, to turn to him.

"You have to do anything you can in this business to stand out," I told him. "You see, most of these people are walking right out that door. Wick Eckert will never know them. And he may not remember me or you. But in the off chance that he does or that we say something to him that resonates, do you think that hurts us in any way?"

He thought about that for a moment. "No, it wouldn't."

"Exactly. Always take every opportunity you can to meet everyone you can. You never know which connections will matter most. You never know who you'll make the impression on that counts. But always put yourself in front of every leader you can and make yourself known."

When I met Vincent, he was 23 years old and was this inexplicably amazing sales rep with no polish and very little business sense. In May 2003, he was promoted to sales manager and we both went to Montrose for 6 months until they permanently closed that office. Shelly moved me there to mentor him as I still had the top team in the unit.

That soon changed.

Vincent started out trying to get his team to like him and trying to take calls for his reps; I remember him camping out in the middle of his team and actually putting himself into the queue so they could listen to him on the phone. They would listen to music together, have meals together, and I think he genuinely befriended them. It was certainly one way of doing things.

But I think his real awakening as a manager was after more personal hurt. We all moved back to Rockwood when Montrose closed and he was forced to work side by side with Stacey after she had decided to stay with her husband. While I know that was hard for him – and for her – he wouldn't show it. In fact, he stubbornly ignored her. He threw everything he had into managing his team. And he took some of the emotion out of it.

He couldn't control these relationships but he could control holding his team accountable. I mentored him on how to walk these reps through the disciplinary process for measurement of work – not following call flow – when they weren't selling. We couldn't fire people for results, but we could certainly grade their calls and put them on plans accordingly. I remember when Shelly purposely took problem child Barbara Allison off my team and put her on Vincent's because she wanted him to fire her.

He tried and tried to make her a good rep – to understand her motivations, to appeal to her career aspirations, to give her support and recognition; she was excellent at first but then started to take advantage of his generosity with her. And rather than accept it, rather than keep giving her more chances, Shelly and I watched as he took it upon himself to pursue the discipline. The training wheels were off.

I remember sitting in that termination meeting and he asked questions like a lawyer. I hadn't even coached him on that! He would ask questions he already knew the answer to, guiding her into her own trap. She had been guilty of hanging up on customers yet her defense was that she was having phone difficulties. Vincent, however, had caught a call where she had tried to hang up on an unruly customer (who became more agitated with Barbara's bad attitude), it didn't work, the customer kept talking, and then the phone system showed, "Rep hung up."

A sales rep could hang up if connection was lost – Barbara had said "Hello?" a few times like she could not hear the customer, but the customer was clearly still there and talking – she did not want to put forth the effort to dig into their slightly more complicated than the norm issue.

He had the proof, but it wasn't good enough – he wanted them to admit guilt. At first, she wouldn't, but he masterfully, skillfully led her into tearfully admitting that yes – she had hung up on the customer. She did it because she was frustrated, having a bad day – whatever. Faced with all of the evidence and Vincent's line of questioning, she had no choice.

But Vincent was also compassionate and empathetic if his team was honest with him. He had a great friendship with Lacy Harvell, a rep on his team who had considerable issues with her boyfriend/daughter's father and a diehard crush on him. During some of her darkest times, she lazily started putting services on customer accounts without their acknowledgment. Our director at the time had zero tolerance for this. Vincent came in on his own vacation to counsel Lacy in the final termination hearing with the director and to be in the meeting with her.

Rather than have her try to come up with any excuse or defense, he instructed Lacy to throw herself on the mercy of the court. Our director had gone through a difficult divorce, and Vincent told Lacy to channel those emotions in our director. It was brilliant. And it worked. Against all odds, Lacy lived to sell another day. She's still there today – 12 ½ years later and has been able to take care of her kids and support them well because Vincent Scott saved the day.

It didn't stop there. My two most prominent pupils had been Vincent and Dick Knoll, who were promoted within two weeks of one another in May 2003. Their rivalry became rather intense when our offices converged in December 2003 and even more heated when Shelly chose Dick over Vincent to be interim area manager when she went out on maternity leave in August 2004.

Vincent did not go looking for these little competitions with Bambi or Dick or whomever else became jealous of his dominance; they would make excuses or lies about why he was better and attempt to diminish his achievements. They'd pick a fight and a still maturing Vincent would far too often take the bait.

While Vincent did things his way no matter what the repercussions, Dick said all the right things and kissed Shelly's butt. Dick came to be known as "The Terminator" as he took firing people to new extremes – no one was safe. He even tried to fire his own friend from church and he fired a perfectly good rep the week of his wedding because he was having a down month and wanted him off the team's sales numbers for the month. Despicable and shameful.

Vincent, on the other hand, wanted all struggling reps on his team – he turned them into Top Gun sales reps (the moniker for the top 5% of sales reps in the company). Dick never seemed to understand Vincent's devotion to coaching and certainly couldn't understand how Vincent would beat him every month without fail. Dick thought by firing every rep not hitting goal that he could lift his numbers, but instead he bred mistrust. Vincent, on the other hand, knew by turning a rep who started out hitting 50% into one that at least hit 80%, his worst reps would still be better than average. By moving the bottom and middle, and building trust and security, Vincent couldn't be stopped.

And it wasn't even close. I'll be honest – I reached a point in 2004 when I lost faith that I'd ever get promoted in this department. Shelly was doing me no favors and I grew tired of seeing her rarely in the office, never in support of us and when she was at work, smoking or shopping with her best friend Stacey. I started making connections in the downtown office and managed to leave in September 2004.

Vincent started putting up ridiculous numbers in the spring and summer of 2004. Dick would consistently produce 125%, 130% to goal but Vincent would make it a personal mission to destroy Dick's numbers. Dick had "called him out" as it were and Vincent took it as a personal attack that could only be answered by destroying him on the sales report at all costs.

Vincent would do 150%, 166% to goal per month at his peak. It confounded Dick. Dick would go out of bounds and monitor Vincent's reps, trying to catch them in bad call flow or cheating. He'd target Vincent's friends, like former peer Bryant Edwards who was on Dick's hit list, was saved by Vincent and then turned into a star. Dick did everything he could to undermine Vincent's success and when Vincent would rightfully get perturbed about Dick and then Shelly wanting him to write up his team members, he'd grow defiant.

Vincent's coach at all costs mentality directly conflicted with the division's desire to remove all reps who were encountered having a bad call. It was a daily grind taking phone calls from pissed off customers belligerent about their bills while being required to sell more and more and he thought his team was entitled to the occasional bad call amidst all that; how dare he, right?

Vincent also felt that with his results, no one should question his decisions to – in essence – take care of his team.

We kept in touch after I left. I know things got testy between Vincent and Shelly, but Vincent produced and she had to put up with his "rogue" efforts. Shelly backed Dick for a promotion that Vincent wanted and Dick wound up getting it. Vincent made the decision to leave the division because he knew there was no future for him there; he got Shelly's OK to leave even on a lateral move. Of course, as soon as he found interested parties, she vetoed the move. It meant he could only leave on promotion.

Vincent did manage to apply to a brand new division that needed sales managers in bulk and wound up promoted into that group in the marketing and advertising division in March 2006.

I found out in January 2007 that I had three months to secure employment elsewhere within ABM or I would be laid off. In the eleventh hour, I did go to Vincent – now a Division Manager in the advertising company – for help. He got me an interview with his boss for a second-line position working directly for Vincent. I got the job and it saved my career.

At this point, though, I'll say I was tired – tired of managing call center kids and keeping up with the ever changing technology. I did well at first, but clashed with the union again when I went after some of the poor performers. Vincent saw it, knew that his boss was going to fire me and he protected me like a friend would; he made the case to – ironically – Dick Knoll, who was now actually half a level lower than Vincent in another section of ABM Telecom, to let me finish my career in his department.

But what I saw of Vincent before I left ABM Advertising in November 2007 showed me what a full circle transformation he had undergone.

Here was this young man – at 29 years old – who was a director level in the company getting up every day in front of hundreds of sales reps and managers, delivering speeches that ended in standing ovations. Once upon a time, he was an introverted sales rep who went about his business, steering clear of most of his peers and any of the office drama and politics. Now, he managed second-line managers and oversaw call center offices in three states that called into nearly 900 directories and campaigns across the country. His office was full of pictures of his beautiful newborn daughter. The executives were telling him he'd be the CEO of ABM Advertising one day.

The next time I saw Vincent was at his book signing in October 2010. Both of us had been shuffled out by ABM; Dick Knoll had orchestrated my forced retirement because he thought I was too old to be there and wanted to replace me with young, ambitious blood. Vincent had been terminated amidst a pretty intense conspiracy. Not long after, in February-March 2011, we talked briefly about me coming to manage one of his retail stores at Cellular Horizons. I had resorted to a cellular phone selling position for a reseller to make ends meet. I met with Vincent and with a couple of the owners and never got a call back.

But I've never blamed him for that. The lunch we had in February 2011 to discuss that position was the last time I saw him.

He reached out to me in April 2012 asking if I'd be a reference for him for a District Manager position at Tel-Cell Wireless, a cellular phone company coming into more prominence. Of course, I obliged.

"Is there anything else you feel we should know about Vincent Scott that would assist us in making a hiring decision?" they asked.

I thought about that one for a moment.

"Yes," I said, with my voice likely cracking just the slightest bit with the hint of nostalgia that washed over me. "Vincent is a great man and the best leader I've ever seen. I had the pleasure of being his manager when he was just starting in his career and I knew even then that he would do great things. What's amazing is that he has surpassed my expectations but he's never finished in his own vision. He's accomplished far more than anyone I know – and he's not finished. He's the best salesperson and sales manager I've ever seen, he has developed discipline and the ability to liaise with everyone in an organization, he's an incredible father and an amazing person. I'm honored to know him. And you'll never find a better candidate."

The Vocational Viewpoint, via Vincent Scott
(Republished with permission)
"The Most Important Component of the Sale: How to Lay the Foundation"

In all my years of sales, a mistake I regularly see is the belief that overcoming objections is the most vital part of the sale.

More often than any other component of the sale, my counsel has been sought on that topic – how to overcome objections – common and rare – from the customers my teams have encountered.

My team members have requested I jump into the deep end of the pool on their sales calls and visits, expecting me to dig them out of whatever hole they have found themselves in. Sometimes I am successful but, other times, I deem this impossible because no foundation has been built. Even when I am successful, I pretty much have to begin the routine all over again because vital pieces of the buildup have been omitted.

What does all of this mean?

Like not being able to skip steps in a recipe, you cannot build a successful sales relationship or visit or call without laying the foundation. This starts from even before the call is made.

First, recognize that this is a game where numbers reign king; it is a contact sport and you have to optimize your time so as to effectively cover as many leads as possible in the time allotted. Too much of anything is a bad thing and excessive preparation can be poison – do not spend so much time psyching yourself out that this lead is of good quality when the majority of the time your knock on the door, entrance into a business or cold call is met with no decision maker on the other end.

In addition, a big stumbling block occurs at the beginning of the call – if you give the decision maker the opportunity to take over control of the conversation OR if you fail to ask the right stuff while putting together your case against the customer's current program's weaknesses, you will lose.

Customers often build up an immunity from the poor salespeople which can adversely affect you if you're not careful. Anticipate it. Your mission is to progress each sales call as far through the cycle toward closing as you can and either land the deal or be able to look back and know the specific reason the customer did not believe in you and/or your product. That's it. Easy, right?

I've often found simplifying what is a typically over-complicated task helps immensely.

Asking yes or no questions, allowing the customer to take control of the call or dictate the conversation without you being able to orchestrate through sales process, or failing to recognize your role asking pointed questions designed to uncover weaknesses in current process you will use later to sell change will lead to your demise.

Don't get me wrong – they should control certain facets like answering your questions and revealing their needs (whether they are aware of them or not). You will do more listening than talking, but your talking must count and have the necessary effect at critical times.

Your introduction needs to state your name, company, your intention and *immediately transition* into a question – the first question on your itinerary. Do not give them a chance to deviate from your process. They will try and, when they do, you ***acknowledge their statement, respectfully address it and put it in its proper perspective*** and then ***immediately move right back on track into your agenda item in the sales process*** – be it your next question or, if you have enough information, **your pitch**.

You will not close them all – no one could. You will not overcome every objection. You will not win over every customer and some will take months or years to make the decision to purchase. However, you will not even make it out of the gates if you fail to set up the right foundation for your relationship.

That foundation begins from the moment you knock on that door or dial the phone. What happens next is always up to you.

The reason this is so imperative is because *if* you actually manage to get to a pitch or you later try to overcome objections from your customer, the process on your end will be half baked. Without uncovering needs and potential weaknesses in their current process from your customer, without being able to use their own words and philosophies and wants to combat objections and sell the reason for change and without knowing anything about their current situation, you do not have a leg to stand on when you are backed up against their innate desire to remove you from the call.

From the get-go, your mission is to create enough value or reason for the customer to keep you talking. This can be achieved by having a strategy, being unique, sticking to your plan and asking the right questions to elicit helpful responses and using those responses to formulate the proposed change.

Focus on finding out what makes your customer tick. Once you determine that, you must show them what their weaknesses are – make them realize what they are – and show them how what you have cures what ails them. THAT is sales. And that, my friends, is what will make you a master of the selling game.

**The Vocational Viewpoint, via Vincent Scott
(Republished with permission)
"The 10 Keys to Exceeding Expectations and Achieving Results"**

Certainly, it is not a simple feat to achieve every fleeting aspiration that materializes in our minds lest we would all be challenge- and worry-free. Yet we all dream of a better version of ourselves: one who accomplishes great things, leaves an enduring legacy and makes the world a better place. Someone who excels at work and home and is revered and can be counted on.

With all of that ambition, how does anyone fall flat? Well, do sports teams take the field without practice, coaching and the huddle? Do politicians mount a campaign sans extensive research and a well-developed platform (hmm... well, it seems some may...)?

There are keys to ensuring success over the long term which can be employed in your every task.

1. The attitude and determination that will carry you through any obstacles. Your attitude will be what forces your hand in moving forward where others quit. Your attitude will be what overshadows the fear and doubt that cloud your mind and judgment. Your determination is what ensures you stay the course despite any hiccups that pop up along the way.

2. Clearly defined goal(s) with a realistic approach. Presumably, you are attempting to tackle something that either can be or has been done. (If not, ideally you have the research to suggest it can be done.) If you are moving, but you don't know where you are moving toward, there is chaos. Sure, you may not be able to calculate the exact trajectory of your path and you may far exceed your goals; on the flip side, you also do not want to set the bar too low and stymie your strengths. Lay out the goals with a strong why behind them and plot out your path to get there.

3. Preparation: Do you have the tools necessary to reach the goals? If you are embarking on a new diet or workout routine, do you have the needed equipment and knowledge and recipes and regimen to succeed? You can have all the drive in the world but if you go into battle without the weapons you need - it's over before it begins.

4. Patience: Very few noteworthy goals can occur overnight. When we make our initial charge, however, we want to see immediate results as reinforcement of our decision. We will rarely get it, however, which is why the virtue of patience is paramount.

5. Be adaptable and open to change and tweaks to your process. We obviously identified the need for a change or a course of action up front, but as we embark and learn the terrain and identify that modifications to process are required, we must be nimble and adjust accordingly.

6. Perseverance! Just when you think everything is going along swimmingly, you'll be caught off guard with a bump in the road and how you react and respond will have a huge impact on the road ahead. Without process, it's just madness; address, adjust as needed, but get back to the process as quickly as you can.

7. Build relationships that are symbiotic, mutually beneficial. Find ways

to make contributions to the journeys of others and they will make investments in yours that will exceed your own expectations. While being an individual contributor may be much of your role or current status, having a positive impact in the lives of others will always pay off more often than not. You can learn so much from the paths of others - do so!

 8. Make the conscious decision every day and at every leg in the race to continue. The decision to execute and carry on rests solely and squarely on your shoulders. You decide if you get out of bed early every day to make time to work out. You decide if you eat right and take care of yourself. You decide if you allot enough time to properly prepare for work and get there with time to spare so you are ready to start the day. You decide whose company you keep, what you do with your talents and what you do when you hit roadblocks. Control every detail that you can control and control your response when you encounter an uncontrollable force. Continued execution can become easier to deliver due to the innate gratification from prior excellence. We want to win because we won before and we liked how it felt. We don't want to lose or fail to execute because it's an unsavory feeling and we regret not doing what we knew we should have.

 9. The ability to take most things as they come, as they need to be dealt with and to fit things into your process or bend rather than break. It means sometimes shutting your mind off to the doubt and continuing on. It means always returning to your process after addressing bumps in the road. Don't let doubts during downward times derail or deter you from a plan concocted by a clearer head.

 10. A continued quest for growth. Learn from all of the mistakes and lessons, but let go of the pain they brought when you convert it into fuel for your determination. You cannot close yourself off to new people or experiences just because your trust was broken or you faced setbacks. Doing so will leave you stunted, incomplete and certainly incapable of achieving your potential.

 Whether you are lining up New Years' resolutions or simply have a project to do, apply these principles and you'll be unstoppable.

The Vocational Viewpoint, via Vincent Scott
(Republished with permission)
"Workaholism: How to Set Limits"

 Workaholism is very real.

 Do these symptoms sound familiar? You're at home and yet compelled to fire up the laptop and check e-mail and reports and progress of projects. It's the weekend and you're hammering away on yet another presentation. You're putting out fires at 4 AM and at midnight and people comment regularly on the lack of sleep amongst your nocturnal activities. A sale happens that doesn't go to you and you're obsessed with finding out why and ensuring such a thing never happens again!

You're not alone.

Workaholics are often a product of traits established in their early environment, often the result of an upbringing where they were taught extreme levels of self-reliance and responsibility. They are constantly in competition but not necessarily with others - with their own potential! They may be obsessed with being #1 or with handling everything thrown at them at once but either way, something is driving them. It's fairly important to ensure they don't drive into a brick wall never to recover.

A workaholic in their 20's differs from those in their 30's and beyond; in our 20's we are establishing the rhythm and foundation of a career. A decade or more in, we have that tempo in place but our motivation is different. Staying ahead, keeping up, setting ourselves apart - the motivations may fluctuate but these are often the goals.

So how do we set limits that will prevent us from overdoing it?

1. Schedule and prioritize breaks/rest. Often, the workaholic is good at making a multitude of appointments and sticking to a plan. This is why it is critical we schedule down time also. Whether you are part of a family that requires your presence at dinner or kids' sporting events or date nights or you're a single in need of the occasional escape into a good book on your lunch break that frees your mind up to do its best work upon your return, you've got to make that time. Specifically when loved ones want to see you or interact, you've got to prioritize your personal life just like you're juggling all of your work commitments. It matters! Make that time, lest you'll be left with nothing but your work! And your work doesn't love you back – trust me.

2. Find outlets that will rejuvenate you. What are your interests? Do you enjoy exercise, reading, writing, films, music, sports or even just some solid sack time? When scheduling for these allowances, keep in mind that if all you ever do is work, your mind will turn to mush (yes, that's the technical term) and your effectiveness will certainly eventually diminish. Sure, you may think you can take on the world all day every day, but eventually it will wear you down. Even if it's just for a half hour a day, you need to get away - and when you do, explore something that also stimulates other parts of your mind and gives you a brief getaway.

3. When you have proven you can do it all and will do it all, expectations of you will continue to rise. So when do you limit that? Many of us never do, unfortunately, because we fear that's when somebody will pass us up as the go-to person, as #1. We think about how much money we are making or how many points we are scoring with the boss, but we rarely stop to think the toll it is taking on us and our lives. Do a personal assessment: are you satisfied with all areas of your life that you have control over? It's OK to compromise with the boss on what projects you will and can handle yourself, what you can delegate or

involve another team member on, and so forth. Ask them: "I'm currently juggling several projects. I'd love to take this one on, but I don't want the quality of any of them to suffer or be performed with less than my acceptable level of excellence. What do you suggest?" Like any "dilemma", turn it around to them and put that ball in their court. It soundly makes clear, sure, you could do it, and you're open to it, but you want to ensure it's done right. They have to respect that.

4. Re-visit your priorities. Are your workaholic ways truly planting the seeds necessary to transform into the garden of goodness you seek? Or are you just doing a lot of busy work that prevents you from exploring new or untapped aptitudes? Career is all about calibration to regularly examine the path we're on. If we are swamped with work that is not adding to the result we desire, it may be time to readjust our focus. It's awesome to have a work ethic and drive, but if it isn't driving you on the road you want to be on it's time to examine that.

Workaholics are admirable in many ways; they get the job done and they do it well. They can be counted on, but they can also be taken advantage of. Ensure that your priorities are in order, that your hard work is paying off or will and make sure that you are making time for yourself and your growth a priority!

The Vocational Viewpoint, via Vincent Scott
(Republished with permission)
"Never Give Your Audience the Excuses They Seek!"

As a sales expert or leader, it is your function to implement and execute upon process while taking care of, promoting and guiding people - your customers and your employees. Much of our work consists of diagnosing what's wrong; like baseball hitting coaches, we must inspect the mechanism and see where we fail on follow through. Like Sherlock Holmes, it's imperative we search for all potential clues, be they lurking in our audience's psyche or self-doubt, being down on some component of the product or the job, or hiding in the inner sanctum of their personal lives.

Coaching sessions for our employees are paramount - not only to the discovery, but also to the collaboration on the plan to take us forward. It is in these sessions where we revisit the documentation from our last meeting, literally re-reading the commitments we made to one another. A renewal of vows, if you will. Likewise with our follow-up's with our customers; over time, we grow to learn their needs and wants, the way they wish to be taken care of in the business sense and what is of the utmost importance to keep the relationship ticking.

Far too often, however, we are the very catalyst for the lack of progress. Why, oh why, do we insist on handing our audience the very weapon with which to kill our sales presentation? We diagnose potential concerns, yet often we blurt out the end of the caper prior to allowing our audience to self-discover.

Realize that your customers and employees don't change simply because you wish it to be so. Once they see - from your prodding, of course - that they should fear the ramifications of not changing more than they fear making a change, they will make their decision. This is the most telling time of that relationship: does your customer make the decision that just because prior attempts at pursuing a product or service of this ilk failed, they'll move forward with you because you've shown them how you are different, of value, and vital? Does your employee note that their current trajectory on the sales charts will lead to not getting that promotion or not retaining their role, and they decide that it's time to get out of their comfortable ways of failing in favor of the course of action you suggested and that the two of you plot together? Ideally, yes and yes.

Yet many coaching sessions are simply managers talking at their employees. Many sales transactions are merely sales people talking at their customers - telling them a laundry list of talking points and simply guessing at or speaking at a general scenario rather than being specific and matching product with needs.

Don't load the gun of their excuses for them! The reason people don't buy or change is because they don't see the urgency! They fear change and they are locked into what I have referenced as the aforementioned "comfortable ways of failing." When you ask a customer, "What's the issue - is it the cost? Is it the economy?," you're conceivably giving them even more reasons to say no. It's like when I ask my daughter – "Why are you in a bad mood – are you tired? Did you not get enough sleep?" I've provided an excuse for antics. State your business, and immediately go into asking about theirs. You're in search of clues - and even if you solve the case early - don't blurt it out! Nobody likes spoilers!

"In my extensive work in your industry, I've been told there is a shift in what you and your competition are doing in this field - do you find that to be the case, and how have you approached it?" It's fine and great to use your hypotheses, but don't give them a reason to shut you down and don't deviate from the tried and true method of gaining all your evidence from their own mouths. There is no better way to overcome objections than weaving in your audience's own words when diagnosing, when pitching, and when closing.

What not to do: "What's the issue out there on your sales calls - why aren't we selling more of Metric X? Are we not offering it? Do you not feel comfortable with the product?" is all over the place; we've demonstrated as leaders that we're a bit lost, trying to prod and trying to get some confession that may never come. News flash: we're not looking for desired answers here. We're not looking to lead the witness. Our goal is self-discovery on their part.

"Joe/Mary Rep - your metrics indicate we aren't closing Metric X near as often as your peers. Why are customers refusing your recommendation?" "At what point is the call going awry?" "Let me hear your pitch of Metric X." Stop there. In this instance, start from the result and trace your way back to the cause.

I believe that every customer wants to be successful and each of your employees do as well. That said, each of us get off track at certain points for a variety of reasons: past failure in the area, the strain of managing multiple priorities, the uncertainty of the future. It's always up to us to rekindle the flame in our audience. They will always give you a myriad of reasons for complacency; like detectives, it is incumbent upon us to wade through the murk, ask very specific questions about the result that are geared to tracing back to the cause, and ultimately decide - can I show this audience why their lack of belief should be altered in favor of the outcome I am offering?

Your audience already has their reasoning, founded or not, so giving them additional excuses or simply being conversational without purpose will go nowhere. Yet this is one of the most common mistakes of management and selling - conversation without purpose. Recall again that people and process must govern all we do; the part of the process in this case is processing why your audience is struggling with the component being analyzed and there's no better way to do so than to ask questions designed to uncover the truth.

The Vocational Viewpoint, via Vincent Scott
(Republished with permission)
"Humble Pie: An Essential Morsel for Team Success"

When you are great at something, you often want the world to know. As human beings, we have an innate, natural craving for recognition and respect, and often we feel it necessary to ensure everyone we come into contact knows specifically what we can do, how well we do it and that we'd gladly do more for more money. From being interviewed for a job or new project to giving a description of your role and contributions to any inquiring party, projecting a team mentality and forgoing over-indulgent self-promotion is best.

Prior to acquiring polish and business acumen in our careers, we often express our love of self in the wrong fashion. We should absolutely be big advocates for ourselves! Sometimes, we may be the only ones out there evangelizing for ourselves so we have to be our own biggest fans. It is vital that we know our strengths and areas of opportunity, our goals and what we are doing to attain them, and ways we can showcase and sharpen our skills. However, no one likes a braggart; some tweaks to your delivery can make your message so much more impactful.

1. Drop the "I's": Think about your dialogue when asked about your job environment or when you send out communications - specifically those where you will be making mention of process you are involved in or projects you have contributed on. Re-read written verbiage and minimize usage of the word "I," and do the same when speaking, always looking for ways instead to illustrate how

you have worked with a team to achieve results.

    Hiring managers, promoting managers, visiting managers, general audiences whose attention you desire - they are looking for someone who embraces and is inviting. They want to be enticed with warm and fuzzy feelings of camaraderie. They want to see that you play nicely in the sandbox with everyone you share space with. They don't want to hear how great thou art. Show through your willingness to help others, don't tell. Your message will get across, trust me.

    2. Not everything is a competition. Do you find yourself feeling the necessity of one-upping others? Do you have to win at literally all costs? If the cost is alienating someone whose support you need, making someone on your team look bad or others having a genuine feeling of inferiority around you, you're doing more harm than good. Remember: find ways to connect with others, add value to your relationships with them and always offer to support or provide service wherever you go.

    Gaps may exist between you and others, but you can bridge as many as possible with genuine addition of value. Focus on process and teamwork, and other pieces will fall into place. Rather than be intimidated by your skills and reluctant to endorse or encourage you, peers and others in your circle of influence will be more open and honest to you and will legitimately look for ways to engage you and sing your praises.

    3. Look for ways to involve others. Sure, you may be the one carrying more weight than others on this project. However, what about the next project when you could learn a substantial amount from others on your team and may need more of their support? When you are talking about your current projects, even if you are the star, find ways to point out the contributions of others, draw them into the discussions and ensure everyone gets input and credit. While you absolutely want to make sure your heavy lifting is woven into that description, do not draw so much attention to yourself that you make others uncomfortable or sound slightly insignificant.

    While you may be looking to impress a certain audience currently and monopolizing the attention may aid you in the short term, you never know when you will encounter these peers or team members again. You may not know where and to whom their circle of influence extends. Do what brings the most value to the largest group of people.

    Other people, whomever they are, look for a variety of attributes in you: work ethic, teamwork, success under stress, ability to meet deadlines, multiple metrics and dependability. While your sparkling results in one or more of these areas certainly can speak volumes, what speaks more is your literal mastery of all and your willingness to learn and contribute even more.

    It's one thing to do great things or have great results. It's entirely another to add enough value to the environments of so many others that you make a significant impact. Focus on how you can best contribute to the team, aid in the success of others and be the consummate team player, and you'll get your just desserts.

CHAPTER 1: MAJESTECH

The flight was only 2 hours, 22 minutes from Minneapolis-St. Paul to Washington, D.C. Vincent would spend his time reading, from his preferred aisle seat over a black coffee and diet cola.

He exited the plane with his backpack and garment bag, hailed a cab and began the trek to his hotel.

It was his third time in D.C. for Majestech-Ware, a prominent hardware and software company selling worldwide. Vincent had held the rank of Regional Business Manager, a glorified player-coach title where he oversaw sales in parts of Minnesota, Wisconsin, Iowa, and North and South Dakota. He had sales liaisons in numerous cities through those five states, disseminated work and he was often the one driving leads and transacting. There were retail locations and business-to-business reps scattered throughout his territory whose numbers rolled up to him. His primary competition was other resellers of their product, of which there were several.

When Vincent left Tel-Cell Wireless in August 2013, he thought he had closed the door on his sales management career and he was perfectly at peace with the decision. Shortly thereafter, he learned the management consultant firm he was duped into joining was a catastrophe. He swallowed his pride, putting daughter Elizabeth's interests first and inquired about his old job even after torching the bridge in an exit interview. They moved on.

He applied to countless jobs again and utilized the outreach and connecting mechanisms he had learned. But traction could not come soon enough.

Able to rekindle talks with Apricot Innovations, whom he had rebuffed in April 2012 for more money and autonomy with Tel-Cell, it was settled that an opportunity would open for him January 2014.

Vincent was hesitantly optimistic but ultimately yielded to the inevitability he would start for this staple in technology. He ceased job hunting and enjoyed the final weeks of the year with family.

January 1 came and went. Calls to his contacts within Apricot went unanswered. "I know, I know, surely they are just on holiday vacations," Vincent told himself, trying to quell the thoughts of doom in the recesses of his mind. They had courted him once, were ecstatic he re-engaged and promised him this role. Vincent was due a break after years of clawing back to relevance. Just a little bit longer…

The first week of January bled into the second and third. Finally, to force a response, Vincent reached out to his would-be boss's boss with new year tidings and expressing his joy at beginning work there during January.

It did force a response, albeit not the desired one. She instructed Nate Schulman, his hiring manager, to reach out and deliver news that the position – once inevitable – was not vacant and there was no timetable for it to be.

In November 2013, Vincent had politely declined overtures from once frenemy Mitch Finkleson – a fiercely competitive peer from his time at Tel-Cell. Mitch had gotten on as a territory manager with Majestech-Ware and had referred Vincent for a role he would later revisit after the snub from Apricot.

Vincent was surprised that Mitch, by whom he had been goaded into trading verbal barbs at Tel-Cell, had recommended Vincent, but as these roles were aligned, Mitch stood to receive a referral bonus and a boost to results. He was not a huge fan of Vincent, but did think highly of his work ethic and probability that he would drive up results in his own territory.

February 2014, Vincent had gotten yet another lowball job offer to return as a sales manager – starting out $40K with small quarterly bonus potential (one-quarter of his earnings in his best year), 50+ hour work weeks and nights and weekends. His decorated resume, while putting him certainly in the ranks of those who could be a sales director or higher, could not crack him into those inner circles. Having not originated in Minneapolis or St. Paul, he had few contacts if any who were high enough to pull him into powerful positions. He had also torched his last three employers upon exit. *Ill-advised, but deserved*, he told himself.

Vincent was reluctant to revisit talks with Mitch. It was a pride thing, it was the fact it was more of a player-coach role. Vincent had not been in charge of his own sales process and results in 11 years! He felt it was yet another step backward, despite the salary being competitive with Tel-Cell and the bonus potential being even greater.

Pride for Vincent at this stage in the game meant far less than it did in his supernova 20's. He called Mitch and the role – which had been filled but vacated in the final background stages – was still available. He interviewed with Mitch's boss, then her boss, then assumed the role in March 2014.

Vincent had been in the telecom, Internet and wireless games, which featured technology in the mediums that utilized these innovations: typically phones, cellular phones and desktop computers. While he could write his own basic computer programs and games as a kid thanks to his aunt's best friend, interest in burgeoning technology waned years ago in favor of writing, reading, selling, girls and alcohol.

It was overwhelming. Excruciatingly overwhelming. Vincent second-guessed the decision akin to his early days at ABM Telecom 13 years prior. It was humbling and especially challenging learning fundamentals and device specs he didn't particularly care about from kids 10-17 years his junior and trying to breathe life into leads that had grown long cold.

Casey Carnes, whom Vincent had dated in recent years when he was not seeing Emily Nance or his daughter's mother Abby Winters, was actually able to make him feel better.

"You're going through what we normal people go through," she proffered. "That's how I feel when I start a new job."

"My brain hurts every day, usually after just a couple of hours," Vincent responded. "I feel old and out of place and out of touch and I can't stand it. I have no idea what I'm doing and I feel like an idiot on these customer calls and around these tech whiz kids who probably wonder what the hell I'm doing here."

"It's good for you," she countered. "You know, I hate giving you too many compliments because I want to keep your ego in the stratosphere, but you're the smartest guy I've ever met. You're brilliant. You can absolutely do this, but it will take some time. Who cares what anybody else thinks, if they think less of you at all. You earned the job, you've dominated at everything you've ever done and you'll do it again."

"But what if I don't? Doesn't the luck have to run out eventually?"

"Think of how far you've come in the last few years. What I admire most about you is that you're willing to take risks and you don't give up. You don't have to be #1 all the time, but I have a feeling you will be here, too."

It was the boost he needed – to hear this assessment of his talents and perseverance. To know that someone who knew him better than most actually believed in him.

Vincent came to accept he was here to be a contributor. He needed to pay the bills and support Elizabeth and the last few years had quieted his bombast. He would come in every day, do the job, be responsive, ask questions, make internal and external connections, perform outreach, follow up, learn, and use time with Elizabeth, exercise and vodka to erase any pains along the way.

It was now January 2016. Vincent had taken this incubational brand new role in March 2014 and had been #1 on their aggregate scorecard ranking out of 71-to-116 total peers every quarter he was in role.

The stay in Washington would feature a welcome reception with him and his peers the first night, seminars on their products and upcoming releases on day two and would culminate with an awards ceremony on night three.

Wedged in-between, the general manager of the entire regional business manager division, Luther Petty, had recruited Vincent for a new position – a market manager role – that would involve him overseeing one of four business markets across the world. Vincent and three other candidates would have final interviews on Day 2 for a position Petty had informed Vincent he was the top candidate for when he talked him out of taking two other potential promotions for which Vincent had been pursued in recent months.

To cap it off, Vincent was the logical choice for the Business Manager of the Year Award for the final night, and was asked to speak to the assembly in the closing hours.

It had not been 2 years of fun and games. While Vincent did learn substantially and enjoyed plenty of freedom in how he crafted his role, there was next to no support outside of his peer group.

His formal training took place six months after he came on board, as he went to D.C. and met the 42 peers who had come on since the last training.

Vincent had been offered the choice of starting a week earlier than he did, which was Elizabeth's spring break week he had made plans with her for. The younger Vincent may have chosen differently, but the Dad chose to be with his daughter.

Vincent was not outspoken nor was he even talkative when he was unsure of himself in a role – he didn't feel he had yet earned the right to speak up or offer feedback. With six months under his belt and already having topped the very first full quarter of this new division's scorecard, he was walking into this session already notorious.

Like all sales roles, his previous ones included, there were already haters trying to undermine his results. Vincent had landed what would eventually amount to a $4 million deal from a travel company who resold the equipment to their subscribing companies and purchased in small increments, meaning Vincent's sales board realized results from this win on a daily basis. Peers felt it wasn't fair he was recognized for these results every day on the sales report.

Furthermore, he had hooked up one of the device sellers who sold Majestech tablets in his market with some amenities at their St. Paul retail store, which was well within his right. When the seller, Mel Sparks, sold a $2 million opportunity to a company that had previously bought strictly through resellers, he threw the sale to Vincent.

Big wins weren't the tale of the tape, though. Like trying to sell every customer he talked to on the phones in 2002 and making 5 times as many sales as his peers, he did not discriminate against opportunities including something as small as a tablet case or a charger or even a single, "old-school" desktop computer. Every sale mattered, no matter how small, and they could and often would beget big money relationships. He would respond quickly to every need, engage the right team for a quote or do it himself if they weren't fast enough, conduct workshops and events to grow knowledge and awareness, develop mutually beneficial relationships with several local companies he could trade referrals with, and he averaged 11 times as many sales as his peers and even 4 times the closest competitor Melton Stein from the West Region.

When a division is in its relative infancy, the rules and terrain are still being defined. A rough estimate of goals is fleshed out. Half-baked processes are the best that can be proposed because they often do not even know what they will encounter yet. The rule of thumb is roll out the regulations (and sometimes the dice) and be nimble in adapting depending on where things go.

Majestech-Ware had been around since 1995. The leadership team was brilliant. The verdict on Luther Petty was still out.

He was a cheerleader; full of chants and generic talking points and empty promises. He told Vincent he would visit Minneapolis six times before he actually did it, and when he did, it was merely to recruit him for this role – which he desperately needed Vincent in if the division was going to start heading toward its potential. He was tough to get ahold of and tougher to get an answer or resolution from.

Because the division was new, many processes were being tweaked along the way and there were numerous gaps in process. Orders were taking too long. Large customers would often have to go through unnecessary checks and balances to get a credit line. The administrative team that was paid to process the work was hit or miss; some of them were stellar (and Vincent was sure to not only utilize them in critical times but also to send their bosses positive feedback and have fruit baskets delivered). It was difficult enough to sell against resellers that had been the market for years in a department open for months with often non-competitive pricing and delayed shipping, but to have his orders kicked back citing incorrect shipping tax (when he was correct), questioning discounts on a weekly basis that had been approved for months, or telling Vincent it would take four weeks for them to build and ship a custom device and winding up taking eleven, even the great Vincent Scott was having a hard time holding it all together.

To top it off, every team in the district had to hit goal or Vincent got next to nothing on parts of his bonus payout. There were quarters where Vincent was tops in the land but being paid less than peers on final write-up or being fired for poor results.

When they provided the feedback of the hurdles they were facing, powers that be in this division – not wanting to ask for additional resources because they were already paid too much and doing too little – chose to ignore it and call these critics negative. It was a fruitless cause.

The division was a no-brainer and was already making more money than initially anticipated with no one breathing down their necks to do so – why rock the boat by admitting they were doing a shoddy job of managing and optimizing it?

Vincent had, however, learned quite well from his previous experience that questioning leadership or being one of those outspoken crusaders wound up nowhere good.

In his training in D.C., Vincent did not need to seek out others; he had plenty seeking him out. They knew he was the top seller every month so everyone at least knew who he was whether they were making excuses why they couldn't catch up or not. His peers fell in one of two categories: those who wanted to meet him and learn from him and those who made up reasons why him being #1 every week was a farce.

Vincent was more passive than usual, not voicing concerns in breakout sessions but quick to answer when asked why he was so successful and what he had done up to this point. He had no qualms about sharing his success stories and best practices. Him driving results in the five states he had a hand in certainly did not take food off the table anywhere else and vice versa.

He roomed with Fred Hampton, a 46-year old former motorcycle salesman from Houston who, like Vincent, had found ways to make shortcuts in process and discounting and was the top seller of the South. They struck up conversations with Drew Cosby from L.A., Mindy Wolsey of Portland, Drake Telemon from Fort Worth, Garrison Reece from San Antonio, Stu Romatowski from Miami, and the list goes on.

The "star" of the bunch was Glenn Timmons – he was the Washington, D.C. Regional Manager. His team got all of the headquarters referrals and sales, he was in the training videos, and had been awarded the first "Business Manager of the Quarter" award for the previous quarter – Vincent's first at #1. He didn't really talk to Vincent apart from barely acknowledging Vincent's "hello." And it was actually his top seller who did most of the prospecting and closing and the team knew it even if the leadership was aloof.

Some things hadn't changed; Vincent's and Fred's room 208 wound up the "party room" after hours where everyone stopped by, rehearsed their presentations, had a few beers and chatted about the state of the business.

It was from this experience that these folks realized everyone was grappling with the same debilitating issues that were going unaddressed by Luther Petty and his incompetence.

Vincent was heartened to attend a CIO summit in St. Paul just weeks later. The speakers were successful CIO's from all over the Twin Cities and it was attended by 11,000 IT professionals from all over Minnesota. While many of the topics were still over Vincent's head, he ran into a handful of his new contacts from his Majestech exploits. The most impactful piece of all was a speaker at the innovation presentation.

"I've never applied for another position, much less one of my promotions, in my life," remarked Thomas Julio, one of the panel speakers and CIO of McHenry Manufacturing in Minneapolis. "I've seen problems and I've become the solution. Period. I've tried to add value in whatever I do. And I've just kept going, regardless of results. They've always come."

That line stuck with Vincent.

His role felt like a dead end step back and far cry from his trajectory to CEO at ABM that was abruptly cut short. While he was quite successful, there was no position between himself and Luther Petty. Roles elsewhere in the company were very niche and being considered for one would require technical competencies Vincent lacked. The rest of the company was also rather oblivious to the goings-on and wins from Vincent's channel; no one was serving as an ambassador for their group and it was looked at like the minor leagues.

He was treading water in complacency and boredom. No more. Come hell or high water, Vincent would make some noise and create a path.

That day, Vincent challenged himself to start a "Dear Abby" of Sales and Sales Leadership called "The Vocational Viewpoint by Vincent Scott" which he would write daily and promote and grow via grassroots marketing.

He saw the problems in his division and he decided to rally the troops from the underground and form a support network. Their boss wasn't doing it, but he would. Rather than join the group complaining about Luther Petty, he would simply be the answer.

Vincent reached out via instant messenger to the aforementioned contacts and then some, just seeing if they wanted to become part of a weekly chat on the business. They would share frustrations and best practices and it would guarantee upward movement of results and would lessen frustration. Vincent would be the hero that could be in the shadows. He didn't need the recognition he wasn't getting – he had boxes and boxes of awards and certificates spanning fifteen years that meant nothing; he desired bringing value to the masses, leaving his mark and making a legacy.

It was inevitable that one of the managers Vincent reached out to would reveal his intentions to Luther Petty.

Petty, who was already more than aware of Vincent's past successes as a director level leading hundreds of folks, public speaking and books, interviews, sales videos and social media dominance, reached out to Vincent right away. He wanted to keep this above board; he wanted control of it. He couldn't let whatever control he did have over this organization slip away, despite the fact Vincent had no intention of taking any.

"I want you to put together a platform for driving peer results," he said. "I thought of you for a project like this and then heard you were having some great conversations about collaboration with your peers."

Vincent had heard it all before. *No, Luther, you heard I was talking to my peers and wanting to help them and you're making it your idea.*

"Absolutely, Luther, I'd be glad to."

"Great, Vincent. You'll present it on our weekly global business calls. Get everyone involved, have guest speakers. Ask me for anything you need."

Vincent tried to involve Luther but never got responses. Luther indicated he wanted control over sending the e-mail questionnaires out every week but when Luther didn't even send the first one or respond to it, Vincent had to do it himself. And he never asked for help from Luther again. He owned it completely.

Vincent crafted a platform entitled Collaboration Station. He would send weekly communication to the entire team of Regional Business Managers soliciting their ideas for topics, their best practices, their advice and tips and tricks. He would take a couple hours per week to compile it all into a presentation. He would fill in considerable gaps when many peers – like the "stars" Glenn Timmons and Melton Stein – would shun every request he sent, choosing not to share their ideas. He would be witty and brilliant and bold and funny and on a stage of hundreds (albeit virtually) like he had once been. It brought him back to life.

Vincent knew that it would take time but it would lead to promotion. Somewhere. Sometime. It didn't matter. He just wanted to feel like he was doing something and not wasting his talents anymore.

Soon after, Jessica Marks – Luther's boss – started dropping hints of a

Market Manager position that would be created in four parts of the world and Vincent was the frontrunner for North America.

Vincent did 23 Collaboration Stations in all. Sometimes, he would be pre-empted with zero notice after spending two hours during an already busy week putting together his usual quality presentation. Other times, his segment would be cut from 5 minutes to 3 to 2 out of an hour-long call. Collaboration and best practices were clearly not that big of a priority!

Luther told Vincent on numerous occasions he wanted other people speaking, but no one had interest outside of a few. Vincent got a handful involved when he could, struggled to put together content when sometimes only three peers would respond but no one seemed to care or appreciate it. His struggling or new peers absolutely did, but no one above. It was the typical predicament that befell Vincent Scott.

Vincent was surprised then when Luther Petty make the trip to Minneapolis to recruit him for Market Manager of the Americas. His first interview was with Zeke Walton and he blew it away. His second was with CeCe Carlisle and it went even better. It seemed like a formality at this point. Even Jessica Marks – Luther's boss – had already called Vincent to talk about what they were going to do together and which markets she wanted him to focus on most.

Vincent was still leaving nothing to chance, reaching out to numerous contacts he had made in his two years that resided in Texas, Missouri, Illinois, Indiana, Washington, California and Florida to write letters of recommendation to Luther on his behalf.

After all these years from his past where he had tried to fight every battle only to lose the war, Vincent was doing everything right – earning political allies, winning people over and influencing the masses. Everything was falling into place. It was perfect. Absolutely perfect.

In the meantime, Vincent had been approached by two other segments of the business to recruit him to either the government or education side for similar roles with significantly more money. Luther Petty had talked him out of both as he was frontrunner for Market Manager of the Americas in this division he had already mastered. Now, it was the final interview with Luther in Washington, D.C. in January 2016.

"Brother, you're going to kill it," Saul Portman, longtime workhorse salesman under Vincent's tutelage, confirmed prior to the trip. Saul had worked with Vincent for 5 years now between Cellular Horizons, Tel-Cell Wireless and Majestech-Ware.

"Thanks, Saul. And, then, what's next?" Vincent found himself asking Saul for probably the fifth time in five years.

"We'll figure it out. We always do."

They fist-bumped.

Vincent had dropped Elizabeth off while his wife worked overnight at the hospital near their home and he made his way to the nation's capital to fight for his right to regain and surpass the standing he had lost 6 years before.

The Jack Johnson Story

Much of my childhood featured moving to different parts of the country. We lived in Kansas City, in Minneapolis, Chicago and then Mankato, Minnesota, as my Dad took on different roles in retail management through the first 11 years of my life. I lived in good baseball towns, grew up a good Midwesterner and our family fit in well in Mankato. They stayed there.

It was my 4th grade year I met Eddie Haskins. Both of our mothers were teachers and we found ourselves with similar interests in the way of 80's music and cartoons and movies. I still vividly recall his 12th birthday party when we celebrated the lyrical catalogue of Tom Cochrane.

Eddie had been lifelong friends with Vincent Scott. Vincent was in 5th grade when I was in 4th and Eddie 3rd; interestingly, because of when I started school, I was a few weeks older than Eddie. We were thick as thieves for the next decade.

This story is about Vincent – he has always been an interesting specimen. I've always understood him where others don't. His passions have always included music, movies, arts – I clicked with Eddie and Vincent because of the intellectual conversations and banter but also because of the unabashed silliness.

Vincent, Eddie and I were inseparable but also quite different; the differences played out even more elaborately as we grew older. Eddie was exactly as he presented himself to be. I used to care quite a bit about what others thought of me and I tried to stick with the popular group – something I jettisoned as I aged. Vincent had people gravitate toward him magnetically, but was always competitive and seemed to care more about perception and being the best. He's changed considerably over the years, but his life has changed him. He's been molded by his battles in his career and personal life akin to my molding at the hands of Afghanistan in the Navy, albeit on different scales and magnitudes. Once we both hit certain points, we were never the same.

Vincent had skipped second grade, so he was already friends with many of the kids in my class. We were the ones he was paired with for age group type stuff, like basketball, like Cub and Boy Scouts, like baseball. Even in high school, he spent the majority of free times with me, with our friends Mitchell Grissom and Julian Cooper from my class, and Eddie. We were on the same teams for Scholar Bowl and when the basketball coach started a golf team we were both on there as well.

Thing was with Vincent, he wouldn't admit it to anyone but he was insecure; he had to be the best at absolutely everything. I love the guy, but he'd shave strokes from his golf score because he couldn't stand to lose. He used to be boastful – only because he wanted to be liked and wanted us to be impressed by him. He wanted to be the center of attention. I know it was because growing up, he was an only child and because the social standing and successes and expectations of his parents were intimidating. He put tremendous pressure on himself to be the most popular kid in the room and the best at everything.

I think some of that went away – he definitely grew more humble in the wake of aging and experience. There are other parts of it that took different forms. One thing that never left was his willingness to do whatever it took to be the best at everything he did.

I've known a lot of people in my day, between the Navy, my smattering of previous jobs, my time in coffee shops and philosophy classes in college and my travels. Of them all, only Eddie and Vincent are the ones who have always been a constant. Sure, we've gone months at a time with zero contact. We've all had times when we've annoyed and been annoyed by another in the trio. We've grown older, have less hair, put on some pounds at times and had women and kids enter the picture (and exit the picture and come back). But of everywhere I've been stationed in the Navy, Vincent is the only friend who's visited me at each base. We've lost touch at times when we've been in relationships or tied up in career but when relationships end or change or we happen to be in Mankato for a holiday, we do everything we can to have even brief visits featuring witty banter, beverages and stories.

Some of my greatest adventures – you know, the ones that aren't classified – have been with Vincent. We saw a lot of concerts in our youth: the Rolling Stones, Aerosmith, Bob Dylan, Brian Setzer, Lynyrd Skynyrd, ZZ Top – and a Beatles tribute band where we had to run to our favorite pizza place when nature called and I set the Guinness Book record for lengthiest urination.

We hung out at a lot of downtown Mankato hot spots, a lot of coffee shops and breakfast joints late at night and early in the morning. We did a lot of writing – mostly poetry, sometimes songs, sometimes short stories. Some were serious, some were spoofs of pop culture that we did with Eddie. In high school, Mitchell's large backyard featured a treehouse we dubbed "The Cheetah Club" where we would listen to Sinatra, smoke cigars and drink whiskey. We were old souls, ahead of our time. In past lives, we were probably Rat Packers or some facsimile thereof.

Vincent's parents had the 15th green of the municipal golf course behind their backyard and he and I would take our clubs through the fence and just start playing (we had memberships, of course). We played golf every day (and were actually really good back in college)! I've seen his best round – a 68 – and I saw his worst…when he shot 72 on 9. He wanted to quit, but he stayed the course (see what I did there? Eddie would like that joke…).

We were in a handful of stage plays together – some with Eddie as well. We were all pretty theatrical. In numerous ways. Vincent was really good – his most prominent role was when he was the lead shepherd in the Christmas production in 8th grade. Everyone flooded him and his parents with excitement to see him in high school plays – and he purposely walked away from it all. In fact, when Eddie and I got in a play together, Vincent was a bit jealous hearing us talk about it all the time and managed to lobby the producers for a bit, non-speaking role. He wound up creating his own lines, which were directors-approved. True Vincent style.

Something I feel, in hindsight, was very telling regarding Vincent's choice to pursue greatness in something he has a struggle with his affection for (like sales) is the fact he didn't declare his business major until his junior year. In fact, up until that point, many of his classes were with me in the liberal arts building! I'd pick him up on the side of the road with my coffee thermos full of the magical elixir with a strong splash of whiskey in the mornings and we'd wax poetic, listen to Zeppelin and ride around before screenwriting class or art of film class. We spent countless hours reading and writing and speaking of philosophy and girls and music while drinking coffee and hitting on waitresses.

My major life events to follow included a summer at Yellowstone National Park when I converted to Buddhism in 1999, moving to Denver for a few years in 2002 and coming home in a few more years when the money ran out. I got married in 2005 and we had our sons in 2007 and 2009. Vincent bailed me out of trouble a time or two, was in my wedding and was there when my sons were born; he's the only person I can say all of that for.

He's said the same of me. Vincent moved away in 2001. His grandfather committed suicide just weeks later. He had some tumultuous relationships with Julie, Stacy (who was married), Abby (whom, yes, he definitely loved all along – he told me so), Phoebe (who he saw when he didn't know Abby was pregnant and who he later saw when she was married), and then for years it was an on-again off-again rollercoaster between Abby, Casey Carnes and Emily Nance. That rollercoaster finally ended in 2015. In the interim, he was also promoted four times at ABM only to have them put the screws to him when he stood up to a corrupt department head. He toiled around in roles afterward where he overworked himself to get back to the level he lost. His dad had a heart attack and a stroke, both which nearly ended badly. He spent years and tens of thousands of dollars in court battling ABM and Abby.

His saving grace was Elizabeth. She changed everything. Vincent loved her more than himself, which achieved a few things: he learned patience, humility, the value of family and that while he had given every ounce of himself to corporate America for years, the real value was in loving his little girl.

In high school and college, Vincent put on this charade of being a cross between James Bond and his *Beverly Hills 90210* idol Dylan McKay. Yes, I invoked *90210*. He acted like nothing affected him – though he couldn't fool me. It was more important to him that he was perceived as a ladies' man or too cool or mysterious whether he had any feelings on the matter or for anything, for that matter. Fortunately, he was never a jerk; he never took it too far. He did have real emotions, but they dulled over time due to the aforementioned.

I still think of Vincent as the carefree guy I had coffee with and played golf with and snuck vodka to my upstairs attic with while we watched *Ghostbusters* on the tiny television. We had these old green chairs that were so comfortable. With Eddie, we'd memorize these films and laugh about them for hours. Vincent was so passionate about creating these musical countdowns we'd put to tape; I thought it was a little silly sometimes, but now that I have a few of these CD's Vincent made for me of us announcing our favorite songs like deejays and telling stories that are now twenty years old, I cherish them quite a bit.

They are also evidence of how much I've changed. As much as all of us figured we'd be out of Mankato, I wound up back there for a while. Eddie teaches at our old high school. Vincent never returned. I worked a lot of different jobs prior to leaving for the Navy in November 2007 to provide better for my family, but only briefly as what I set out to be: a college professor. Go figure. Vincent has pushed me to write more, which I really need to make the time to do…

Ironically, in 2007, I even interviewed with Vincent's bosses for a sales rep job in his department. I didn't get it, and didn't really expect to. Frankly, I don't think Vincent wanted me there; but *not* because he thought I couldn't do it. It was because he didn't want to wish that life on me.

If our journeys have had parallels, I'll say what has changed my behaviors and outlook and perspective the most was my seven months in Afghanistan. Sure, I wasn't in combat and I won't claim to have had the most harrowing experience of all time, but things I saw, things that occurred right next to me, memories of that time that still keep me up…and the fact that I returned and just felt out of place in my own life…it forced transformation for me.

What forced transformation for Vincent's outlook is this: while Elizabeth was his saving grace and the reason he was able to ensure everything he encountered, the culmination of the end of his three-way race of females altered his longstanding perspective permanently.

He met Abby in 2006 and became entangled in a workplace fling that resulted in her pregnancy. For 2007 he was torn between Abby and Phoebe. In 2008, he was caught up in Phoebe who was ultimately coerced to forsake him for her job – and she all too willingly accepted despite Vincent doing the opposite when he was faced with the same decision. After Vincent lost his job, he found solace in Casey Carnes, who had come off a very brutal divorce and custody fight with an abusive ex. And, that was his pattern for years…

Vincent refused to commit – to anything – outside of his career and Elizabeth. Greatest salesman ever. Phenomenal father. But when he and Kacie pledged "no relationships" and she wanted one not too long after, he shied away. Sure, there were some other girls in the mix, but it generally went Abby-Kacie-Emily.

It was October 2005 when Anita and I were planning our wedding that we matched Emily and Vincent together to walk down the aisle. Emily was single at the time and we figured they'd be a perfect match. She was in school with Anita to become a nurse. By the time our wedding rolled around the following summer, Emily was in a relationship. The two thought nothing of it. Vincent saw Emily again at the hospital when our boys were born. They made small-talk.

In the advent of Facebook (which I slowly adapted to – hell, I didn't even have a cell phone until 2001!), Vincent sent a friend request to Emily in 2010 toward the end of the year. Emily's marriage was on the rocks. Vincent was post-Abby and post-ABM. Another two wounded birds connected. After Emily's separation was official and divorce filed for, the two took their harmless Facebook messenger chats about life and kids to spending time together and playdates for the kids. They also both liked *90210*. Gag.

In 2011, they became closer and became intimate – but, of course, it was "no relationships." Emily was Anita's best friend, so it did make for some enjoyable time together the four of us. Inevitably, Emily fell in love with Vincent and wanted to take it further. Not only did commitment to a relationship scare Vincent, but he avoided conflict at all costs and typically upon a wrong turn in these female entanglements, he'd run for the hills.

One of the three was always waiting in the wings. Vincent never led any of them on, but would float to Abby until an old issue would resurface. He'd disappear for a few days and she'd rekindle with an old flame, sending him reeling into the arms of Emily. Then Kacie. Then Abby would invite him in after an Elizabeth exchange and the cycle continued.

Kacie lived in Mankato and after some pretty epic arguments about their future, or lack thereof, in early 2015, they cut off communication and both were too stubborn to talk to the other again.

Emily and Vincent had a falling out shortly thereafter when Vincent chose to propose to Abby. It didn't work out. Months later, out of the blue, Emily missed Vincent and on a whim invited him to a movie. They caught up and started spending mostly platonic time together for several weeks. Vincent had been through the ringer with Abby once more and felt he may have finally come to a conclusion; he was ready to be in a relationship with Emily.

Emily and Anita, on the other hand, had a bit of estrangement. It was a cycle with them; they were very strong-willed women and were opinionated and – similar to Emily and Vincent – Emily and Anita would take time from one another rather than swiftly solve their conflicts.

The morning of January 28, 2015, Vincent called me at 7:38 AM. I was on the naval base in Millington, Tennessee, but just prior to reporting to my shift.

"Hello, Vincent! A bit early?"

"Yeah," his troubled tone came from the other side. "Jack, I just wanted to tell you that I just learned Emily died in a car accident last night."

There was forced silence, like the wind being knocked out of me. Little shocked me anymore as my experiences had significantly muted my senses, but learning that a longtime friend I had been close with since college has suddenly died certainly conjured up any bit of surprise I had left.

"Wow – Vincent – I'm so sorry to hear this. Does Anita know?"

Anita was back living in Mankato near her and my parents with our two boys while I was stationed here.

"I left a message with her just before calling."

"Let me know when the visitation and funeral are. I'll be there."

I flew in that Friday evening to Minnesota and Vincent picked me up at the airport. Anita was coming in by car and was staying with Emily's family. We all went to the visitation; Vincent brought Elizabeth and we were all ushered in first like family.

Certainly a somber evening; not unlike any other wake.

Afterwards, we went back to Vincent's apartment. Elizabeth went to bed. Vincent and I engaged in the only kind of therapy I know to work (he and I have tried plenty): we watched *Ghostbusters*, drank copious amounts of vodka and beer, respectively, and just talked. About everything.

Vincent still speaks vaguely of this time as when he drew his line in the sand and made the decision to live every day as it comes. Sure, there are a lot of clichés written like this, but for him it meant bringing his "A" game to the table every morning and wiping out what was past. It meant not obsessing about past or future but focusing on the present day while making every attempt to make positive deposits in his bank of life.

I haven't seen Vincent much over the last several years. He makes a point to visit when he can and we see one another in Mankato when we both happen to be there once or twice a year. In 2007, we e-mailed quite frequently. We dubbed it the "Dangling Conversation" due to my obsession with Simon and Garfunkel in my youth. Then it became the "Sunday Conversation" when we would just book time on Sunday afternoon whether I was making a long drive home or to the airport or just sitting in my hovel alone and away from my family.

Our children met July 26, 2009: it was an epic visit of my sons, Eddie's son and Vincent's Elizabeth. We met at the Lincoln Park near our childhood homes where we played frequently as kids. As frenetic as our adult lives get, with my time in Afghanistan with death right outside the door, Eddie working his tail off teaching at our old high school and Vincent enslaved to the man, these moments where we can step outside our current lives are surreal. Our kids were standing around talking about *Star Wars*, for crying out loud.

These temporary but needed blips of life, like watching Eddie direct the pep band at halftime of a basketball game from our high school alma mater (featuring "Don't Stop Believin'" to Vincent's delight), having impromptu James Bond marathons at Mitch Grissom's, revisiting and eventually retiring The Cheetah Club, trick-or-treating with Vincent's and Eddie's kids, Vincent's trips to visit me at the base when we played golf and watched movies, and dinners at La Terraza – our favorite Mexican place, where Vincent and I once had a contest to see how many chips with the spiciest salsa we could eat without drinking water (we called a draw at 55) – take me outside of myself for a moment. Life has a way of just going along as we plow through our never-ending responsibilities but these moments provide temporary solace.

The last time I saw both Eddie and Vincent together was July 19, 2015. For me, it was moving time again – this time en route to Rhode Island for a brief stay prior to Virginia and then California.

Vincent had been at Majestech-Ware for over a year and had been #1 in his role every quarter since starting – no surprise. Eddie was working his summer job answering calls at the Mankato Dewey Hotel and prepping to begin another year of teaching high school.

They were helping me move stuff out of my parents' house in Mankato. Anita was staying in Mankato until I was going to be in one place for more than six months – ha! Sad, funny, and true. And, here we were, all together again in this upstairs room I was spending the weekend in prior to shoving off the following morning.

We didn't have to hide the whiskey in the secret panel I had discovered in the side of the wall anymore. We had all recently seen the first one, so on this night we took in *Ghostbusters 2* while we reminisced and went through a bunch of my old stuff – all of it bringing up ample memories. (And for the record, I like *Ghostbusters 2* – it doesn't deserve the bad rap and still has plenty of quotable lines – the litmus test of any classic film.)

When we were younger, say in high school and some of college, and got together for the evening, the typical constants were drinking and a roundtable discussion we dubbed "a forum." On this night, we may have had the last one for a while. Then again, we've said that so many times and we've always managed to re-convene.

Hilariously, there was one we had in 1996 – I have evidence on tape! – where we sat around talking prior to any of us going to college. Eddie talked about his desire to move away, his girlfriend at the time Mimi, and a potential interest in getting into politics. I talked about my girlfriend Moira, my desire to be an English professor and silly stories about how Mitch and I used to antagonize the janitor at high school. Yeah, yeah. Now Mitch is a county judge! And Vincent figured he would somehow get involved in business, commenting on the unlikelihood of his real dream that Eddie pointed out: getting involved in the movies somehow as a writer or producer or director.

Nearly twenty years later, here we all were – family men of various sorts. Vincent the single Dad, Eddie the teacher and husband and Dad, and me the Navy man with a wife and two kids. The dreams weren't dead but they were mere flickers left in a life that could have been. I don't think any of us had regrets.

"Do you think you'll be in the Navy forever?" Eddie asked me.

"You know, I never thought I'd say this, because you know I joined because I had to," I responded after a moment of thought. "But I love it. As nice as it was to come home after Afghanistan and see my family, I miss elements of it. I miss being needed in that capacity and being really good at something."

"Your turn, Vincent," Eddie indicated.

"Eddie – will you stay in Mankato?"

"For many reasons, I hope so," Eddie answered with a smile on his face. "It's funny, because I never thought I'd come back, but it just made sense. This is my home. As for Lucy, I know she wouldn't mind moving, but I like the school that Marty is in and I like my job and our life."

"My turn," I said. "Vincent – will you ever settle down?"

"Hahaha – touché," he responded. "Gee, well, the last time I was engaged it went so horribly awry that three weeks later I dropped the money I was going to spend on the wedding on an Aston Martin. That's kind of my ode to eternal bachelorhood."

We laughed. It was kind of true. Vincent ran every time.

"In all seriousness, it's not that I don't want the happily ever after. I just don't know if I've got it in me. I know I'm moody and not good at apologizing, especially when I did nothing wrong. I know I'm a loner. I know I can't love anything or anybody more than I love Elizabeth. My career was my whole focus for so long, and unfortunately it meant that most of the ladies in my life came into it because of my jobs. Janie, Becky and Julie were from Cooke's, Stacy, Phoebe and Abby from ABM. Hell, I've been dating a girl lately that dated a guy who worked for me at Cellular Horizons! I went out with a girl that worked for me at Tel-Cell before her. It's kind of atrocious. The only girl I didn't meet at work was Emily…"

Vincent took a strong, contemplative drink of whiskey.

"You guys know, ABM beat the shit out of me. I mean, it was like I peaked at 27, then lost everything – my career, friends, my girlfriend, my income. It was 1,229 days until there was resolution and to get what was relatively just I had to wait months while the people paid to bring justice did nothing and sit in multiple day-long depositions and be absolutely degraded like I did something wrong. They drudged up everything they could trying to paint me in a negative light, creating some story that *I* conspired single-handedly to unseat my corrupt boss while they tried to wash their hands of years of psychological and emotional damages they caused to me and dozens of others from the acts and tolerance of retaliation. Sure, I won, but I never got back anything I had. I'm 36 and still haven't reached the plateau I was on ten years ago."

"You're a better person," Eddie offered.

"The years of doubt and uncertainty certainly humbled me. And maybe I needed that."

"Maybe?" I laughed.

"Ha ha," Vincent responded. "Yeah, yeah. I don't know, it's just you see your life going on a certain trajectory and you do everything the right way. I know I did some stupid things. It's just a tough pill to swallow when you don't deserve it. And I've spent the last five years just struggling to ascend higher than my peak. If that's the best life can ever get, that's pretty depressing. There isn't a day that goes by I don't miss aspects of that old life."

"But much of it was fake; a propped up sense of security, fake friends, people who were attracted to your status and money," I reminded him.

"I know. But what a ride," Vincent said, then looking across the room to ensure we got the *Ghostbusters* reference. Eddie smiled, but groaned. I laughed.

"At this point," Vincent concluded, "I look at life in a totally different way. Back then, it was all about 'what's next?' and planning my rise to CEO of ABM. It was imminent, until it wasn't. Now, I just take solace in my routines. I get up in the morning, work out, get Elizabeth ready, take her to school, eat the same breakfast sandwich, have the same lunch and read Bond or Sherlock Holmes, do my best at a job that doesn't challenge me, pick up Elizabeth and take her wherever she needs to go if she has cheerleading or baton or gymnastics, come home, eat popcorn and either read or watch TV until I go to bed and repeat the process. I've marginalized everything down to a process – eating, working out, work. It's like everything's a science. I've almost found a semblance of peace in hiding in the things I can control while taking the occasional drastic adventure – like just flying off to Washington, D.C., or Dallas for a weekend. Life on my terms. I make it look like I'm having fun, but honestly, it's lonely. It's tired. So, to answer your question, if the right girl comes along I would imagine it's possible."

"Maybe she has," I proffered. "You have to face the fact that somebody who puts up with you is sometimes what you get. Who gives you your space when you need it but who challenges you and makes you want to be a better man. Thing is, there is no perfect scenario. There is no complete control. You won't find it until you relinquish control over the situation. Yield to it. Stop expecting perfection – it won't happen. Hell, if you can find somebody with whom you are 51-49 in favor of being with you've got a winner."

We laughed, but it was true.

"It's funny, I always thought my parents had this perfect life and relationship I couldn't possibly live up to. But, honestly, the balance of power in their relationship isn't one I'd want in mine. I now accept that my relationship wouldn't be what theirs is, and I'm OK with that. They are amazing people, but I'm quite different than they are. I don't believe they understand my life or why I've made some of my choices, and that's OK, too. I just want them to be proud of me, and I know they just want me to be happy.

"I don't know anymore where I'll retire from, what the next step is, or anything else, really. I know that today, right now, I'm good. And Elizabeth's good. And that's enough."

Little did we know, more major change was coming for Vincent quite soon.

Two things I always tried to teach Vincent. One was that when negative feelings or emotions surfaced, acknowledge their presence and consciously refocus your attention on dismissing them. We spend so much of our time obsessing over the things we have no control over and much of what we fret never comes to fruition and these worries are merely obstacles to our moving forward.

The second was the contents of the Serenity Prayer. Certainly, it's well known for its use in Alcoholics Anonymous, but I really dig the part about accepting the things we cannot change. I can say with certainty that where this was not one of Vincent's strong suits (he always wanted to drastically change the world, and a part of him still probably does) but he is better because he has grown to accept the facets of his life he cannot control. He has chosen to accept each day as it comes and make the most of it. He has learned to forgive, to leave the past in the past. He has continued to effectively evolve personally, which has helped him professionally as well.

The Vocational Viewpoint, via Vincent Scott
(Republished with permission)
"How do I effectively network, for my job and career?"

From today's mailbag: "I've taken on a new role and know I need to network to make new connections, but it's not really my thing. How do I go about it?"

No matter what type of business role you are in, it's extremely probable you will have to network at some point. From networking and utilizing your network effectively to land a job to prospecting and creating new network, the people you can connect and collaborate with play a vital role in your success - and theirs! Do not forget it can often be just as important that they know you! You likely offer value and service, and it's important they know it, too.

If you lack comfort with networking, fret not - some of the greatest salespeople and sales managers I know are introverts. The fact is you likely do not enjoy being in a room filled with strangers and having to force conversation - right? More people feel this way than you probably think. Furthermore, those who appear to be social butterflies often either do not want to be or they had to learn how to master this part of the dance. Like any type of business or personal relationship, you cannot start a fire without a spark. We will never find new connections without making effort.

Some of us are more comfortable behind the screen of our computers, and, honestly this is not a bad way for the whole process to start. Utilization of social media is a magnificent way in this day and age to find the people you should be connected to, making an introduction and setting up the initial meeting. It makes it easier to find who we need to meet, make an introduction and briefly present why a meeting would be valuable. Asking for advice or guidance, explaining why their expertise interested you and assuring them you are not seeking an interview or a job (by not mentioning either!) can be great ways to get yourself to the table the first time.

Preparation is another key for success in networking. Whether you are going to a networking event or using the web to meet new connections, having a game plan is crucial. Sure, we may still fumble at times - specifically if we are *too* rehearsed - but being observant, listening for key words in conversations, talking to the guest speakers after they deliver their speeches, or even simply saying, "Hi, I'm _____, what brought you here today?" is a great way to begin the process.

At networking events, others are there to network also. Listen for cues of how others start conversations! They are likely doing the exact same thing and have once been in your shoes. Do not over-think it: others are there to find value in the room. You may not meet your next mentor or customer while you're there, but you are establishing a presence as a resource. Like any process, if you consistently apply the proper principles, results will follow. As you continue to plant seeds, seek out ways to be a value to others and establish yourself as a resource, others will introduce you to more people you need to connect with... and the dance continues and it becomes easier.

Are you comfortable talking about your value - great! If not, focus on this first as your initial goal will be to feel good about your process. Once you have a process, like anything else, you practice it, evolve it and be consistent with it. From there, you will build and grow the foundation of a network that you will engage in many often very fruitful ways for years and years to come.

The Vocational Viewpoint, via Vincent Scott
(Republished with permission)
"What fact-finding questions should I ask during the needs analysis?"

From today's mailbag: "My manager tells me I need to ask 'fact-finding questions' but I'm not really sure where to get started. What questions should I ask?"

Your success in any given sales transaction that hopefully begets a business relationship hinges quite a bit on first contact and how you choose to follow (or not follow) a selling process.

Once you are granted access to ask questions and have a conversation, thanks to maneuvering through the gatekeeper as a friend rather than foe and by capturing enough attention to advance from the decision-maker, it is time to start gathering clues. Like Sherlock Holmes and Doctor John Watson, you must advance stealthily but methodically; one false step and you're toast.

Proper and proficient use of your time, however, in ascertaining your customer's needs and wants, their current method of doing whatever you're trying to convince them to change (either non-existent or a competitor) and what they do and don't like about that current choice will determine practically everything going forward.

1. Don't ask a question just to be asking a question. Many times, I've heard sales reps just ask a myriad of questions with no real purpose or because their work script calls for it and they never use the information gleaned. Certainly, it does help to know how long they have been in business, where they've been and want to go but right now I don't necessarily need to hear a litany of their entire life story. Be able to inquire without interrogating; be able to figure out what you really need to know to uncover specifically how you can be the solution to their problem.

2. Think big picture. Where does this customer want to go? What are potential new forays they can make? What's something they are missing in their current arsenal? To uncover these, think about what you have to offer. What does your solution often cure? Try to find any potential holes or points of discontentment in your customer's current way of doing business. Then find out what they have done to address it, or why they have not addressed it. Not only will you need to overcome objections like lack of belief and price, but you will need to uncover hidden objections as well - past failures in the very line of work you're in - to actually proceed.

3. Ask the questions that will allow you to prove return on investment. Find out the worth and value of a proper solution for your customer. Utilize this information when you are justifying the price and cost of your solution - "Mr./Mrs. Customer, you indicated previously that landing a new client/

remedying your efficiency issue/ the cost of acquiring a new employee, etc., was $$$$. By applying our tried and true strategy, you increase the probability of landing that client/ resolving that issue by XXX% for a mere $$$$$ investment. That said, just how quickly do you make a profit?" Work with them to uncover the solution you want them to uncover.

 4. Realize that a customer's primary objection is lack of belief. In reality, it's the only one; it's the very reason they throw obstacles like price and partners out to you. If they believed this would work, they'd be selling their partner and they'd be spending the money to fix a problem they have already identified (or that you've helped them find! Elementary, my dear Watson!). Knowing this, and knowing you don't really sell anything - they make the decision to buy! - ask the questions that will lead the horse to the water that they will be enticed to drink. You want them to draw conclusions, so make them see the inadequacies of their current comfortable (or uncomfortable) ways of mediocrity or failing. Show them that it's possible to "have it all" - to dive into the new forays or ventures they want to eventually pursue.

 5. Check with them along the way. Remember, we don't close every customer the first conversation. In fact, we rarely do. That said, ask the questions that show you're there as a trusted advisor. Point out the current state of the union and ask, "How may I be of additional value?" "How may I further support you at this point?" "What additional questions exist, or what can I shed further light on so we may provide the added efficiency we discussed?" Open-ended questions, not questions that end in a yes or a no, that position you as someone with their best interests at heart and make clear you are offering respectful service rather than a hard close will make the environment conducive to the sale.

 Ask the questions that will enable you to overcome stated or hidden objections before they even surface. Use your experience and mistakes in sales conversations to figure out where you stumbled before. Odds are, asking more questions and having more facts would have and will enable you to solve the case of what specific combination of facts prompt your customer to respect you, trust in you, and buy from you.

The Vocational Viewpoint, via Vincent Scott
(Republished with permission)
"How do I make my resume stand out?"

 From today's mailbag: "How do I get my resume noticed when I'm applying to jobs? How do I make it stand out so I actually get a response?"

 You have likely heard the phrase before that you have to sell yourself -

your most valuable commodity. People buy from people, so when you are marketing your attributes and skills it is important to mirror other selling processes; namely, be unique and stand out by any practical means necessary.

1. Avoid the clichés. Frankly, double-think all of the adjectives or statements that make you out to be a team player or driven or goals-oriented or hard worker and discard them in favor of finding ways to illustrate these strengths with numbers (see next point). Think about it from a hiring manager's perspective - everyone is telling them that they are the best candidate for the job. *Show* them what you've done to merit consideration. Don't just tell.

2. Use lots of numbers. One of the most frequent things I see missing in resumes is numbers. You can rarely have too many. From percent increases you provoked in your previous roles to percent of goal and total number of dollars generated and people you impacted, your mission here is to show a potential employer something that makes them say - "Hey, I want this person working for me and doing these things for me!"

3. Be creative. Again, think about what other resumes look like or what is relatively easy to present (namely, a basic, generic synopsis of a role you fulfilled). Make your resume stand out. Make a video resume. Hand-deliver it. Make different versions that are easy to digest, such as in a slide show or web page format. Do the work that others won't so you are the one who gets the attention.

3. Strength in numbers. Send your materials out feverishly, to the right people in a superior way. Anyone can apply to a job online. Not everyone looks up the company or the hiring manager on LinkedIn and connects with a gracious, humble message to be followed by a request for an advice meeting. Not everyone is willing to do what it takes to meet and connect with decision makers outside of the online jobs that are posted for all to see (which prevents them from ever knowing about the jobs that *aren't* posted). Not everyone is willing to tweak their resume regularly with new accomplishments and accolades.

To get attention from your resume, make your presentation stand out. Consider what your hiring manager will want to see. You are playing a numbers' game, so the only logical approach is to tip the odds in your favor by any means necessary. Don't allow yourself to be the world's best kept secret by creating a resume and not doing everything you can to get it in the hands of those who can hire and promote you!

The Vocational Viewpoint, via Vincent Scott
(Republished with permission)
"Nobody is motivating me. What do I do?"

From today's mailbag: "I'm in a sales environment where no one is motivating me to do better or be more. It's really depressing. Morale is low and I'm trying to tough it out, but I'm not sure what I should do. Please help."

While it is technically the responsibility of your leadership - all the way to the top - to find innovative ways to adapt and influence, to train and support you and to create an environment conducive to happy customers and employees, you will find if you have not already that offices, departments, companies - like relationships - are not perfect.

Sales managers often take a lot of blame for not motivating teams, but if no one is motivating them, training them and showing them how it's done, who is really to blame?

You're in an environment where no one is leading you or coaching you or developing you, and many of us have been there or are there; many people use this as the excuse to lay down, to be lazy, to underperform or to constantly job-hop.

However, as I pray I have illustrated in many of my writings to date, your goal should always be to stand out, not follow the herd and to challenge yourself to be great. Not being motivated? Motivate yourself! Want things to change? Be the positive, permanent change! Morale is low? Work with your peers to improve things! Make proposals to leadership to form committees to improve morale - be the solution to every problem around.

It's very likely your manager(s) know the problems exist and they are either so caught up in the daily minutiae to fix it or they don't know how. Don't complain about or rebel against leadership - propose to help them, work with them and for them to improve the state of the union.

If you wait around for someone to motivate you, you may be gravely disappointed. Not a lot of people know how to motivate others because no one has shown them how; they have not taken the time to get to know their teams to know what motivates them! That said, what motivates you? What are you trying to achieve? What is your plan to get there? What are you doing every day to head in the right direction? What do you do when you have setbacks? Even if you are a one person cheering squad, you've got to do it. What gets your juices flowing? What makes you feel you can move mountains? Relish your routines and your motivating music and inspiring quotes and whatever you need to keep your mind focused on the prize and off of the dismal decay around you.

You cannot control those around you and you cannot force them to be happy or do their best or achieve. You can contribute to it, but you cannot make them follow your lead. Some will, some will merely bask in the excuse of low morale and use it as their crutch as they are mired in mediocrity and misery and ultimately lose their jobs. You cannot control your supervisor and their supervisors; you can certainly communicate your needs and wants and gauge their level of interest in getting you where you need to be, the level of support they provide or fail to, and if they are accepting of your solutions. You cannot control many of the factors and variables set forth by upper management. But you can control your response, your reactions and your resolve to produce results.

Take every day at a time. Every day completed is a day achieved. Master each call, each meeting, each day as best you can. Don't worry about motivating yourself for a long period of time - just maximize each portion of your role and your tasks as they come. You can do this. You hold a lot of power - more than most people give themselves credit for. And no one controls your attitude and your motivation but you. We allow outside stimulus to impact our inspiration and motivation, but we can also keep negative forces from impacting them if we try hard enough.

Stay focused on your prize, keep working on the steps you know will get you there, and do not let the obstacles and roadblocks keep you from continuing on the path to what you want, no matter how many steps it takes!

The Jimmy Sander Story

Monday, May 15, 2000 was my first day with ABM Telecom. I worked in Chanhassen, a bit southwest of Minneapolis.

I loved it, and life was much simpler then. It was before the wives and kids, it was just me being young and making money. Not that I have regrets, but it really was another lifetime ago.

My role back then was fielding calls from internal ABM resources regarding their need for technical work – both for telephony and later and more prominently, broadband. That office was rife with new friends and girls to date. I was single and made good money – it was everything I needed.

Unfortunately, as my life and the lives of many I have encountered over the years have illustrated, it's quite uncommon to spend the duration of one's career with the same company – no matter how hard you try. It was Friday, February 17, 2006, when I was informed I was being laid off.

One of the few worthwhile things our union had established with the company was that we were first to interview for other open requisitions if we took any interest. Typically, we had sixty days to find another role within the company with no guarantees that we'd find one. Sure, sometimes my colleagues would have political alliances elsewhere that helped them land something. I had nothing of the sort.

It was April 14 when I went in to interview for my last hope. The job was a sales representative role for a new division of ABM Advertising – one which would call on businesses nationwide attempting to market print and online mediums. Despite technical knowledge and skills, I had no sales experience, no advertising experience and the half dozen others from my office that interviewed for this job were denied. It didn't look good.

It was my first time in the downtown Minneapolis ABM office. The first person who greeted me was the HR administrator, Phoebe Wells. She was overly friendly and took me up the elevator to meet the sales manager conducting interviews, Vincent Scott.

Phoebe opened the door to the interview office and ushered me in. A 6'1" man with slicked back blonde hair and a black and grey suit and tie combination greeted me.

"Jimmy Sander, this is Vincent Scott, the hiring manager," Phoebe indicated.

"Thank you, Phoebe," Vincent acknowledged. I accepted his outstretched hand. "Jimmy, nice to meet you. Vincent Scott."

"Nice to meet you, Vincent."

Phoebe exited the room and Vincent ushered me to a couple of seats at the desk near the window. The view of downtown Minneapolis was striking.

"So, Mr. Sander, tell me a little bit about yourself and why you feel you would be a fit for this position."

"Well, I have a wife and a little boy. He's 2. I've been working for the last 6 years in the telephony/broadband division in internal field resources."

"Chanhassen, right?" Vincent asked. My resume was nowhere to be found.

"Right – did you need my resume?"

"No – I never use them. Please, continue."

"I'd be a good fit for this position because, first and foremost, I love this company. My Mom works for the company and plans to retire from here. I believe in the staples we have created with telephone, Internet, broadband and top flight advertising over the last several decades. The story is rich, and our company has endured because of strategy and critical thinking. My passion for the company makes me a great ambassador for it, whether I am helping link the chain for sales behind the scenes or talking directly to customers about it."

"Cold-calling businesses to sell them advertising is a far cry from serving as liaison to internal field operatives. Why would you be successful doing that?"

"I'm confident. I'm a people person. I've got a lot of potential small business and entrepreneurial type ideas myself and I know how I'd need to be reached and connected with in order to buy."

"Give me an example."

"What are they doing currently? My bet is they've tried a lot of different things, maybe been burned. We're going to have an uphill battle, we'll have to get them to listen and understand why we're different. The name ABM is going to open a lot of doors, but I can't dilly-dally once the door's open. Just like when I diagnose an internal issue, it's about the questions I ask and what I do with the answers. What's the return on investment? If I can bring them paying customers, what's that worth to them? Once I know their current methods of advertising, what's worked and what hasn't, their average job worth and can show them results we're getting, it's a compelling story."

"Currently, you're linking internal field team members, answering questions, and not facing any rejection. How will you react in the face of rejection if you can even get someone on the phone at all?"

"I've dated a lot, so I know about rejection," I smiled wryly. Vincent laughed. I was feeling good – hell, what did I have to lose? It was like a sales adage I heard about later – if you get them to laugh, you've got them. "But, seriously, I believe where most people fail in the face of rejection is just spouting out talking points. With these business owners, people who have poured their blood, sweat and tears into their business, they don't want that. They want empathy, they want understanding. I can talk to them like a human being. I can get to know their business, even in that brief cold call, enough to make a proposal that makes sense."

"Jimmy, it all sounds great," Vincent Scott continued. He was cool as a cucumber; he sat somewhat reclined in the chair opposite me – far from the picture of a typical interviewer. I would come to find out there was nothing typical about this man. "Thing is, you don't get much time to get to know these folks and they often tell you just enough to get you off the phone thinking they're interested only to never answer the phone again. How do you find success in a scenario like that?"

I leaned in, and in that moment, I was as serious as I've ever been.

"Vincent, if there's a sale to make, I'll make it. I'm not fazed by rejection or the brush off or the hang up or the unanswered ring. I'll do whatever I have to do to stay with this company and take care of my family. I'll do whatever I have to do to make my Mom who has spent most of her life here proud of me. If it's 100, 200, 300 calls in a day, I'll make them. Somebody will answer, and when they do I'll do what telemarketers won't: I'll talk to them like a person. I'll actually show I understand where they're coming from – that I understand their frustration with the economy and other failed marketing practices. I'll make a pitch and I'm not afraid to call them on the fact that I may never talk to them again. There's no need for either of us to waste our time. But I've got to ask you something."

"Yes?" Vincent asked, fully attentive with a slight smirk and a twinkle in his eye.

"I've had a dozen folks from my office interview with you, and you've passed on every one of them. Am *I* wasting *my* time?"

Vincent now flashed a full on smile. He leaned forward in his chair and did not answer right away.

"You know the difference between them and you?"

"What's that?"

"Every one of them came in here like I owed them something. Like they were entitled to a job in this department because they were losing their other job. No one had any respect for me or for my responsibility to hire the people who will take this department forward. Sure, I feel for every one of you – I do. But – like it or not – I was hired to hit a number – to demolish a number. I was hired to do what's right by the company and our customers and our internal partners. I'd be irresponsible to do anything else. But what you've done that they didn't do is come in here and show me your true self. No attitude, no entitlement mentality. I have no doubt you can do this job. Jimmy Sander, you're hired."

I thanked him and we shook hands. On Monday, April 24, I started in my new role in the ABM Advertising division and was able to continue my career with this company. And the adventures ahead certainly dwarfed any behind.

My training class was a motley crew to be sure. The most prominent cast members were, of course, Vincent, Abby Winters, Chad Willman and Sahim Saundura – each of whom would play a major role in the years to come.

What had started out as a little test project in November 2005 to see if this division could successfully sell remotely in the local field reps' offseason to a couple of markets was truly taking off. Nancy Wilkes trained our class and then many of us became members of her team. She was pretty emotional and quite territorial, as she was one of the original members of the department, and she absolutely hated getting beaten by the neighboring crew managed by Vincent Scott.

She was highly competitive; Vincent's team would create names from DC superhero comics and dubbed themselves the Justice League, so Nancy made us all mob nicknames and pictures. They were regularly one-upping each other on floorwide e-mails about various topics, as Vincent was heavy into sales strategy and Nancy was into the details of each product. The managers sent e-mails out for each sale to build momentum and these two made them more and more elaborate. Vincent bought an air horn that would sound every time his team got a sale – which was more than any other crew. I could tell he was having fun, and I could see why he was always #1.

While most of the managers had come from other departments and shied away from the phones, Vincent got on the phone – he showed his team how to fearlessly cold call, get decision-makers on the phone, talk on their level, and utilize the nuggets he gleaned in fact finding to pitch, close and overcome. You could hear him, because we were merely separated by tall cubicles, and his aggression was contagious. I wanted to work for this guy.

He also mingled with the people, which, looking back, may have been his downfall in some ways. Knowing him, I know that he threw so much into his work and was not overly outgoing in other social settings with people he did not know, so to allow himself to mix with a bunch of 20-something's that worshipped him was very easy. He didn't have to meet anyone new or risk being rejected by a group – these kids all wanted to latch to his rising star.

Thing is, in a department of this ilk, it would be difficult to always be #1. So many factors, like extremely large sales that would catapult a team past numerous other teams and attrition through both turnover and appointment into our inbound team of our top reps (who most often came from Vincent's team) dramatically changed the landscape. However, against many odds, Vincent could tell you the only month off the top of his head that he was not #1 during the 12 months he was in that role. A very large sale closed on the last day of the month that had to be cleared via a waiver because it had no credit check and was only allowed for morale purposes.

Vincent was smart. Our division manager, Derek Walters, was tapped to temp run a telephone division of advertising teams that was also housed in Minneapolis that fall. Vincent was our top manager but he also went to Keith, the director, and took on as many extra responsibilities as he could. He was the one sending the daily sales e-mails and recaps – and he did it better than Walters. He was the one we went to for answers and who was our liaison to Keith. He was the one who started managing our developmental programs, meeting with Labor, tracking metrics, overseeing the department's inbound inquiries and sitting at the head of the table. We all even called him Mini-Walters. He saw the writing on the wall; when Derek was promoted, so was Vincent – over former advertising people like Mark Rogers and Danny Boyd – because he had made himself so valuable and was the obvious choice.

It was also that fall when our collective gravitated more toward him; we'd wind up at Finley's Bar drinking beer and vodka and shots galore, the likes of Vincent, Cal Riley, Sahim, Ronnie Collins, Chad Willman and later Abby. We called Vincent the Godfather – and they even put it on his tabs…for years to come.

For the record, I knew something was going on with Vincent and Abby long before anyone else! The two of them started canoodling in October 2006 and Abby confided in me; we even had a codename for him. Because Vincent loved James Bond, we called him Sean Pierson – a mesh of two 007 actor names. (Eventually, Vincent found out and he even sent Abby flowers under that name to remain anonymous.) So I knew when they were on and off, Abby was pregnant and when they were on, off, on, off, on, off, on throughout the years to come.

It was a tough situation; I mean, Keith told Vincent, "Don't fuck the help" on this first day on the job and just when he was about to be promoted, he finds out his fling with Abby resulted in her unexpected pregnancy. I think he did what he thought was right by everybody, but he shelved his want at the time – Phoebe Wells – who certainly came back and factored into the future.

The money was flowing like water, too. We started out making 15% commission; like any new department, you either over- or underestimate. You could make $70K and not even be that good. Our top rep made $190K. Chad Willman went out and bought a new car just a few months after we started. We were living large; lavish lunches in downtown Minneapolis every day and nights on the town every night.

The teams were re-drafted in 2007 and I got to work for Vincent. He needed me more than ever when he lost the top third of his old team to our inbound group. Fret not, readers – we were still #1. Jane Daugherty, who worked for Vincent in the telecom division, and I were his top reps.

I feel for my friend, looking back. He gave that place his everything, even though it didn't deserve it. While I didn't approve of Vincent's involvement with Phoebe, I understood. I was always there, whether it was venting about Abby or Phoebe or Keith and there was always plenty of bourbon and beer and video games around. I played mediator going to Elizabeth's doctor appointments with them when Abby and Vincent weren't speaking. He did everything he could for Abby – getting her jobs even when they weren't together and he was the best Dad he could have possibly been. He is the best guy I've ever known. Not perfect, but he has taken every loss – fair or unfair – and risen above it like nobody else I've ever seen.

It was January 17, 2008, when Vincent made the greatest decision in his career. He promoted me.

In seriousness, it was something I had wanted for a long time and, in earning that promotion, I had come a long way from the nearly out of work layoff victim I nearly became just two years prior. The two years to follow were the best of my career so far and I – like nearly everyone there – have painstakingly spent the years since trying to recapture what I felt back then.

When you're at the top of the mountain, everyone's looking up at you. Some choose to cheer, others choose to throw stones and – even worse – some choose to take anonymous potshots from afar. That's what started happening to Vincent with a vengeance in 2008. Looking back at that time, it was definitely the beginning of the end.

It's funny, because people weren't even leaving our outbound team to go to the inbound team, which some viewed as a promotion, solely because of what Vincent was doing at the helm of our division.

Vincent was literally told by our boss that he'd get rid of Vincent if he heard another rumor about him hanging around with Phoebe – whom Vincent truly was in love with. I totally understood that it was messy; Abby was working in the department, albeit not for Vincent, and Phoebe was getting divorced and was cavorting with her interview candidates' hiring manager…but I think a lot of it was that Keith wanted Vincent for himself. He had a crush on this guy he viewed as his protégé.

Nobody had never seen anything like Vincent. Heck, he'd be leading the same types of teams as his counterpart Mark and whipped him by 30% to goal each month. There was just no explaining it; our old boss, Derek, visited to sell our division on selling freelance deals elsewhere in Minnesota – the reception was so-so, lukewarm. Vincent got up there and put it in perspective, told us what was in it for us, how easy it was, how well we'd be compensated and he got a standing ovation! I've never seen anything like him or it before or since.

When I think about those times, I most fondly remember the breakfasts. Each morning, Vincent and Mark met with our entire leadership team. Vincent would typically let Mark open the dialogue, which was good, because it was dry and by the numbers boring. Vincent let him say his bit and then he'd take over – getting our attention, getting our feedback, caring about our concerns, providing solutions and answers and guiding us to solve the problems of our division.

He managed every single day to sell all of us on being the best we could be. Then, he'd do the same thing in a room of over 200 people – Mark would bore and Vincent would score. The reps and managers absolutely loved him. I loved him like a brother. When things went awry with Abby or Phoebe or when these higher-ups would put the squeeze on him, he'd stay at my place or we'd play video games and I saw him for who he really was: a vulnerable guy who wanted everyone to like him.

He killed himself for these people – it's why he worked all day and obsessed about it at night. He couldn't control the chaos with his personal life, but when he was planning our daily dialing schedules, researching the markets, writing scripts, giving speeches and parading through the office mid-month to "Don't Stop Believin'" while we were whomping our way to yet another record-shattering month it was clear he was in love with his career. When he and Elizabeth would go trick-or-treating with my son Dylan and me, take time off work solely to be with his daughter and the way he was so proud of her, took care of her and put her above anything else – including his career – it was clear he was in love with being a Daddy. I saw the guy hit 7 three-pointers in a row from half court and do things on a basketball court in his 30's that a teenager couldn't do.

Vincent didn't let most people see his inner workings, but I knew it bothered him when the big bosses questioned him or when some anonymous bullshit would surface and paint him in an unfair, negative light. I knew it bothered him when a sales rep he was trying to help got defensive and acted like Vincent was bullying him solely because the rep couldn't cut it. Heck, I did the job: I know it was difficult. But if we bought into the process and believed in Vincent Scott, we were never led astray. Of course, that was until the whole department was given the shock of its life.

We were all transformed by that place. None of us wanted to or enjoyed terminating people, but it came as part of the game. We went through thousands of people to get the several hundreds who worked there and it was a hell of a grind. There were cut and dry processes that Keith and Derek had put in place and Vincent was paid to execute – that's all. He didn't like firing the former teacher who just barely missed goal despite trying his ass off (especially when Keith simply moved a VP's son to another department when he was on the chopping block). He didn't like firing people he had been social with in previous roles. But when these reps would lie about why they missed work or tried to get over on us, he gave it no second thought.

Vincent did everything he was asked to do and then some, but his fatal mistake was standing up for us when he disagreed. He also responded and reacted to his detractors. His personal life was rife with ammunition that could be used against him and the fact it played out on the business stage meant his enemies could use it to destroy him. And they did.

It got to the point it seemed like the operations and clerical managers were against us, which we later learned was because they were intentionally shorting us for increased profit margin and their bonuses by mishandling our work.

Keith would throw up roadblocks all the time, but Vincent plowed through or scaled over them. Keith wanted Mark to be better so badly, because Vincent was overpowering when he ran the show. But they had no choice but to sit on the sidelines and watch him dominate. They were going to shut down the customer research team that called existing advertisers because they never did better than 78% to goal. Vincent took them to save those jobs and doubled their output in a month. He came with new ideas constantly to give us new life: I remember in January 2009 when he started us out calling our dog shit leads for the first two weeks of the month before feeding us the Glengarry leads. We'd try our asses off starved on the bad stuff and would just come out swinging for the fences on day 15. It worked every time. We started with $10 million annual goals and eventually the guy did damn near $60 million.

We were *too* successful. We started out as a potential cleanup crew for the bigger advertising groups and wound up making them look bad. Their excuses as to why they were dropping billions of dollars in revenue made no sense when Vincent Scott and Co. was coming in and stealing headlines. It got to the point Keith would purposely schedule meaningless, tedious trainings on stuff we already knew during peak dialing times like he wanted us to sell less so his buddies in the other units didn't look bad. Keith would institute these phony revenue audits, using a fraudulent missing contracts report to attempt to steal hard-earned money from his subordinates and wouldn't listen to anyone trying to talk reason. Rather, he put a target on their backs and took them out one by one: Ronnie Collins, Andy Simpson, Jackson Kerr, Chad Willman, Jack Taber, Leslie Warner, Jeff Ranken, Lloyd Meridian, Warren Treble, Kip Connors – the list went on and on. It's just that no one expected Vincent Scott to find his way on that list. He was too valuable.

But when Keith realized it was either him or Vincent, he set his star player up for a fall and took him out, using his off-limits personal life to seal his fate.

I can't tell you how many times my friend had to face a firing squad because he was like a king and was surrounded by these jealous, petty pricks. There were anonymous letters attacking his relationships. There were anonymous callers to the HR line who made up lies about how he conducted himself in meetings or on company trips. He'd have women throw themselves at him and then spread rumors that they had slept with him or that he had come on to them! I don't know how he put up with it. Elizabeth and vodka were the only things that really kept him afloat – and, back then, me.

Senior leadership would rip into Vincent about these claims while Vincent was the only reason we had success. Keith could hide his buddy Mark's bad numbers in with Vincent's fantastic numbers thus hiding the impact Vincent was having on our department. He was the reason we expanded, he was the reason hundreds of people had jobs, he was the reason we were successful and he was the reason we stayed. Vincent came on board when we called off spreadsheets and manual dialing; he oversaw expansion with an auto-dialer, created call flow processes and scripts, and met with our team members himself so he knew them, watched our coaching and coached us in the process.

The bitch of it all is that Vincent stood up to these clowns and kept us safe as long as he could, but when he sided with us to take down Keith for his countless HR crimes, illegal activity and horrendous abuse of all of us, he was the one who fell. And he didn't just get reprimanded – even Labor only supported suspension at most for a text message he sent Abby after a huge fight when she didn't even work for him. Keith fired him out of revenge and plunged our whole department into chaos – he undid many of the policies and processes Vincent created that made us successful. In just one year, we dropped 50% of our output, headcount started to collapse and eventually our division was sold off.

We were unfairly seen as a sideshow distraction – a fraternity, and I get it. While we actually made fun of that categorization, even making shirts with our faces on the likenesses of *Entourage* characters and walking around like the Mod Squad, the reality was our circus was blowing out numbers and making kids filthy rich but we were lumped in with the poorly performing Mark Rogers parts of the business and came out looking like a mediocre product causing drama and ruckus.

While many of us lost our jobs (I was targeted for my friendship with Vincent and eventually demoted), Vincent did lose everything. He refused to stop seeing Phoebe when Keith threatened him, but she dropped him the second she sniffed possible promotion pending on her distancing herself. She reappeared after his demise only to leave again when another promotion hung in the balance – and they never spoke again. Keith threatened every single one of us: if we sided with Vincent, it was our death sentence. "Don't let what happened to him happen to you."

Keith learned in late 2008 that Vincent had all the power. He knew he couldn't replace Vincent but he also couldn't control him; Vincent no longer blindly did his bidding – he stood up to him when Keith cursed him out and threatened him. When Vincent showed it didn't faze him, he turned the tables and Vincent was running the show. When we mutinied Keith, the ending was obvious: HR promised Keith's removal and Vincent was the only one who could take the mantle. He was already doing the job. Keith knew it, pulled his political strings and got his way: he destroyed Vincent maliciously and completely.

Vincent ruffled feathers when he dated whomever he wanted, said whatever he wanted, did whatever he wanted. He poked the bear when he waged war with Keith and the clerical managers over their fraudulent reports and our teams not getting paid properly. He signed his death warrant when he signed on to Clyde Barton's "Brotherhood" which was our band of managers hell bent on unseating Keith.

He did everything it took, despite the sacrifice, to protect our reps and us, even going so far as spoon-feeding the Union evidence of commission fraud.

Making the decision to cut myself off from Vincent at that time was not an easy one. It was corrupt politics the likes of *House of Cards*; that son of a bitch completely destroyed my friend and took pleasure in it – but that wasn't enough. Vincent lost his career, his girlfriend, his friends in one fell swoop.

I didn't feel like I had a choice. I had a family, I had debt and I knew that Keith meant it: if I publicly sided with Vincent, I would be destroyed and I could not take that chance. Thinking back on it, I could have and should have reached out even in private. It's just that Vincent was also waging a very public war and I couldn't gamble that my name would stay out of it.

We went from being at each other's kids' birthdays and together nearly every day or few days to nothing – and I had nobody to blame but myself. Both that I lost my friend but also that he didn't want to talk to me when I attempted to make amends and that things were never, ever remotely close to the same again.

Vincent gave me a loan and was in my wedding and he trusted me with his daughter and we'd cut work to go to movies and hang out and he was my family. But January 22, 2010 was the end of all of that.

It also signaled the death knell of the department and all the trust that existed in our leadership team previously was destroyed.

I'll never forget that afternoon. I slipped outside for a cigarette and the chatter was overwhelming.

"Did you hear?"

"About what?"

"Vincent. He got fired this morning."

"What? No way. Are you serious?"

"Yeah, they took him downtown and fired him."

"I heard he got in a tiff with Keith and quit."

"No, he left Greenfield this morning and no one has seen him since. The light was still on in his office and I saw Kinsey in there for a while with the door shut going through his stuff."

"Oh, wow…what's going to happen to this place?"

"I don't know. Nothing good, you can bet on that. He was the only person with the balls to stand up to Keith."

"I heard they had to call the police on him because he created such a spectacle."

"No way."

"No they didn't. A friend of mine that works downtown saw them walking him out."

"Wow. So this is real."

"Yeah, it's real."

"Who's going to take his place?"

"Who knows."

The small assemblage of sales representatives at the Greenfield advertising office stood around in their coats, puffing on cigarettes as the latest gossip got its legs. Shortly thereafter, the management team was summoned into a meeting in our conference room by our director Keith and we all reported promptly at 1 PM.

Keith took just a few awkward sentences to flippantly eulogize the man who was the biggest reason we were all there.

There were gasps, looks of shock and murmurs. Eyes darted from one person to another in panic. A couple of the ladies cried.

A few of the folks in the room were already in on the conspiracy and three of them had even been promised Vincent's job to keep quiet – "interviewed" before any inquiry of Vincent had even taken place.

The truth was obvious: the literal heart of this department had been ripped out of its chest. And the future was uncertain at best.

The initial fallout of the Vincent Scott termination was complete shock, awe and panic. Vincent had been the crusader for all things rep-and-manager related, but he was also the advocate for better efficiency, optimized sales results in every category, employee committees for sales and office betterment, scheduled campaigns across the country that not only made sense for the business but also put the reps in the best position to win. These things were certainly the first to go.

Nobody did anything. Reps would talk to each other much of the day. We as managers did not hold them accountable anymore, because it was mass chaos. None of us had any idea how to keep the control. And it was glaringly obvious very quickly that this was going to be a bumpy ride.

It was Tuesday, January 25, 2011, over a full year after the fateful day that destroyed my friend's career, before I saw him again. An assemblage was gathered at Cullen's, the popular Greenfield hangout across the street from our office, for my birthday. There were several ABM Online faithful as onlookers: Cal Riley, Eric Aames, Johnny Slade, Cathy Schumer, Karen Kennedy to name a few.

The drinks were flowing, good times being shared and time ticking by into the evening.

In the midst of it all, the door opened and, entering fashionably tardy, came a man wearing a sleek grey suit and loosened tie.

"Look who it is," Cal Riley said in near-disbelief.

"There he is," I said, beginning to smile.

As he emerged into the light, one could see a familiar yet changed face. Vincent's appearance had changed dramatically; his hair was quite long – nearly shoulder length. He was wearing a suit with his tie loosened and had a beard. He was drinking diet sodas throughout the night having been sober for months and while Johnny Slade, Cal Riley and I shared our stressed out stories, he seemed worry free.

I was demoted three days later back to a sales rep on the phones and, because Keith Dickhauser despised me and my friendship with Vincent, he put me in the outbound, cold-calling division as opposed to letting me go to the inbound group like Adam Sandberg, Mark Rogers' buddy who self-demoted.

The times I've seen Vincent since have been just as sporadic. He had a Cellular Horizons store not far from our Greenfield office and he lunched with a handful of us a few months later when Frankie Rivera went to work for him there.

As the years went slowly past, traction would finally be made on his lawsuit. I was contacted by the EEOC and later I gave my story to Vincent's attorney. What was at fever pitch in January 2010 had fizzled out into foregone conclusion by the time it finally ended in summer 2013.

Vincent won, but he had lost so much that I don't know if he felt like a winner again until years later.

I've had hopes in the years since of latching on with Vincent in his endeavors at Tel-Cell and when he was slated to start at Apricot but it never happened. Nothing I've done since has compared to those days at ABM with Vincent; it was in 2012, after being a rep for as long as I could stomach and realizing I wasn't going anywhere that I finally accepted it was time to move on.

I'm far from the only person who feels that way. Vincent touched so many people over the years – literally thousands. One day, I have no doubt it will be far more.

When I'm lucky enough to see him, we play the NCAA Basketball video game – he's always '82 North Carolina and Michael Jordan takes over the game – or we watch television or just talk shop. But he isn't the same open book to me; he is the same person to me he used to be to everyone else – guarded.

Never does too much time go by before I fondly remember cutting work with Vincent, Cal Riley, Johnny Slade to see *The Dark Knight*, watching movies in Vincent's office, going to the VIP box at the Twins games every month with the top closers in the office, when Phoebe surprised Vincent with his 30th birthday party at Cullen's Bar, all of the nights grilling over at my place with the kids and the different ladies that went through our lives, when Vincent took me to his Top Gun trip to Las Vegas because he was forbidden to take Phoebe, and the January 20, 2009 awards banquet where Vincent called me his "brother from another mother." Standing up there, emceeing that event, he stole the show – he had our visiting Executive Director Cesar Fiorentino in stitches and ran that thing like a talk show host with music, nicknames, energy, jokes, everything.

I remember how excited Vincent was on January 25, 2009, when he had met with Keith and Mark and revamped the whole department – giving him a hand in everything, finally. See, some observers thought Vincent was just after power, but that couldn't have been farther from the truth. He was after influence; he and everyone else knew that he possessed the Midas touch. He knew these other struggling facets of our division could be healed and made great, but only if he was the one governing them.

I remember a day in March 2009 when we were having a rough start to the month; we always called the lowest propensity to buy leads for the first couple of weeks before Vincent fed us the more lucrative ones. Keith demanded Vincent give us the good leads early, and Vincent refused; instead, he gave us one of these trademark morning speech rallies, instructed all managers to forego any administrative tasks that day (to clerical managers' chagrin) to get on the phones and be on the floor, had me blare "We are the Champions" and we hit 130% to goal that day calling dogshit leads in Detroit in a recession. The guy was a magician.

The most magic thing the guy ever did was leave his mark on so many people; I've been in awe of him since the day I met him and I owe him so much of the good memories and successes I've enjoyed.

The Vocational Viewpoint, via Vincent Scott
(Republished with permission)
"Lead Generation: How can I get in front of more customers?"

From today's mailbag: "I'm at my wits' end trying to get in front of more customers. I get some leads from my company but for the rest, I'm on my own. What are some good methods of lead generation?"

The best way to view the multiple ways of generating leads is that there are numerous oil wells for which you have established drilling mechanisms. You do not want to discriminate against any of the possible fields and there is no telling which one will strike and how lucrative it will be. This is why we have to continue to pursue success in each individual potential lead source.

(1) Consider your industry. Who are your target customers? Where are they located geographically? What industries are they in? What do your competitors do to market and who is currently picking them? What can you do to metaphorically place a billboard between your potential customers and the competition? This can help you start to formulate different potential leads and sources.

(2) Consider the mediums open to you. Do you get leads from your company? Have you worked with current and past customers to obtain referrals? (Setting up a mutually beneficial referral program with them can be quite helpful.) Are there industry specific or noteworthy networking events and Chambers and meet-up groups that you know of or have researched? Are you engaged in social media? Just on LinkedIn alone, you have the capability of geo-targeting customers in any industry you like, seeing their title and reaching out to them. There are websites like Hoover's which will allow you to find companies in the size and territory you sell into. With the resources available to you, the networking groups and events, marketing methods and the ways you can conduct outreach (even picking up the phone and calling from an online search in a pinch), there is no shortage of ways to research and reach out.

(3) Lead with value. So many sellers fail to pinpoint exactly what they want to lead off with or promote. Many of them try to cram way too much into a call or e-mail and it gets ignored. When you sound like every other marketer out there, that's when you are treated like every other one with the hang-up or delete bin. What is in it for the customer to talk to you? And what do you have to offer that actually provides them the most return on investment or value without too much risk? If you are selling an appointment, focus on selling the appointment; don't skip steps in the sales process. You can't try to sell the end result before you get the buy-in or appointment.

(4) Sell an appointment. Whether you meet a potential lead at a grocery store or Chamber meeting or you get their number from an online search, your primary goal should be to set the face to face. Social media and the multitude of outreach methods available to you are fantastic as connecting devices. From there, you should use these awesome tools to set up the irreplaceable face-to-face meeting. Nothing will ever trump the handshake and the physical meeting - putting faces with names and discussing your roles and how you can develop mutual synergies. What doors can you open for them? Continue to focus on the value you can bring - and you may not establish all of the ways you can partner up front. In fact, sometimes these meetings will feel like duds. Then, 6 months later, something pops up and one of you will be top of mind with the other because you...

(5) Follow up strategically. Find ways to get multiple, quality touches of that account whether it is reaching out within a few days with the answers to questions you committed to obtain to adding them to your newsletter so they see your name often or sending them articles via social media that would be of interest. Following up isn't just about calling and leaving a voice mail or sending an e-mail asking if they are ready to buy yet. It's about staying top of mind by continuing to connect, attempting to add value or being a resource.

The sales circle of life will continue; as you build a book of business, as you continue to connect with others and obtain referrals from them, as you reach out with a newsletter or articles or other means of contact. Start to prioritize your lead generation methods by what gleans results but do not neglect other methods that can yield; you never know when a well will run dry or another might start to gush.

Getting in front of customers is also about ensuring you are selling the next step - not two steps ahead. Focus on the immediate attempt at an appointment, always lead with value and try to find ways to collaborate and partner that are mutually beneficial. Finally, take great care of your customers, communicate effectively and diligently in a timely fashion when they ask anything of you, build your reputation and you will really start to grow your network based on a strong personal brand.

The Vocational Viewpoint, via Vincent Scott
(Republished with permission)
"My job training is insufficient. What do I do?"

From today's mailbag: "My training at my job has been insufficient; borderline non-existent. What should I do to make sure I am adequately trained?"

The discussion of training begins even before the job offer is accepted; in the interview, one of the best questions to ask is what the training will look like. It is my firm belief that when a company and candidate enter into a job offer and acceptance, a contract is negotiated. You are pledging to be the person you committed to being on interview day - that plucky, proactive, productive protagonist who will bring your talent into this new arena and deliver results. Your new company has committed to giving you the training and resources and support necessary to succeed. From that moment, you have entered into negotiations on how this relationship will go and it is incumbent upon both of you to continually revisit the agreement to ensure the promises are kept and the relationship sound.

It is quite often that one or both of the parties may falter a bit in their commitments. Like any relationship, it is key that we work together to address concerns that exist and provide solutions to any and all problems that ail us.

When it comes to training, the onboarding experience is one that sets our early foundation for success; like the formative years of youngsters, it is the experiences we have early that will profoundly impact how we handle and work through future encounters in this role.

1. What resources are available to you for continuous growth? Even if your training was paltry, surely there are some types of materials available to outline your proposed process, there are plans on which you must execute and there are various sources of reading material or job aids that can assist you in formulating a plan. Certainly, we may not all get the quarter-long classroom training that meticulously spells out every possible outlook and outcome of our role, but even if we just get handed stuff to read we have something to start with.

2. What are your peers doing? If your dilemma in a role is that you feel you do not have enough training, have your peers encountered the same obstacle? What have they done to address any shortcomings in their own experience? What are the best of your peers doing to overcome this roadblock? Where there's a will, there's a way, and if people are achieving despite the obstacle of little direction, you can too. Don't let lack of training or support or guidance keep you from being successful.

3. What have you done to address the situation with your leadership? How often do you have a touch base with your supervisor? They are paid to be there to help and guide you - if you are having an underwhelming training experience and do not feel you have the support and resources necessary to be effective and productive, your boss must know about it. However, it's all in the delivery - rather than chastising your training or lack thereof, find constructive ways to come to a solution. Ask them if you can partner with a top performer. Ask them if they will ride along with you on your sales calls or show you how it's done. Ask them what additional materials you should seek out in order to bridge any gaps in your process and understanding. Get their feedback on how you are

performing and ensure that you are coming up with an agreed-upon plan together on how to combat any shortcomings in your experience.

4. Follow up, and re-visit. The most important facet of any training is continuous training that adapts to the changing environment. What you were once trained on can become obsolete. Even the fundamental training you receive needs refreshing and revisiting to ensure that process and basics are always top of mind. Training also must broach modifications in your environment - if new variables have introduced themselves, new competitors, changing situations - all of these require being addressed by leadership so you can cohesively move forward in the most effective way possible as a unit.

Even if your company lets you down, don't lay down - a lot of the issues of faulty or fruitless training can be overcome with how you accept and adapt. Take it upon yourself to seek out the people and resources that can make a difference in your learning experience and your success. If they have a vested interest in how you perform, it's likely they will do what they can to help. No matter what, there's always something you can do to better yourself, your knowledge of process and your execution and results. Do everything you can to make that happen!

The Vocational Viewpoint, via Vincent Scott
(Republished with permission)
"How do I follow up with my sales prospects without losing them?"

From today's mailbag: "I can get the meeting and present my product, but I lose them after that. What is a good follow up process?"

Ah, yes... the disappearing act dance that many of our prospects engage in. We have success in setting the meeting, make an effective presentation, they commit to thinking about it, talking about it, investigating it, etc. and then we wait. And wait. And sometimes wait a little more.

It helps to realize that our customers DO actually have a lot of other stuff on their plate like, you know, running their business. But we also want to make sure they are thinking about us, right? So how much is too much?

The follow up process is - like anything related to selling process - a delicate one that requires finesse. Upon the meeting's conclusion, send a quick note or e-mail simply thanking the customer for their time along with any items you promised to send during the meeting that you have on hand along with summary of any additional questions that may have arisen in the interim. Next, go to work on any additional commitments you made in the meeting.

All the while, be aware that this is a numbers' game; I've seen far too many people throw far too much of their time "chasing whales" or devoted to a few customers to their detriment; they chase big whales they often don't catch while several very hearty fish swim away.

Keep tabs on your CRM or make a spreadsheet of who you are working with, what you are working on and when you last made contact. Keep things simple, give them breathing room but don't let too much time elapse between contacts and focus on the words you choose to use.

As with anything in selling, stay unique! Avoid the pitfalls of the typical language that befalls most salespeople; remember that customers have figured out the process of the average salesperson so you have to evolve here. Don't say I'm "checking in" or "following up" or anything cliché. Keep it to the point, draw up something relevant from your conversation and keep closing the sale.

"Mr./Mrs. Customer: Good morning/afternoon! It is my hope this note finds you well. The intent of my note is to ensure I am operating on your timetable." At this point, depending on what you are selling, it helps to reference past conversations - for instance, if they initially said they would be purchasing around now, and any steps you would need to take prior to making the transaction that have not yet been made. "Please let me know how I may be of further service/value!" Remember, your sales is a service and your role is supporting them and providing value. Take that tone in everything you say and do and you will not come off salesy.

It is another issue entirely when you have politely followed up multiple times for weeks, at once per week or biweekly intervals and you continue to hear crickets. Frankly, I have a "flash it or flush it" policy; if you are spending too much time chasing someone who isn't responsive and is taking time away from obtaining new quality leads, it's time to get a definitive answer! "Mr./Mrs. Customer: Good morning/afternoon! It is my hope this note finds you well. The intent of the correspondence is to gauge the current status of your needs and ensure I am operating on your timetable. Your inventory/current slot (if you are scheduling something for them)/ current whatever you can come up with that is pertinent to what you sell) is on hold for you pending your decision and I am working to line up the necessary resources to fulfill your order. Please let me know how you wish to proceed, so I may coordinate appropriately. Much appreciated!"

It can also help if you mention you have other interested parties ready to buy if they wish to release their order. If you show them they have skin in the game and that resources are aligned for them, it's more likely you will receive a response. Let's face it, a lot of customers don't want to be the bearer of bad news. They don't want to break up with you. So, if you still do not get a response from that last contact, let it go.

I've found success by finding ways to continue to at least stay in touch, like newsletters and events - things that continue to soft sell you and keep you in their consciousness. When they are ready, they will reach out - don't worry! You cannot win them all, but knowing how and when to follow up and when to cut

bait is winning in itself.
Happy selling!

The Vocational Viewpoint, via Vincent Scott
(Republished with permission)
"I'm burnt out in my job with nowhere to go. Help!"

From today's mailbag: "I'm completely burnt out on my job! I've been passed up for promotions and just feel like there's nowhere to go. I've applied to jobs inside and outside the company but get nowhere. Help!"

Your affliction is common, but fortunately it is often misdiagnosed as burnout. Help is on the way.

Believe me, there is a possibility you have achieved everything you believe there is to achieve at your current role. This is why it is so important to have regular career conversations with others who can aid you in getting where you want to be. Your manager is also partly responsible for your success - hopefully they know that! It is not anyone's responsibility to promote you; you've got to make sure to engage and initiate these conversations with supervisors and other influencers in your organization. If you are turned down for a job, did you reach out to the rejecting hiring manager and request advice or guidance on how you may parlay your skills into their department or into this role?

Michael Jordan, probably the greatest competitor ever, achieved quite a bit of success early and often in his career - but (as books about him attest) he constantly presented new challenges to himself and requested that his coach, Phil Jackson, did the same in order to keep him motivated and hungry. He even left and came back - twice - because he had something to prove both times. Are there metrics you are NOT currently doing well in? Are there areas of the business you are uncomfortable with that you can learn and therefore make yourself more valuable? Ask your manager to work with you on a plan to get you ready for the next level. Once you have truly accomplished everything you set out to do together, the proof's in the pudding.

As for being passed up for promotions, always remember that when a promotion occurs you literally have to be the #1 choice in all areas being sought out of however many people applied. You may very well be qualified or overqualified! But we all have to pay our dues - sometimes, multiple times. And you will certainly learn that a variety of factors – some you cannot control – are taken into consideration when the other job or project is filled.

Are you truly "burnt out"? Or are you just out of love with the job you promised to love when you interviewed for it? We must constantly transform ourselves back to who we were on interview day. We entered into a contract with our company; they agreed to train and pay us. We agreed to be that eager beaver who would take the world by storm. Are we still holding up our end of bargain? And - yes - I know that sometimes companies fail to live up to theirs. But is the grass truly greener starting all over at another company and moving down the ladder or staying on the same rung for even longer? Or can you grin and bear it, weather the storm, stay ahead in the race and ensure you are the obvious choice the next time a better opportunity comes along?

In my experience, I've always found that when I feel "burnt out" in a role, I create or find a new challenge to assist me in becoming more valuable, I continue to perform at a high level and I ensure that I'm a candidate every time a promotion comes up. Eventually, you will get it. Don't give up. Monotony in a job is better than the misery of not having one! And if you do leave your company because there literally is nowhere to go (sometimes this can be the case!), be smart, leave on good terms, don't burn bridges and make sure that the new role you go to offers the longterm plan you desire. Don't settle.

Hang in there! These types of situations have a way of working out, specifically when you have followed the proper processes in the way of networking and conducting yourself in your role. While you may not get the opportunities you initially think you want, you'll likely look back and things will make sense when that next challenge is upon you.

Rather than dwell so much on your current state of affairs, focus on making the most of each day and creating new challenges; it will take time, but investing in your future every chance you get will pay dividends. Approaching it on a day-by-day basis also makes the whole situation more palatable. Each day you survive is a victory and every gain you made leads you closer – even when it's inch by inch – to your next goal.

The Vocational Viewpoint, via Vincent Scott
(Republished with permission)
"How do I keep my personal life from hurting my work?"

From today's mailbag: "How do I keep the disaster that is my personal life from destroying my work life and career?"

This predicament befalls us all in one way or another at some point in our career. No matter how hard you try, your personal life will affect your mindset while at work in some way. However, it is vital not to let it affect your output because if a dreadful personal life is allowed to ruin your business life, you've got yourself a catastrophe.

Tragedy in your life, end of relationships, trouble with the law, drama: they all serve to take your mind off your work at given times in the day. Depending on the severity, you most certainly should pursue resources available to you through your work or insurance to receive counseling and support through a difficult time. Most every company has these options and, if they do not and you have the means, you should seek professional treatment to assist you in coping with these challenges.

While I would love to say you should also be able to confide in your boss, I must warn to be careful and selective with whom you allow to see you bleed. I've known bosses who will use these sensitive subjects as ammunition against you later; even a boss that tells you they sympathize and are there to help. Furthermore, this rule goes with your co-workers and certainly with any employees you have. When keeping your personal life separate it means not talking about it in the workplace.

Finally, there is the emotional anguish that these things can cause. As best you can, "throw yourself into your work." Focus so intently on the things you CAN control. We often cannot control these happenings in our personal life from spiraling out of control yet we have control over our business process and that can be very comforting. Exerting control over what you can control aids and soothes in whatever healing processes we must undertake.

Most personal drama passes, but the impact it might have on our careers can be everlasting. This is why it is so vital to separate the two as best as you can. Take the frustrations and anguish you have out on the obstacles you face (constructively, of course). Because you cannot control your personal drama, control the energy you put into those reports or overcoming your customer's objections. You'll find you can very much turn negatives into positives. And, I truly hope you find positive resolution in any struggles you face!

The Vocational Viewpoint, via Vincent Scott
(Republished with permission)
"How do I address the brick wall I've hit in my career?"

From today's mailbag: "I've hit a brick wall in my career because there's really nowhere else to go. I've had success in my role, but my boss isn't going anywhere, I am not mobile and I'm growing stagnant. What do I do?"

The short answer: always look for ways to add value for yourself, your clients, your employees, your peers - anything. Nothing lasts forever and when there is an opportunity or a role you have to be the obvious top candidate or someone will pass you up.

Here's the thing: A little known secret to success is that no matter what your station and situation, you have likely realized a problem out there. It could be in your office or organization, but wherever it is be proactive and be the solution. Find ways to make your peers' lives easier. Gain the buy-in from your team members and your boss to take on new projects that improve processes. Make your name synonymous with teamwork, innovation and improvement.

Michael Jordan won 6 NBA Championships and was the greatest NBA basketball player of all time and that will ever be. He even left to play baseball and star in *Space Jam* and then came back. (Guess which one was the better decision of the two?) Then he became an owner and his best decision was to activate himself yet again at age 40 for the Washington Wizards. All of that said, one of my favorite books is Sam Smith's *Jordan Rules*. It and other interviews with Jordan detail how Phil Jackson had to create new challenges for Jordan on a regular basis to keep him engaged, striving for something new and continuing to chase new levels of greatness though he was already the best. Sure, he can score - can he pass? Can he rebound? Can he engage his teammates? Can he anticipate the moves of a defender, offensive player or team?

Sure, you are successful in your role. Are there other metrics you can master? Are there areas you could stand to learn that would add value? Does your job pay for you to continue your education? Can you offer more to your peers and your hierarchy? Have you formed a plan with your supervisor to get you ready for the next level? Frankly, your promotion may come long after you're ready, but you have to make sure you are that obvious choice.

The role that's right for you may not even be created yet, either. Find areas where you can impact your business and if you make enough impact and a strong enough case, they may create a new role just for you. We live and work in a new, more innovative age and companies are adapting and evolving with those times. It's cliché, but be the change you want to see and be the change your company needs. It will pay off, whether financially, with a new role, or even with just new experiences and learning that make you more valuable wherever you land next. I promise you'll get there.

The Vocational Viewpoint, via Vincent Scott
(Republished with permission)
"How do I earn my way past the gatekeeper to the decision-maker?"

From today's mailbag: "I've had a really hard time getting past the gatekeeper and reaching the real decision-maker. What tips do you have on accomplishing this?"

Like practically any facet of selling, there is a process. There is a sales food chain consisting of the various links of relationships. Prior to connecting with the decision-makers in a business, you will need to reach "the man or woman behind the curtain."

People have gatekeepers for a variety of reasons - to field initial queries, to disseminate the work and to filter what reaches the top brass. Just like you have a sales process, they often have a process: of minimizing, or completely keeping out, the "solicitor."

It is important to point out that often to prevent from being treated like the solicitor or the telemarketer or the dreaded salesperson, your aim should be to differentiate yourself from the rest of the pack. It's just like winning a romantic interest: you stand out from the crowd, you offer something that they need or want and you utilize charm and wit and confidence to steer through the initial awkwardness.

Most gatekeepers only seek to stop you in your tracks because of the poor presentations that have come previously. They are used to the salesy lines and those who are only out for themselves. Break from this mold and you can break the pattern.

1. Treat the gatekeeper like a human being. Remember that they are an important part of their business and a trusted advisor of the business owner or other decision makers. Showing them respect can garner you a reciprocal approach.

2. Be direct. Don't beat around the bush or try to over-complicate the first step. They have likely stated their name if we are phoning or you can see a name badge or placard if not. "Good morning/afternoon, Gatekeeper's Name! John Smith, please." Don't ask if they are available, don't talk too much. "Is he expecting you?" could be their likely response; "He very well may be - I'm here about your account. May I please speak with him?" Keep addressing their response while fashioning back into your desired direction.

3. Expect the initial objection, and be prepared with a response. If you know you are shot down at a pivotal moment in the sales process, have a solution. "Well, he's not in right now. Would you like his voice mail?" "Certainly, but what number should I reach him at right now? It won't take long to update him on the account." You will not make it to the next leg of the sales process every time, but it's all probability. The most effective approach at each stage of the game will give you the best odds at advancing. You'll go farther if you are more effective at each stage of the process.

4. Go ahead and leave a voice mail. Often, you are being screened (sometimes even by the decision maker masquerading as a gatekeeper!) solely to get a glimpse into your pitch without any sign of commitment. Be concise but to the point. "Hello, Mr./Mrs. Decision Maker, this is Jane Doe with XYZ. I'm calling because many in your industry are taking advantage of the services/customers/offerings we have. Please give me a call to let me know

when would be a good time to discuss how we may best collaborate / I may best be of value."

5. Seek and take their advice. It's OK to say, "Hey, there, Betty, we've chatted a few times and I've had no luck reaching The Big Cheese to update him on the account. When is the best time to reach him? What number should I call right now?" There's always a chance you'll get that cell number. Persistence paid off when Bud Fox wanted to meet Gordon Gekko - be confident and charming but clear about your goals and adamant in achieving them.

If you can earn your way into the gatekeeper's good graces by being respectful and honest, the chances of them granting you access to the dance increase exponentially.

The Waiter's Story

For five years, I was a waiter in a popular chain restaurant. It's quite difficult to remember the vast majority of people I waited on. Sure, there was the couple who came every Thursday that sat in the same booth, ate the same meal, tipped well and wanted to set me up with their granddaughter. There was the eccentric elderly gentleman who was a veteran poet; he'd stay for hours late into the night after his meal just drinking coffee, reading and scribbling in a notebook. However, of all the customers I waited on, the most significant was certainly Vincent Scott.

It was Friday, August 17, 2007, the night I waited on Vincent Scott and Abby Winters. Of course, I don't recall what they ate or drank; the process of the meal itself was rather mundane and blended in with most meals before and after. It was when I returned to the table after they departed and picked up the check envelope when I discovered the note that would alter the course of my life and career.

Inside the check envelope was Vincent's business card, face down so I could see what he wrote on the flip side.

"Ryan: Thank you for your exemplary service tonight! I've never done this before, but your personality and character are unique. I manage an advertising sales call center where someone like you could make a lot of money. No pressure at all, but if you'd like to just discuss it, let me know. Sincerely, Vincent T. Scott."

My initial reaction: I was flattered. No, I did not want to be in food service for life. But my aspirations didn't really fit into sales, either. My goal had always been to save enough money to go to school for a nursing degree.

Vincent made a good point when we spoke: everything's selling, one way or another. You can either get paid well for your knack for it, or not.

"I really try to avoid referring people to or for this job," he said when I called him a week later. "Friends or previous employees wanted to follow me here and they've had mixed success. I would never put the tough sell on you and frankly, I won't be offended if you don't want to do it. Look, you're personable, you're assertive, you've got charm – those types of things can't be taught and they can make you very successful in selling. If I can offer you a better way of life or a portal into something that improves you, I'm glad to do it. That's my job."

I was taken with the guy's words, no doubt. Working for barely minimum wage was not doing much to further my ambitions. Vincent, and subsequently tougher conversations with Phoebe Wells, Gina Baker and George Flaker almost trying to talk me out of the role, solidified my plan to take on the challenge. What did I have to lose? There were millions of chain restaurants to choose from if I ever missed complaining customers and memorizing orders. At least my new customers would be more lucrative.

September 4, 2007 was my first day at **ABM Advertising**. I won't lie; it was overwhelming to be surrounded by these Wall Street wannabes in suits with their slicked back hair and "glowing" resumes of either years of sales experience or bouncing around to different car warranty places. They could barely pay their rent but they had the latest smartphone and a nice car. "Slow and steady wins the race," I kept telling myself.

November was my first partial month on the selling floor and December my first full – I actually hit sales objective in December.

While a lot of these guys were boisterous and they whooped and hollered when they closed deals, I was never that guy nor did I have the inclination to be. I was there to collect a better paycheck. It legitimately excited me when I was able to close a sale and realize how much it equated into my paycheck.

These customers: I felt for many of them. They were small business owners who had tried various marketing mediums with meddling success. They often had good concepts but weren't reaching the masses and I wasn't always sure I could help them.

So much of we did and so much of what Vincent Scott mastered was selling a concept…a potential reality…an ideal situation. Certainly, there was method to it; we'd go in armed with our collateral about results our products had gotten in certain situations or headings. We'd find out enough about our customer to recommend a program and we'd be able to combat any objections using their own words and return on investment information. It did make sense. But the dialing for dollars was brutal.

Every morning, we'd come in, log into our PC's and check e-mail. Vincent would send out a dialing schedule for the day along with a quick synopsis of each city or campaign we were calling that day. It was spaced out dependent on time zones; we'd call into the east coast in the morning and move west as the day progressed. Depending on availability and time of the month, he would also move us into campaigns that were existing advertisers, customers we could upsell from free listings, winback campaigns, and just gobs and gobs of non-advertisers.

I don't care who you are: sitting on an auto-dialer attempting hundreds of outbound calls every single day, the majority of which result in a voice mail or disgruntled gatekeeper is not glamorous. But if you follow the process Vincent puts in place, you get farther and farther in the sale. Eventually, a light bulb goes off and confidence surfaces. Once that happens, you can do this.

There is an inevitability in sales: you will eventually straddle that line between skill and will. The time comes when you realize you can do something, but your desire has to be there to carry you through the times you don't want to do it anymore.

While I did hit goal 4 of my first 6 months and qualified for the semi-promotion to the inbound group, spent a quarter in there before finishing in the bottom half and returning, and made a fair amount of money – the best W-2's of my life were from ABM – I made two tear-filled journeys to Vincent's office toward the end.

It was difficult to face him because I knew he believed in me. And what some may find surprising, he couldn't have been nicer or more supportive.

"Ryan, if this isn't for you, I completely understand," he said.

"But you never once pressured me. You gave me the choice of coming on board, even detailing the ups and downs. I came here and committed and I feel like I'm failing you."

"Stop," he said, calmly, leaning forward in his chair and giving me complete attention. This man who, as everyone in the department knew, was regularly embroiled in career and personal battles and was likely going to run this company someday genuinely cared to have a conversation with me rather than push an agenda. "Ryan, you're a human being. I'm a human being – until proven otherwise." He chuckled, and I couldn't help but smiling. "This job is brutal. It's being married to the phone. Hell, I don't even know if I could do it anymore. Thing is, you came in and you were willing to give it a shot. You did better in this role than 90% of the folks I've seen try it. You can stay or you can go, but I don't for a second regret giving you the chance to decide. You decided then and you can decide now."

I stayed. But not for much longer. It was only a couple of months later when I returned to that office with my manager, Frankie Rivera to concede that this was not for me.

Fortunately for me, the position put me in a place financially where I could go to nursing school. I got married while I worked at ABM and was able to afford a honeymoon. January 20, 2009, was my last day with the company and while I have not seen Vincent Scott since then, he has checked in on me on social media from time to time. I know he had high hopes for me and I'm glad that he still thinks highly of me.

It was evident Vincent was a conflicted character. Most of the people in the department very obviously latched on to him because they saw the opportunity and wanted him to promote them. Obviously, he had undergone a relatively public split from his daughter's mother, had a relationship with the HR manager in plain sight and was romantically linked at various times to a handful of women in the department – true or not.

But what I saw in Vincent Scott was a guy who went out of his way to help me. It would have been one thing had I been this sales rock star or had he held any selfish motive in my selection and hiring. There were over 200 people in the office – it's not like adding me to that mix was life-altering for him. At least, probably not. He merely took a chance on me that changed the trajectory of my life, without expecting anything at all in return. For that, I will always fondly

recall Vincent Scott.
    I had a birth as a salesman, even if it led to a completely different path.

CHAPTER 2: FINAL INTERVIEW

Vincent Scott had been in this situation so many times before: interviewing for a position that was his birthright while reserving that slightest bit of doubt in his mind that would assuredly be subdued by getting his rightful promotion.

It had been nearly exactly 6 years since his career had crashed and burned. When he took on this new mantle, it would all have been worth it.

Night One: Vincent checked into his room. He had, of course, checked with Fred Hampton in advance of the event and ensured they were rooming together for the third of three times the assemblage had collectively gathered.

Fred reached out to Vincent almost weekly. While Fred was seasoned and accomplished, both in this role and previous, he legitimately looked up to and respected Vincent's resilience. He recognized the thwarting Luther Petty threw at him. But it was refreshing to see that Vincent would finally get his just due from a man who undoubtedly knew Vincent could single-handedly save the entire global operation from its many difficulties and aid in it reaching its massive potential.

They reminisced and had a drink from the mini-bar prior to descending to the ballroom to meet up with their peers. It was a great time, culminating in a welcome speech from Luther and one from his boss, Jessica. Vincent went through all the motions, as he had for the almost two years prior. He had played the political game to a tee, even telling Luther how eager he was to learn from him in this new role.

For, as anyone familiar with Vincent knew, his Achilles' heel and downfall was his unwillingness to play the game. Vincent challenged his inept superiors, fought for his teams, attempted to eradicate poor policies and was the candid campaigner for revolution. No more.

In this role, Vincent had stayed silent when ignored for what was now five "Business Manager of the Quarter" awards. They had gone to Glenn Timmons of D.C., Melton Stein of Colorado, Tip Lucas from London, Joey Christianson from Vancouver, and Allison Truman – also of Washington, D.C. – who was an Assistant Regional Manager and was awarded because (1) she was actually the one doing all the work and (2) rather than reward his top player Vincent Scott, Luther Petty named an Assistant Manager.

Vincent had been shunned too long but was now finally going to shine. His accomplishments from the Twin Cities, while nothing to shake a stick at, were not as heralded as lesser wins from what top brass deemed sexier locations.

The majority of the Regional Managers ended up in Vincent's and Fred's room that evening for conversation and cocktails. Everyone knew of the pending final interview and upcoming decision this week of the Market Managers. It was consensus that Vincent would be the manager for the Americas, Cheryl Montoya would lead Africa, Fong Cheung for Eurasia and Noah Archer in Australia.

Day 2 featured seminars on Majestech's current and upcoming offerings in the way of tablets, laptops, monitors, software and applications. There was a virtual office they were launching to the public in the coming months. There was a television offering. There was a new software package for education. Vincent mostly tagged along with his group of Fred, Mindy, Drew and Garrison.

It was 5 PM when he walked into the conference room with Luther Petty for his final interview – the one last hurdle standing between him and destiny.

"Vincent, good afternoon," Luther Petty boisterously boomed, rising from his chair behind the conference room table and walking toward Vincent with his hand outstretched. Vincent took it.

"Luther – good to see you. Thank you for your time."

"Of course. How has your trip been thus far?"

"It has been excellent. Hoping to continue that trend," Vincent smiled. Luther chuckled.

"Yes, yes, I'm sure," Luther responded as he sat and motioned for Vincent to do the same. "Well, Vincent, as you know, we are doing the final interviews for Market Manager and will announce them at the awards banquet tomorrow night. Are you ready for your speech on sales excellence?"

"Absolutely," Vincent responded. "I was flattered Jessica asked me."

"Well, you've done lots of sales speeches before and your material is all over the Internet. We're all looking forward to it."

Vincent could never tell if Luther was being genuine or intentionally calling attention to things about Vincent he was jealous of or wished to hold him back over.

"I appreciate that."

"Well, Vincent, let's get started. Why are you interested in the Market Manager position?"

"Luther, first off, thank you so much for your consideration. I'm honored. This role speaks to me – the potential, the power of our products, the purpose, the plan. I subscribe to your vision of driving forward with innovation and that the future is always just a double click away."

Luther smiled. Vincent was weaving magic.

He continued, "My greatest passion is helping others. I've found a great deal of joy making an impact for our customers, be it in wins in education that have put devices in our schools or wins in medicine that have put them in life-saving situations. We have a tremendous team; it has excited me to learn so much daily from you and my peers. We have amazing products and a great story to tell. And with my experience leading teams, track record of success in multiple verticals, will to win and ideas for taking our division to the next level with your blessing and insight, I'm ecstatic at the possibilities. This role is the next logical step."

"Where do you want to be in five years?" It was an overused, too obvious question that surprised Vincent, but he launched in unfettered nonetheless.

"Learning, Luther. Whatever I'm doing, I want to be learning. Let's call it what it is – the roles we may have in five years may not even exist yet, and I find that exhilarating. Whatever I'm doing I want to be making a difference. First things first, I want to master the role I'm in and earn passage to a role where I can make the most substantial impact I'm allowed to make."

"Great answer, Vincent, great answer," Luther replied. "So, we have 116 Regional Business Managers across the world. We have about sixteen of them hitting goal. How do you come in and get them where they need to be?"

"Luther, we work for a dynamic company. My peers and I legitimately believe in Majestech-Ware – it's why we're here. We are passionate about the technology and innovation, we believe in the company, we are excited to make a difference where we can and truly want to succeed. For our customers, for our company, for you and our leadership team.

"That said, what I find to be the best thing about this role has caused struggle for others. I had the opportunity to go to Apricot Innovations once upon a time and I declined mostly because it was a cookie cutter program with limited opportunity to be entrepreneurial. Don't get me wrong: they've earned the right to do business however they please. However, I believe the very reason of our prominence in industry since 1995 has been because of the entrepreneurial spirit.

"Some of us do well by entering into a position where we are free to set our hours, work from wherever we please, prospect how we see fit and by being 100% in charge of our business. We have made so many strides as well, but I have numerous peers who merely want to use our opportunities to improve as their excuses for failure. I tell them every time: 'Look back six months and tell me we haven't come a long way in every regard since then.' We're brand new! We're headed in the right direction, but this department is the youngest in Majestech-Ware. You can't hurry love – it takes a little time to get a new division where everything is running smoothly. But you guys are making the changes we need all the time. Things are getting better. Success is an attitude and a choice.

"If I am fortunate enough to be selected for this role, I would spend time with my team. At first, it's most essential to analyze their process and get to know them. Furthermore, I don't want to clone myself – there are different geographies and idiosyncrasies and variables I know nothing about. I need to know what makes them all tick individually – what they are looking for. We can develop a plan together to get them where they want to be. At the onset, I can discover their strengths and areas of opportunity for improvement and we can make plans together to improve their processes that lead to leads and appointments and devices and warranties and software packages.

"We've done so many things in Minneapolis because of that amazing team that I believe can be adapted elsewhere with our events and outreach and volunteerism and follow up protocol. The wheel doesn't need to be reinvented. This is an awesome, well-intentioned team and I will kickstart and reignite it by showing them how it can be done. I'll communicate. I'll be responsive and transparent. I'll share best practices as I see them and send daily sales reports and recognize their achievements and agree on plans with them and ensure they are being carried out. Luther, in short, I'll be your solider in the field holding them accountable to the vision you preach every Tuesday on our calls. It's time to fly."

"Wow, Vincent, wow," Luther bellowed. "That's fantastic. Why are you the right choice for this role?"

"Luther, it is a blessing when you are able to be part of a team where you learn every day. When your sales team teaches you things constantly. When ideas are free-flowing and you can look back and see the fruits of your labor.

"These things can happen on a bigger stage. The things we have done in Minneapolis to be #1 in the world can be replicated everywhere. Other markets can do the events and marketing and outreach and selling and metric focus and reports and coaching and training and collaboration that we do. I can be that liaison.

"For, again, it's your vision," Vincent stated yet again, knowing that egomaniacal Luther Petty would only be more likely to hire him if he stroked his ego. Ten years ago – heck, two years ago – Vincent would never have uttered these words. But he was willing to play the game to get into a position where he could actually make a difference. He had come full circle.

"Luther, I'm the right choice because I've learned what it takes to achieve these team results in a large market here at Majestech-Ware. I've managed through ambiguity and tough situations and departments that were just beginning – not only here, but also at ABM. My teams in my history have been all over the country so I can lead remotely. My ideas of betterment committees to aid in adoption of necessary change and best practices and newsletters and communication and collaboration and conference calls will drive the team initiatives and lead to results. While I accept and respect that this is new terrain because it's a new division and different company, I've led 1st and 2nd level managers to far surpass goal in the past because I know how to build a team, recognize a team, get the most out of a team and work with that team and with peers and with leaders to optimize our processes at every stage. And, finally, because I want to do it more than anything I've ever done."

"Awesome, Vincent. Awesome. So, what do you dislike most about your current role?"

"Great question, Luther," Vincent voiced with nothing but flattery. "There is only one thing to dislike, and it's that we are barely scratching the surface of what we can do as a division. But what better to do with that dislike than to turn it into the fuel for our fire to do the very things we set out to do? I'm blown away by the potential and possibilities here. There are 1,000 small businesses within a mile radius of my office. There are half a million in Minnesota alone! My team sold to 5,000 of them last year. That's 1% - and that's more than any other market in the world.

"When I started, we didn't have much to go on of a process to generate leads. Our processes on the back end have improved, which means we have a better value story to tell. Our product line continues to improve. All signs point to dominance. I dislike the fact we haven't reached our potential but I love the fact we will because of enhancement of your vision by Market Managers in your tutelage."

He was too good. Everything Vincent had done or experienced or endured had led to this seminal moment. He was wading through this interview like Neo in *The Matrix* dodging bullets and performing Kung Fu countless times faster than virtual agents trained to kill him.

Luther continued to throw standard interview questions Vincent's way and Vincent proceeded to crush this interview out of the park unlike any interview he had ever been in.

"Last question," Luther said. Everything up to this point had been simple mastery from Vincent and he was more than ready to put the exclamation point on it. There was a gleam in Luther' eye. Vincent considered himself ready. "Vincent, I got a report today that you've applied to 329 jobs outside our department since you've started working here. Why would I take it seriously that you want this role over anything else?"

Vincent was knocked back by this breach of confidential personnel information, but only paused momentarily.

"Absolutely, Luther. As you know, my primary passion and desire is to lead sales teams for this great company. Every role I applied to over 2 years was a promotion. I didn't start applying until I was six months in and already #1 in the company for six months straight. I cast a wide net geographically, meaning I was sometimes applying to the same role in different cities. This role just became available after being discussed but not made formal for a year and a half. I even backed out of two of the jobs because you told me I was going to get this one. I haven't applied to a single job since then.

"Please understand that I have led at the senior management level and my goal is to have that impact in this organization. I informed my direct HR liaison Jason Maxie of every single job I applied for per guidelines.

"That said, this is the role I have wanted all along, have waited to come available even though there was no confirmation it would and have forsaken other avenues to pursue. You should take me seriously because I am serious. Pursuing a promotion in the meantime only reinforces and reiterates my desire to revolutionize the business."

"OK, Vincent," Luther said, noncommittally. "Thank you so much. Do you have any questions?"

"First, thank you so much for your time, Luther," Vincent responded.

He was a bit rattled with the final question, but still confident considering the months of courting him for this role until it became real. "When will the final decision be made?"

"Well, I will confer with Jessica this evening and tomorrow and take her insight. The final choice of Market Managers is mine and I will announce them tomorrow."

"Excellent! We've come a long way and I look forward to continuing the journey. What will onboarding look like?"

"Good question. We'll be meeting here in D.C. for a week to plan our go-do's and then the Market Managers will make their travel plans for wave one of meeting each Regional Manager in their markets. I will be joining each Market Manager on the road for different legs of their trips. The Market Managers will shadow me in some of the meetings, we'll meet with some top clients in each geography and we'll meet with the local sales teams."

"That sounds like a very good plan," Vincent said agreeably. "I suppose the only other question I have is with everything you know about me and our discussions today and previously, what would prevent you from selecting me for Market Manager?"

"Oh…well…Vincent…" Luther stammered. "You know, I have other folks I have to meet with and talk to. You're a good candidate. We have lots of good candidates."

"Has anything changed since you told me I was the frontrunner for the role, and, if so, what can I modify to improve?"

"Oh, nothing! No, you are a good candidate. I have four other interviews to conduct and will inform you of my decision tomorrow before the announcement."

"That sounds great, Luther. Thank you."

Vincent and Luther shook hands and Vincent left, headed to the team dinner festivities to cap the evening.

With the pressure off, Vincent was ready to relax. But his mind kept wandering back to the "what if?" Why did Luther ask that question? Specifically after wooing him to this role he had been talked to about for a year that almost seemed like it was never going to happen.

Certainly, Vincent had pursued other roles. Working through the chaos and madness and Wild West of this division had been extremely frustrating, specifically for someone of his caliber. But he had waded through each day as best he could knowing each one put him one day closer to the next move. He planted lots of seeds along the way – perhaps excessively – in an attempt to be promoted. But why on earth would Luther have instructed HR to pull such a report? Who pulled it? It was supposed to be confidential and Vincent was displeased with the breach.

His peers' confidence that it was in the bag and a couple of mojitos soothed his nerves and he was able to relax into the evening. Many of the band again made it back to Vincent's and Fred's room to commiserate over the day's events and speculate on the following day's awards and announcements.

Vincent greeted Day Three as he would any other; an hour and a half in the fitness center, a shower, breakfast of an egg white omelet with asparagus and mushrooms and turkey bacon with fruit and coffee. On this day, it was wrap up; sneak peeks at some of the upcoming product launches, a look at advertising, guest speeches from some prominent customers and the closing ceremonies.

It was roughly 4:30 PM when Vincent fielded a text message from his direct HR liaison, Jason Maxie requesting his presence in one of the conference rooms. It was the moment of truth.

Vincent found the room tucked away in a corner of the conference center. He knocked and heard acknowledgment from Luther Petty on the other end.

Opening the door, Vincent found a small table with chairs surrounding it. In the room were Luther Petty, Jason Maxie and Jessica Marks. They stood and pleasantries were exchanged prior to all taking seats.

"Thank you for joining us, Vincent," Luther greeted him. Vincent could make heads nor tails of the looks on the faces in the room.

"My pleasure. Thank you for having me."

"Vincent, first, I appreciate you being a candidate for the Market Manager of the Americas role. You interviewed well and brought a lot of great ideas to the table. However, I have decided to go in another direction."

Thud.

The immediate shock to the system was buffered by the fact Vincent – despite what he was told by Luther, Jessica, Jason and everyone who had ever discussed this role with him – never felt this was a sure thing. His last "sure thing" – Apricot Innovations – had fallen through. Sure things before that, like a promotion to Midwest Director for Tel-Cell Wireless or a spot with corporate Cellular Horizons or the CEO spot at ABM had all gone this very way, so whatever disappointment he was experiencing he could quickly cover with the years of being overlooked and unappreciated and knocked down.

"I see. May I ask why?"

"Uh, yes," Luther stammered. "It was a difficult decision but Jason and I are going to coach you to get you ready for the next round. We will need more Market Managers within the next six months." Not surprisingly, this was not true and another Market Manager would not be hired in this geography.

"Of course. Might I ask what you will be coaching me on, specifically?"

"Well, uh, Vincent," Luther managed, clearly unprepared to deliver this news. "We will schedule some time to discuss a plan of action and develop some more stretch roles for you."

"Absolutely," Vincent responded emphatically, now with nothing to lose. *More stretch roles? After putting me on these committees and projects that mean nothing, you're going to put me on even more?* "I just meant what specifically will we be making a plan to coach me on? What specific items prevented me from getting this job that all three of you recruited me for and told me I was going to get and that you convinced me to turn down other roles for?"

"Uh… uh… Vincent," Luther continued. "Well, Jason and I are committed to continuing to work with you to get you ready for the next level."

Vincent nodded. He was finished here. "I appreciate that." He stood. "I have no further questions. Thank you for your time." Vincent bowed slightly and departed for the door, leaving the three speechless. All three looked as if they wanted to say something, but Vincent abruptly exited what was an awkward situation for everyone.

He was furious, but not surprised. Every fiber in his being told him to put on the brakes, shut down, quit on the spot, tell these fools off like he would have in years past.

He did none of those things. He looked at his phone and thought of his daughter. His wife. He had responsibilities. He wasn't a kid anymore. This was real and a reaction was not warranted nor was it desirable.

Vincent retreated to his room. He had a vodka and diet soda, talked to Fred and then to his small group of close peers and he counted down the hours until his speech. At the very least, he would surely win Business Manager of the Year and be recognized for his unbelievable contributions.

The Saul Portman Story

When I first heard of Vincent Scott, it was right after Jeff Gemini had been fired as our Regional Manager for Brink Wireless in Minneapolis. Jordan Wallace, who was the CEO of Brink and worked alongside CFO Lyle Caminiti and their owner Paul Gemini – Jeff's dad – let a few of us know that this new guy was going to take his place.

The first call I made was to De-Metre Jones. He was the Store Manager at the New Brighton store and I ran the downtown Minneapolis store; we had been tight since coming on board at Brink the year before. So, when we Googled this guy Vincent Scott and realized he had a book and had made several sales videos, we did everything we could to poke holes in him. We figured he would come in and start barking orders and making changes right away. We dreaded another ego without a clue.

Our preconceived notion of Vincent couldn't have been farther from the truth.

To give some perspective, I was 23 years old when I met Vincent on February 8, 2011. The last 6+ years of my life have seen significant changes in my personal life and career. One constant has been Vincent Scott.

Vincent came to my downtown Minneapolis Cellular Horizons store on that cold day in February, along with Jordan Wallace, who was giving him the grand tour of the market. Our busy times of day came in spurts and you could literally find us catering to businessmen and women dressed to the nines all the way to homeless folks wanting us to untangle their Walkman cord while they took their teeth out at our desk. One time a guy peed in the corner. Definitely what you'd call a mixed bag.

I had met Jordan Wallace when the Brink Wireless project had begun two years prior. He had promised what he came to call "blue skies" – a utopian outcome. Under the market management of Jeff Gemini, who led through incompetence, fear and intimidation, we were struggling as a collective unit and, in fact, very isolated. Most of us were searching for other jobs. I had actually found one potentially and was about to bolt myself.

It took a number of us repeatedly providing feedback to Wallace that Jeff was the reason for our lack of success and the turnover in the market. The turmoil was solely because of him.

Vincent came across as different right up front. Sure, there was the usual initial meet and greet conversation and line of questioning – how long had I been there, how did the store perform, who were my top players, etc. But it was what he said there in our first meeting that really struck me.

"Well, Saul, from my vantage point, you've earned the right to run your store and I'll let you do it how you see fit. Of course, if numbers are off, inventory's off, and the like, we'll examine it and come up with a game plan we agree upon. But I'll let you run the plays." He knew I had played college football, and he could do that in every conversation – just weave it into what was personal for us.

Vincent would spend some of his time in my store just staring blankly across the street through our sliding glass door where a 45-story ABM building was located. He didn't talk much about it, but he did indicate that they were his previous employer. It wasn't until much later when we made a road trip together to a wireless dealer convention when we spent the several hours of car time discussing exactly what went down when he was there.

Brink Wireless was a trip. We were surrounded by folks like Dustin Rollins, who ran the Greenfield store I eventually had to help resuscitate. He would sexually harass his employees and show up mid-day in gym shorts after a workout just eating and talking about absolutely filthy things that made everyone around him uncomfortable. I'll never forget when he stole thousands of dollars worth of inventory that technically belonged to our parent master agent Moriarty Wireless and Jordan Wallace actually made Vincent meet him to pay him for the loot with the cash in an envelope.

Looking back, I don't know how we did it. I don't know how Vincent did it. Frankly, I did it because I saw him doing it – saw that he could do it. There were times I wasn't getting paid properly if at all. There were times when Wallace's debts in his Texas stores prohibited us from getting new inventory so Wallace pushed refurbished phones on us that he wanted us to sell like they were new. There were times when he wanted to stop hiring new employees, so he made us bring on nothing but 1099's with zero base, which did not attract the best salespeople. There were times when each week there was a new rumor of who was buying us out and each day we wondered – will I have a job tomorrow?

Vincent pushed through it all. And he always took care of me. He was genuinely interested in my growth and development like no one I'd ever seen save my parents. The two biggest influences on my life have been my high school football coach and Vincent Scott. It's why we continued to work together at two more places of employment after Brink.

While the wheels were coming off at Brink, I connected closely with Vincent and with Terry Bunche, who was a late 40's scrapper and workhorse. He was a bit out of his league with the technology, but he had grand ideas about what we *could* do if given any resources or support. Unfortunately, those items never really came to fruition.

My fondest memories of Brink were sitting in the deli in Eden Prairie that has since closed near the store Terry ran that has also since closed. We would eat sandwiches and just talk about what we needed to do to move forward. We would strategize about the marketing that would propel us to stardom. We would discuss what we needed to force onto the Jordan Wallace radar in order to survive and thrive.

Vincent did things big. Prior to his arrival, the interview and hiring process would consist of scheduling time with a candidate and making a decision to hire them or not; typically, we had to bring them on even if they weren't great because Jeff wasn't giving us many candidates to choose from. Vincent would take the work off our plates so we could produce! He would invite every candidate he received online to show up to an open interview and then just figure it out. It was like herding cattle, but like he said, we were already working in an inexact science. What was the worst that could happen?

I remember one day at the Golden Valley Store, which was kind of our hub, when over 50 people showed up! We just jumped in as a team and conducted interviews – some lasted as little as a few minutes. We chided Terry because some of his were over an hour! He was always a talker.

When the dust settled, we hired 16 of them and had no remaining vacancies in our roster – we actually had a bench. That was the epitome of what Vincent did – he removed legitimate barriers to our success, he made sure we had the foundation vital to doing our jobs and moving forward, and he brought the thunder in everything he did. We couldn't control much, but what we could, Vincent made sure was the utmost quality.

Forced to hire 1099's? We laughed about it for a week. Jordan Wallace celebrated the fact that Vincent's peer, a relatively lazy and hapless Aaron Hartley in Dallas hired a couple of them, and then Vincent just said "The hell with it. If we're forced to hire these folks, we're going to do it best." We brought on 32 one day and 75 in the first *week*. Sure, they flaked at an alarming rate, but it was Vincent's way of taking a directive from senior leadership he didn't necessarily agree with and rather than fighting back, accepting it, doing it incredibly and then being able to say, "See? It didn't work."

Vincent never had to tell me this, but I know his experience with ABM changed him dramatically. I wonder what I would have thought of an unfiltered Vincent Scott leading a leadership team. The guy could drive sales like nobody I had ever seen. He won a Cellular Horizons Superstar contest nationally without even practicing or trying against "the best and brightest" of the retail stars who did the job every day and spent countless hours prepping. If we were short-handed and struggling to finish out the day, he would take the floor and close business. And while he would sometimes pump himself up in jest in conversation or meetings or conference calls, he honestly would defer on compliments; he was far more humble than anyone would ever guess.

Those days taught me principles I continued to use. Finding ways to know my salespeople – what they care about, where they want to go, what's stopping them – and using that knowledge to eliminate their barriers and come up with plans *with them* so I could sell change. It seems so simple but nobody else leads like that.

Personally, I can't ever understand how people don't hand the keys of any kingdom over to Vincent. But he would meet roadblocks from all over from folks who didn't want to see him succeed, people who were jealous of him and people who were afraid he would do their job far better than they could and displace them. The thing is, he would have made their jobs easier. He would have made them a ton of money. But they held him back – and I saw it at Brink with Moriarty Wireless stifling him, I saw it at Tel-Cell Wireless, I saw it at Majestech-Ware.

The guy had immediate, immense impact. Within literally two months of his arrival, our metrics and revenue skyrocketed. Our market would have 50-60% better metrics in each category than other markets. Again, it was because he looked at things differently. A Jeff Gemini or a Doug Wilson from Moriarty or Susie Wilson from Cellular Horizons or a Justin Rollins would say "sell more phones, sell more protection plans, sell more accessories." Vincent Scott would say, "Why are customers refusing protection plans?" It was because we weren't offering them. "Why are we not offering them?" It was because we didn't know enough about them, we weren't using personal examples of phones crapping out or being dropped and damaged. We weren't minimizing price to the pennies per day people were paying to protect this device they were married to.

"We spend more time with our phones than with any person on this planet – why don't we protect them? We rely on phones more often than vehicles and we pay thousands of dollars over their lifetimes to insure them – why are we so cavalier with our pocket-size datebook and computer that connects us with everyone we love?" Vincent would say.

He had a line for everything. He had a way of making everything so simple, so understandable, so relatable. He showed us what was in it for the customer and for ourselves and our company.

Vincent called that his holy trinity of selling – I have always held that one dear. If the customer, our company and we don't personally benefit from every transaction, then it either needs to be modified or scrapped.

Vincent looked at why customers weren't switching to Cellular Horizons: existing contracts and higher prices. Well, it wasn't too tough to sell our quality over that of our competitors because we didn't drop calls and the other guys did on the regular.

But he came up with buying people out of contracts before anybody else did! We operated fully on margin; we bought the phones from Moriarty and knew the cost on each device. Vincent would make and approve deals all the time provided they made sense. While $1 profit wasn't ideal, his philosophy was turning someone into a loyal customer – provided there was profit – was worth the effort to get there. He would buy folks out of their contracts, would adjust prices on accessories – whatever needed to be done to earn their business.

He and Terry devised marketing strategies that utilized fliers and a toll free number and a web tool that captured leads both from the hotline and online. It allowed us to get far-reaching audiences both from having our folks put fliers on cars in down time or posting the discount codes to their social media pages but also to track the outcomes and the promotions that were working rather than just blindly putting our message out there. It was brilliant.

He was patient with lackluster results and limited power. When a kid who skipped college and used Daddy's money to buy a Cellular Horizons store either didn't care or didn't follow Vincent's advice, Vincent persevered. Even staunch and outspoken advocates against Vincent, like Chris Jeffries who owned a couple of stores east of Minneapolis, eventually ended up loving the guy.

Jeffries was one who researched Vincent, knew of his book and videos and wanted to knock him down a peg. He would fight Vincent tooth and nail on every single initiative Vincent tried to implement or any time Vincent tried to get his employees to actually work. In the end, though, because Vincent kept supporting his stores, kept helping his stores despite the frosty reception and remained loyal even after Moriarty's Doug Wilson stabbed him in the back and showed his true colors, Chris came to very much respect Vincent.

That was another element that was new to me but to Vincent seemed like old hat: being betrayed. Keep in mind, I was a kid. Even now, I know I still have lots to learn. I bought into Brink and Moriarty because they did a great job at selling the dream – the "blue skies" – of what could happen if we were firing on all cylinders. Sure, it was all possible. But the problem was they weren't there as a safety net; there was no real security or support from those who sold us on doing their bidding.

When Vincent turned our market around in two months, they were singing his praises! When their system of mounting debts and politics and trying to fire us for issues out of our control and not giving us new phones to sell and not paying us properly reared its ugly head, Vincent stuck around and through it while these folks paid to support us treated us like lepers. They were nowhere to be found. It was very telling.

The things these folks would tell us to sell us, especially looking back, is pretty mind-blowing. I remember Jordan Wallace telling us he envisioned this 100-store expansion that would lead to Vincent overseeing the sales process and conference calls for all of these folks nationwide. We would market our process to these other owners and profit from them, taking a percentage in return for our tutelage. Of course, nothing remotely resembling this ever came to fruition.

I credit Vincent for always keeping me in mind and giving me opportunities when they existed – he lobbied to get me a District Manager role when he was Regional VP over Texas, Missouri and Wisconsin locations as well as our own. But these pie in the blue sky pipe dreams were laughably ludicrous.

What was real was the motivation Vincent drove in us and taught us to administer. When we made a road trip together to the dealer convention in Iowa, Vincent was asked to be on a panel containing an author and motivational speaker Moriarty paid to be there along with several of his peers. He sat at the end of the table, graciously accepting the role of being the last to speak on every single topic because he was the last added to the panel – literally only added because of the insane results he had garnered in just a few short months. That said, the panel turned into the Vincent show.

The others on the panel were various Cellular Horizons store owners in the Moriarty family of business from across the country, store managers and Moriarty account managers, all attempting to share best practices and insights on successes in their respective markets. For the most part, the other 7 folks on the panel would spout the usual talking points they thought others wanted to hear – the generic "We offer," "We bundle," "We ask questions" general bullshit. The paid speaker talked generalities about sales that were not industry specific. Vincent, not only being a sales and sales management expert and author but someone with real success in this game many were failing at was the star attraction. Everything he said was spot-on gold.

He talked of his management style consisting of removing all legitimate obstacles, talked selling change to employees and getting their buy-in, talked marketing concepts that worked, talked his plan on where we were headed. These guys were captivated! Afterward, everyone wanted to meet him. Everyone confirmed with me that I knew him and worked with him and wanted to know what it was like. I told them all: he is the real deal.

Vincent also stands his ground. Moriarty and Cellular Horizons put a ton of pressure on him to fire De-Metre Jones because of complaints coming out of his store. Vincent fired some folks at the store but he refused to fire De-Metre; De-Metre meant well and, like me, was young and in his first leadership role. Vincent stood by his people even though, in the end, that's why Moriarty did not bring Vincent on when they bought out Brink Wireless. And it cost them. Of the 36 Brink stores Moriarty purchased, 26 of them closed within a year. They sold the remainder within three years and another five closed shortly thereafter.

We survived as long as we did because of Vincent Scott. The thanks he got was being callously dumped and laid off without any prior tipoff or heads' up that it was coming.

It was his perseverance that taught me the most: one day, there would be a customer complaint about a tenured employee dry-humping a phone display stand while singing and dancing to sexually explicit music in the store. The next, an employee would text message pictures of himself in his boxers to three customers he helped that day whose numbers he only got because they had to provide them so he could get their account accessed. The next, rogue owner Dustin Rollins steals everything inside two stores and flies the coop only to be rewarded $7,000 for his crime. Then it was a sexual harassment claim from a brand new employee, having next to no inventory while employees aren't even getting paid on time, accurately or at all and being told you're no longer growing the region enough, killing yourself to come up with all kinds of new marketing initiatives that no one will properly execute. We could have fired every last one of them, which means we'd spend all day every day recruiting and hiring only to hire people into an inferno that we could barely convince ourselves to stay in.

We went through the final three months literally every day wondering "will this be the day we are bought out?" "Who will buy us out?" "Will any of us have jobs?" Jordan Wallace would share with Vincent who the alleged multiple suitors were; we would research them and weigh our options. We all stayed through the bitter end as we grappled with the uncertain future with potential buyout from any of six different parties.

Vincent felt bad because of the way it all ended, specifically because he had convinced me to stay in November 2011 when he got me the District Manager role. He was disappointed because the vision he had for me was dashed by others and was out of his control.

The classiest thing he did was perform his job until they literally took it away from him, despite the uncertainty and despite their cold shoulder toward him. He was slated to do interviews for three days straight from open to close. Rather than scrap them in the face of pretty imminent doom, he fulfilled his duties until the end and made recommendations on who to hire into the new regime.

He called to order his final meeting with us, simply to go out on his terms.

"This is my last act as your leader," he literally began. "Working with you guys over the last year has been a real pleasure. When we started this together, I'm sure we all had completely different opinions on how it would go. What we've been through these last few months has been...utterly unbelievable. Years from now, I believe we'll all look back on these days and remember what we did fondly, be better leaders for it and be better people for it. I'm better to have known each of you and I want to thank you for an incredible ride.

"Literally, any day, Brink or Moriarty or Cellular Horizons will remove me from my position. Because of that, I wanted to say goodbye to you guys on my terms and tell you how damn proud I am to have worked with you on this project. To have endured what you have endured says a lot about your character. I didn't get a chance to leave my last job on my terms, so I'm making certain I can do so this time and I want you to know that I have made recommendations that Moriarty keeps each of you in leadership roles when the buyout of these stores becomes official."

Then he took us out for wings across the street on his corporate card on one of the rare days toward the end when it actually worked.

His "replacement" if you can call it that was a kid younger than me named Linus. His idea of coaching was playing "accessory hot potato" where we would throw a mobile accessory to each other amongst our employees and name some benefit of the product before throwing it to someone else. And yes, I'm serious.

He was rarely in our stores. He fired anyone who spoke up against the incoming regime, like Terry Bunche. I went from a District Manager training multiple store managers all the way back to where I started – managing the downtown store. He was pathetic. Most painful of all is after all the gains we made under Vincent – actually believing we could make this half-assed operation work – we crashed and burned from there.

It led me to look elsewhere, which is when I came across Tel-Cell Wireless; the opportunity was for another Store Manager role and it actually paid double what I made with Brink and Moriarty.

It's cliché: they say everything happens for a reason, and when we look back on things we often believe it. Had it not been for my experience and resume from the Brink experience/experiment, I would never have been qualified to join Tel-Cell as a Store Manager. To provide perspective, I went from managing monthly budgets of $10,000-$30,000 to as much as $60,000-$70,000, leading real people getting real paychecks at corporate stores.

When I was in the process for Tel-Cell, it made sense to involve my brothers-in-arms. Every Store Manager from Brink in Minneapolis interviewed at one point or another at Tel-Cell. I also recommended a gun-for-hire District Manager all-star: Vincent Scott.

Vincent, Terry and I kept in really good touch during those few months. I stayed on with Brink until the day I was able to give notice to go to Tel-Cell. Terry, Vincent and I had a cigar bar we'd frequent where we could keep each other in the loop of goings-on. We mapped out our new game plan: takeover at Tel-Cell with more structure and better stability.

Terry, sadly, wasn't along for the ride. Tel-Cell job offered him, but he didn't take the role. Instead, he opted to be an account executive at a mechanical company; despite his lapses in operations, Vincent gave him the recommendation of a lifetime.

As March 2012 concluded and April began, the process was moving smoothly. Again, looking back, it was a relatively quick process but when we were living it – especially combined with those last few months at Brink – every single day was a rollercoaster beyond any proportion I was used to. I grew up in tough neighborhoods with my own safety in question from one day to the next, but at least I grew accustomed to that feeling. Brink wouldn't let you grow accustomed to anything.

Vincent was up for the District Manager role; there were two already in place in two segments of the Twin Cities area and one vacancy that they interviewed him for. Vincent relayed to me that every interview was a walk in the park until he reached the VP of Sales, Jonas Stewart. Jonas and our Director of Sales, Shawn Kirk, conducted his final interview and Jonas gave him the business.

To his credit, Jonas was concerned with the revolving door that was this District Manager role in the Twin Cities. Rightfully so. The market has been through no fewer than 11 market managers in 2 years occupying the 3 slots. But for anyone to look at Vincent's resume and grill him like he did, I'm awestruck.

"Yeah, so he asked me about the most challenging situation I've managed through," Vincent told us while we puffed on Punch cigars and sipped cocktails. "I told him everything about the last few months with Cellular Horizons, Brink and Moriarty – the uncertainty, the lack of new phones and the lack of paychecks. 1099's, the buyout – you name it. This Jonas character actually told me he didn't understand where my challenge came in; he asked me what I actually did to try to solve the problem!"

"No!" I protested against the lunacy of the line of questioning and reactions.

"I told him about how we went to Cellular Horizons and Moriarty for support and help, but also had to pledge allegiance to our employer," Vincent continued. "Not sure if he understood it all, but it was the toughest interview of my life. He interrupted me like ten times saying he didn't want to hear my philosophies, just results and examples even though I was explaining examples. I could do this job in my sleep, but I did not do well in that interview at all. I don't think I'll be joining you, Saul."

Of course, he did. But Vincent had done a really solid job of teaching himself how to network, how to not just apply to jobs but to reach decision makers through social media and get meetings and how to make his resume really pop. He caught the attention of three other companies while interviewing at Tel-Cell; one of them being the highly regarded Apricot Innovations.

As Vincent's fortune would have it, the week we started training together at Tel-Cell, Apricot came knocking.

"Saul, what am I going to do?"

"It's a tough one, brother," I responded. "I mean, you're talking about one of the most innovative companies in the world. A great long-term play. And here, you're talking about a situation we've mastered where we can go hog wild. What are you thinking?"

"The thing with Apricot is…they're Apricot. They pay $65K a year for that role and no more. There's some small team bonuses possible quarterly, but it's half what I made at ABM. Here, the base is $85K and with bonuses monthly…there's potential to add another $40K-to-$50K. It's not perfect, but – like you said – it's a place we can dominate. Apricot is a great potential long-term play, but the manager of the role I was offered lives in California. Moving isn't an option. And I'm tired of taking steps back just to step forward."

Vincent turned down Apricot, despite the fact he had to perform 11 interviews and an on-job assignment with them to garner the offer. The District Leader he broke the news to revealed he was the first person ever to turn down her job offer. That's Vincent Scott.

Vincent was entrepreneurial, liked to have enough control to make a difference, wanted to leave a legacy and wanted to use his talents to their fullest. Could he do that at a company who employed people to carry out a defined, cookie-cutter process? Or would he rather make more money where he could come in like a wrecking ball, tweak process and take a team from rags to riches? You know the answer to that.

It's also funny; when I signed on to Tel-Cell, I wasn't in the market Vincent was given. However, he quickly made sure that I was when they re-mapped the regions.

Our first impression of Tel-Cell was training in a pretty dingy back office for one of the oldest stores in the market – and it looked it. Our trainer was George Zazzle, a portly gentleman with a potty mouth who had come from shoe sales and fancied himself the best store manager in the market. George had some good knowledge, but his disdain for any sense of potential impropriety from higher-ups was so thinly veiled he was casting insults toward management in the training. He was the antithesis of politically correct.

Vincent and I felt the same way in training; the more we heard, the more we compared it to where we had just been. From the sound and appearance, we'd have more support, more room to play and grow and more money. We were chomping at the bit to get out and make our mark.

We met the other district managers who shared control of the Twin Cities Region – Alice Kirkpatrick and Mitchell Tyler.

It became evident up front that there was little leadership above – Shawn Kirk didn't even give Vincent a game plan for his two-week ramp up period between training and officially taking over our market – but Vincent liked it that way. It meant he could create and execute the game plan all by himself.

The first time I ever saw any vulnerability in the man was while with Brink when we made the trip to the dealer convention for Moriarty and Vincent told me the tale of ABM and of Abby Winters. The second was when he called me during a trip to Chicago, a target rich Tel-Cell Market where he was assigned to spend a weekend with the major players of their market. The Chicago market was highly heralded for Tel-Cell, was led by Alejandro Silva – a go-go-go, high octane nephew of the CEO – and was praised for their contribution in the company on practically every conference call, like they were Camelot.

"I can't even describe it," Vincent said, while he sipped a vodka and soda in his hotel room. I had just put my son to bed and was on my laptop studying for one of my college classes as I was going back to finish my degree. "Literally baptism by fire. I was just standing in one of their stores and it was fifty times busier than I've seen our stores on the busiest day. I was trying to help customers – everybody was there for upgrades. Totally in over my head. I don't even know what I'm doing here, Saul. I couldn't care less about cell phones or accessories or any of this crap. I don't know these plans – I don't *want* to know these plans. I feel like an out-of-place, old idiot. This is not how my career was supposed to go."

"I understand, brother. I'm in the same boat. Listen, you know why we're here. It's better than where we were. We're on a mission. Trust me, I stood in my store these past few days and it was like a whirlwind talking about these plans and seeing all of these customers who were complaining about lack of coverage. It's like we took a dip in quality but have a lot more quantity. There's money to be made here, and there are experiences to have."

"You're so right," Vincent responded. "One customer, one sale, one day at a time."

Not many people have ever seen doubt out of Vincent Scott. I've seen it, which I believe makes him more human, more relatable. I've had my fair share of doubt in my business and personal life. When I tried to leave Brink and Vincent fought to get me a better role and pay – that was a tough decision that, looking back, I know I made the right one to stand by him. It might have been a better short-term play, but the guy I was going to go work for back then has changed jobs three times since while I followed Vincent and again increased my income and prospects.

But over those coming weeks and months after that conversation those first weeks of Tel-Cell, he exuded zero doubt to the naked eye. He took the helm of our market and did no small task: he stepped into a position that had been a revolving door into a district that was 2nd-to-last in the company and he did it like a boss.

That first meeting, he met with our market in the back of the same store we trained in. Many store managers were late. I heard the grumbles: they all expected Vincent to come in, promise a "clean slate" and make a lot of drastic changes. He did nothing of the sort.

If anyone ever tried to peg Vincent as just like anyone else, he'd defy every one of them by doing the complete opposite and he'd revel in it. And he'd flaunt his unique status.

"Team, good afternoon! Thank you for joining me and your new teammates today.

"First, I want to establish the groundwork of a team. A team is built on mutual respect for one another. You have earned the right to be in this role, one way or another, and I will never tell you what to do or how to do your job. These daily status reports you have to fill out end today." I could see them perk up already, specifically as he picked up a printed example and ripped it in half. They looked at each other, smiled and a few chuckled.

"The bullshit paperwork – gone. But this is also the last time you show up late to one of our meetings. I'm going to show you the utmost respect and do my best to earn yours. I'm not going to change a thing today or hopefully anytime soon – without your consent and agreement and us deciding as a team that *we* want to change something for *our* market.

"I've seen managers come and go in my day, and I understand you haven't had the same boss for more than 6 months at a time for the last few years. My sympathies, but neither I nor you can change it so let's move on. While I can promise that this experience will be different than anything you've experienced in your careers, my words mean nothing and I can respect that. It's about my actions.

"That said, all I wish to do is remove what stands in your way. I want to know where you want to be in your career, because it's my sole goal to get you there – to chart a course with you and help you every step of the way. When barriers to success are removed, there's no choice but success. Want to take my job? Awesome – I want to teach you how to make your team so successful that you can manage a bigger team. Our team success will get me where I want to go and my job will be yours for the taking. Want to make a ton of money? Awesome – we'll learn together how to best master the scorecard and the commission structure.

"I've heard from you guys that the commission has changed numerous times and often not to your advantage. Sure, we'll take hits and we'll lick our wounds, but we'll adapt. Business is business, and I've seen twelve years of commission changes and inconsistency and things not panning out as expected. It sucks, but we can either complain and suffer or we can solve, shift and succeed.

"I'm passionate as hell about leadership. At one point or another, you desperately wanted the job you're in. Think back to that day. It may not be our dream job every day. We may not always get what we want or what we feel we are owed in our career. But I'll tell you this: if you give me your trust, if you do your absolute best in your role; if you work with me to overcome any impediments that stand in our way, I swear we'll all get what we want out of this place – be it employment, be it money, be it a career stepping stone.

"All I want out of each of you is the solutions to fix the legitimate problems. I don't want complaints, I don't want excuses. But if we have legitimate issues, we will work together on solutions and we will fix them one at a time. I can't promise you I can change every one of them, but what I will do is fight to get every one of them fixed."

After the meeting, George Zazzle cornered Vincent for quite some time, and the rest of the team cornered me – wanting to know what I knew from working previously with Vincent Scott. "Is he for real?" "How is this guy only a District Manager with Tel-Cell at this point in his career?"

Yes, Vincent Scott was for real. He may have gotten the screws put to him, as he liked to say, but he accepted a long journey back – and this was just one of the steps along the way.

If and when employees would call off, leaving Store Managers alone in their stores, Vincent would head that way and help them close down the store. Vincent believed we needed to hire enough people to make the managers actual sales managers rather than player-coaches or glorified reps, and he fought this battle the whole time he was at Tel-Cell. Of course, it meant he had to spend more of our P&L on headcount and commissions, but it paid off – we went from 2nd-to-last in the entire company to #1 in the company on the scorecard within 2 months. Vincent ran the most profitable market in the region within that same timeframe.

One thing we certainly learned about Tel-Cell was its contradictions and complacency; it was like nothing was ever good enough. They made endless changes, even when things were working. Especially when things started working. Unless you were a relative of the owners or in a market they cared about, you got no love.

I could understand the frustration of those who had been around the market for the long haul. It was also almost like we were in a silo; everyone praised Chicago, other markets got the visits from the big brass but it was like we were completely written off no matter how dominant we were on the scorecard.

Sales VP Jonas Stewart was actually let go shortly after we started. Personally, I think it was to save money and because there was so much turnover under his regime. For ten months, we had no VP of Sales and it was pure bliss.

There was shuffling of Directors and our Region wound up with Alejandro Silva's brother, Luke Silva. Initially, he said a lot of things we found insightful, like that we needed to focus just on moving boxes or kits (phones) and focus on metrics… but then we realized he said the same thing no matter what, only praised us and gave us no constructive criticism, had no real clue what we were doing and didn't understand the pain points Vincent was relaying. Luke peppered his speech with calling everyone "bro" and "baby" while just spouting off generic talking points. He wasn't a leader. But Vincent Scott was, and we were rolling.

The most interesting thing about the time with Tel-Cell was the arrival of Mitch Finkleson from the Denver market; we expanded our territory and Mitch arrived to take over the fourth Minnesota district.

Mitch was originally from Minneapolis; he had started as a sales rep and became a store manager in the Monticello store. He had been known for some questionable sales tactics when it came to mobile broadband; our team liked to say "Every customer left with a puck in their bag whether they knew it or not." It was "part of a bundle." He'd send customer service issues to other stores, especially if he could redirect the customer calling in to avoid them from becoming a click on the traffic count. He'd also activate lines on phones he didn't have in inventory and tell the customer to go to a store that had it – he'd claim the sale while the other store did the work.

Anyhow, I had never seen Vincent face any type of competition when it came to sales numbers. At Brink, he immediately took a commanding lead and squashed Lee Christian and Aaron Hartley with zero effort – then he became their boss. Here, he passed up Alice and Mitchell his first week and they never beat him on profitability or metrics or revenue the entire time they worked together. But the arrival of Mitch, while it had no immediate effect, certainly got the rise out of Vincent when Mitch attempted to go right for him, call him out and trash talk him every chance he got.

I remember an interview blitz we did a few months in; we'd often go to the Eliot Park Store where we were initially trained together as it was centrally located and had the largest back room. It harkened back to the 50 interviews we did in a day at Brink; the most I ever saw Vincent do by himself in one day was 38 here at Tel-Cell. Given the chance, I accepted the additional challenges as often as possible – anytime I could be involved in something above and beyond, I saw the chance to grow and learn. Having a hand in hiring our market's employees was certainly something I was interested in.

The district managers were present for the blitz – which was Vincent's idea, borrowed from the success he had with it at Brink – mostly so they could snatch talent right away before their peers could. Vincent saw that the current hiring method was broken; candidates could apply online to an individual store. The store manager could call them, interview, etc., and had to have another store manager present with them – meaning that a store manager would drive from their store to another store for a solitary interview that may or may not even take place if the candidate didn't show. Because they saw so few candidates, they were more likely to hire them out of desperation. Totally inefficient.

Vincent again wanted to take as much work off our plate as store managers as he could to free up our time to coach. Seemed like common sense, but common sense certainly isn't common in retail or sales.

Vincent constructed a form that each candidate could fill out regarding which locations they were willing to work in. This form could be used so the candidate could be placed where the business needed them, rather than in a location that may not even be desperate for them. Candidates would check in, be interviewed by two people working the blitz and the decision would be made on whether or not they would be hired or if another set of eyes was needed. Rather than have good candidates never contacted again once one position was filled, they could be utilized to fill a spot at another store in need. Plus, interviewing in bulk allowed us to quickly plug all the gaps in our region's markets.

Mitch Finkleson was at this first blitz; it was the first time I met him. Apparently, his market had actually beaten us for a week's results for the first time in the two months Mitch had been in town. It was the first week of the month so technically he was #1 for the month.

Mitch introduced himself to a candidate as the top district manager in the Twin Cities. Yeah...

"By what calculation?" Vincent asked, showing no emotion but raising his voice loudly enough to ensure the conversation gained attention.

"What do you mean? We won last week!"

"'Won last week'? So the last eight weeks didn't count?"

"We killed it last week! We're ahead so far for the month!" Mitch responded enthusiastically.

"Hmmm.." Vincent pondered. "Well, don't get used to it. Besides, I've heard of your mobile broadband antics as a store manager so who knows if those numbers are real?"

Mitch turned red-faced, and Vincent revealed to me that he later pulled him aside to relay the offense he took to the comment.

Mitch's market did beat us that month in percent to goal. The following month, there was fraud discovered in Mitch's market by traveling, impartial auditors and a few people got fired. Mitch's market's results never again approached ours and there was always suspicion he at least knew of and potentially authorized the fraudulent activity.

I have always seen the disappointment in Vincent when he is not recognized or received for what and who he is; I do believe that Jordan Wallace knew how impactful Vincent was but there just wasn't anything more he could afford to do for him. Cellular Horizons and Moriarty took him for granted. Tel-Cell praised the Chicago market and nothing we ever did, despite our immediate ascension up the sales ranks, ever seemed to be a blip on their radar. Our market had more stores because of the licensing agreements (they had agreed to open more stores in the Twin Cities than other markets), and we did more revenue than Chicago, but they would have better per-store averages and it was a huge Tel-Cell market so they had far more built in renewal business. In essence, the phone service actually worked there.

Thing is, inept leadership never praises their stars – they are intimidated by them. Vincent mastered this job within months and had us at optimum performance, but he had to constantly ward off senior management's whims – trying to change our hours of operation nonsensically, saying they wanted to be transparent and pay us on renewal business and residuals… which they did for literally one month before reverting, trying to cut our headcounts after we finally got necessary headcount, became effective and had room to coach our teams. I think Vincent took these things harder than the average manager would because he knew what he was doing. He was big picture, and they were not. What he did was working, but nobody wanted the Twin Cities story to be bigger than Chicago or Los Angeles or Dallas or Seattle. He could either accept thankless anonymity or he could voice his concerns, but he knew where that road led.

Ironically, much like Brink had locations near his former ABM stomping grounds, there was a store in Montrose that used to be a Pizza Hut and it was right across the street from the office he first managed in for ABM. There was a store literally a block away from the ABM office he started out at as a sales rep in 2001. There was even one in the same complex as a Cellular Horizons store he managed in Eden Prairie near where we met Terry regularly for sandwiches. Reminders were everywhere of his old haunts, and I could tell he was haunted by them – haunted by not necessary regret but certainly reflection.

We had those amazing ten months without a VP of Sales. It seemed Tel-Cell was never happy with constantly trumping their best month ever – they had to keep making changes despite the fact things were improving from a performance standpoint. The changes paid us less while scraping away more and more money for the higher-up's and they really forced us backwards on a lot of the gains we made on hiring and inventory and selling and metrics. In April 2013, Stan "The Excuse Killer" Keller (a self-pronounced title) came in.

Vincent and I both saw this as a good thing at first. Vincent was #1 in the company the first time he met Keller, which is sitting pretty when you meet your new boss – so we thought. We had some of the oldest stores in the company in our market, and Keller would chastise dilapidated stores in rough parts of town rather than marvel at the 400% year over year revenue growth. He would question internal management promotions Vincent had made recently simply because they had not memorized every step of convoluted processes that had changed three times in as many months; Vincent was so busy, he literally didn't have the time to spend with everyone on our team. We helped and coached each other by committee, and it was working. But Keller wasn't having it; he did everything he could to poke holes rather than praise the insane improvements.

Luke Silva was a disaster – his best coaching was "turn the music up in your store a little bit" – but he had survived 8 years with the company because his uncle was the unit CEO. Keller demoted him within six weeks.

Vincent applied to his job. Sure, Vincent had only been in position for a year, but considering his past with ABM and Cellular Horizons and his unparalleled results here, he was the obvious choice. However, rather than being taken seriously, Vincent didn't even get an interview for his year at the top of the company standings after taking over the 2nd-to-last-place market and modifying the recruiting and hiring and training processes for all of the Twin Cities Region – not just his own market. Keller had a "touchbase" call with him, asked why he felt he should be Director, barely listened to his response before telling him that despite the fact he was the most influential person in the market (turns out, he told that to multiple people) and that he was going to "bring in a Director who could get him ready for the next level."

"I'm done, Saul," Vincent said. I was the first person he called after the call with Keller.

"I hear you, brother. What's he thinking?"

"I'll tell you what he's thinking," Vincent responded. "He's already brought in two of his buddies from his last company to run other regions. He's going to do the same damn thing here, regardless of what we've done, regardless of what's best for the business. It's bullshit. I can't take this shit anymore."

"There's got to be something we can do. Can't you go to Samir Silva?"

"Samir put Keller in the role and Keller's clearly calling these shots. The only thing that would do is put a target on my back."

"It's settled. There is no growth here. The money is good, but just look at these changes Keller is already making! He came in day one and told me I was ineffective because I was working seven days a week; then he tells every district manager in the company a week later that we all *have* to work seven days a week!

He asks us to create store hours for all of our stores based on traffic patterns, and then overrides all of our decisions and just makes his own blanket change. He says all of the right things, and then does whatever the hell he wants. And the way he is riding us to write up our teams for minutiae means there will come a day I'll either have to comply or get written up myself. I just can't do it. I won't do it."

Within weeks, Vincent left for a partner role with a management consultant firm owned by a guy named Joe Downey. Vincent was a bit skeptical, but the guy promised six-figures and it wasn't Tel-Cell, it wasn't retail and it wasn't conventional sales. He took it.

We had lunch a couple of months later and Vincent was actually second-guessing himself; he hated Tel-Cell – the 60-to-70-hour work weeks and complete buffoonery above with zero career path – but the money was good when they weren't jacking our quotas up so high we couldn't hit them. It was a paycheck. Joe Downey had lured Vincent into a trap that at this pace probably wouldn't pay six figures across ten years. Vincent's new peers were dropping like flies and his fellow partners stealing leads. Vincent found a potential strong lead through prospecting and submitted it on the nightly report; at their next weekly progress meeting, one of the partners presented it as his "whale." He subsequently went in to pitch the sales program (Vincent's job) and lost the deal.

Vincent didn't rest on his laurels; within a couple of months, he had networked and made moves and had four companies looking at him and Apricot Innovations – the king of them all – told him they wanted him to come on board January 1, 2014, to the role he turned down the year prior.

In November 2013, Mitch Finkleson of all people reached out to Vincent regarding Majestech-Ware. The role was similar in scope to the Apricot role; while surprised to have his frenemy refer him to the job (Vincent's numbers would have been pooled into the same regional numbers as Mitch's and Mitch would get a $500 referral bonus), Vincent heard him out and politely declined, being transparent about the Apricot role and its imminent timeline.

Vincent followed up in December about his start date…and heard nothing. January 1 came and went. A few weeks in, he kept at it – finally going over the heads of the folks who had said he would be starting by then. Taking it to their level resulted in a call from a VP that revealed the role he was promised was not vacated as planned. He had waited around for this promised role only to not receive it.

The day he called Mitch Finkleson in February to rekindle talks for the Regional Business Manager role was the day after the person hired for the role actually backed out – he had received more money from his employer. The interview process was a formality; Vincent was overqualified in some aspects and uniquely qualified in others: he would be managing a retail location as part of his jurisdiction, but would be more of a player-coach driving results in all sizes of business, government and education.

Vincent brought me on board shortly thereafter.

Looking back now, as that was a few years ago, Vincent accepted a role with a decent base and a lesser role than he was used to. It was Majestech-Ware; a known software/hardware business, in a brand new role that had just been created that really had no roadmap or existing strategy. Vincent wasn't managing hundreds of sales reps and managers across numerous states, but he had a territory where he sold against numerous resellers of our product.

71 Regional Business Managers were initially hired across the world and the number grew to 116 within two years.

Vincent Scott was #1 every single quarter he was there for over two years.

He averaged roughly 3,000 unique business customers per year while the next closest was 1,200, average was 500 and some in his role had 100. He was getting me involved so I could take on his role when he moved on. This was a glimpse I had never seen: Vincent in direct sales, and he was the best there's ever been.

A few months in, he was asked to rewrite the training book on how the job was done. He was called by nearly all of his peers and their business teams as the point of contact for their entire global division – they couldn't get any response from their "leadership" team so they called him. He knew the answers and he always responded. He was working on kind of an underground support network for these unsupported folks when their division boss found out and – to keep control – put Vincent on the weekly business division's conference call presenting a peer collaboration best practices segment he created himself. He was presenting a slide to hundreds of business managers and sales managers and reps across the world every week. It was something. And he owned it and dominated it.

Vincent was told for months that they were creating a promotion for him where we would train and manage those who were now his peers. When the role became open, the head of the business division visited Minneapolis (for the first time ever) to recruit him. Weeks later, he gave it to someone else who was ranked 8th – someone who spouted the talking points rather than someone who would drive results and shake things up like Vincent Scott.

Once again, it was an incredulous situation where nobody wanted the Minneapolis story to trump that of New York City or London or Dallas or Los Angeles or Hong Kong. Once again, it was a situation where somehow, Vincent had found the utmost success in a situation with terrible, half-assed processes and procedures that made no sense for customers or company, and yet he received another slap in the face. He was #1 every single quarter he was in the role, and every quarter "Business Manager of the Quarter" was given to someone in a more politically desirable location who couldn't hold his jockstrap. The division boss was frankly inept and absolutely terrified that allowing Vincent a leg up would mean the end of him. Better to put in someone who had no ability to overtake him.

Knowing Vincent's ABM story, knowing him at Brink and Tel-Cell and working with him again at Majestech-Ware, I can tell you this: he was the most refined and controlled I had ever seen him after the latest unfair occurrence.

I know he had some more tragedy in his life during that time and he told me one day in 2016, "Saul, I learned about a year ago to literally just take every single day at a time. It's all you can do. The past doesn't matter and some days it's all you can do to limp to the finish line. But if you make it, even if you failed that day, you'll be rewarded with tomorrow – a new chance to make brushstrokes toward your masterpiece.

"There's no sense in thinking too far ahead – that was the mistake I used to make. I got so consumed with what was next, what was years down the road, that I totally lost sight of the here and now. There's so many things that don't matter. And so much of our lives is just about acceptance: accepting things how they are, what we can and cannot change, and choosing to make the best impact we can every day. When you look back on your body of work, if you always did your best, it will be something to be proud of.

"Ten years ago when I was told all the time I'd be CEO of a huge company, I was obsessed with the next step and the long-term play. Now I just want to be a Dad and make it through the day – leaving a mark every day. Every day completed where you're still standing is something you can build on."

I didn't see Vincent much after that.

It's funny, though, because I know that after he didn't get that promotion he had some of the biggest days of his life!

A guy like that – so confident on the outside but conflicted on the inside, so strong on the outside yet sentimental, so firm in his resolve but so careful in his planning – he's the most influential, impressive person I've known. It was sometimes hard for me to watch because the better he got, the more he was held back by politics and by bosses who were terrified of his influence. How he held it all together in the face of what he went through personally and professionally, I'll never know. He endured tragedy, empty promises, lack of recognition despite being the best, and yet in the end, I believe he just decided to accept everything he couldn't change for what it was while still doing everything he could to make his presence felt. He definitely made his presence felt.

No one will have as profound an impact on my life and career as Vincent Scott did. He believed in me when no one else did and he actually took the time to truly show me how to improve. He coached me, motivated me, mentored me and just being on his team made me better.

Now I have my own mark to leave.

The Vocational Viewpoint, via Vincent Scott
(Republished with permission)
"My boss told me to cheat. What do I do?"

From today's mailbag: "Lots of people in my department cheat and add services to customers' accounts they know nothing about. Even my boss has indicated that this is common and they would look the other way if I did this to boost numbers. I can't believe I'm even considering it to be able to compete and earn a bonus. What should I do about this?"

Cheating is a line that - once crossed - there is no way back from. You're tainted. Trust me, I can tell you that you can be the best without cheating. These times are temporary, cheaters will be exposed eventually and when the dust settles, you'll be the one standing proudly behind real numbers.

Look at major league baseball as a prime example. Those who have cheated over the last couple of decades posted inflated numbers and celebrated false victories in the moment. But, after all that's said and done, how do we currently view these fallen heroes? They will never make it into the Hall of Fame, their legacies are destroyed, and they are a punchline. Furthermore, if you cheat, like the trainers who get interviewed and turn them in, the likelihood is your boss will not have your back if you're caught.

If any manager tells you to cheat or condones cheating, they are weak and an extremely poor, unethical leader. They, too, will eventually find their way out of the business, believe me. Sales results are all about people and process. If you are struggling in any key metric of your bonus plan or your compensation, look at the reasons why customers are declining. Look to people who are being successful without cheating and find out what they do. Birds of a feather flock together - link up with the winners in your department and share best practices.

Unfortunately, doing things the right way and living a career of integrity can often be a lonely road – at first. You will see accolades and praise given for people that are completely undeserving and will be flavor-of-the-month folks who throw up phony numbers. A career is a body of work. You don't have to be #1 every month, and - frankly - sometimes you have to keep your head down and nose clean and do your job while everything else takes care of itself of its own volition.

The moral of the story: Never, never, never cheat. There are a variety of ways to produce results in any metric without breaking rules; learn best practices from others. Analyze your process to ensure you are asking the right fact finding questions to form enough return on investment ammunition to pitch the product and overcome any objections, and, if your own boss is not going to be a resource, seek counseling from others on your coaching needs and career.

It is frustrating to watch others be praised in an arena you cannot currently compete in - but that's the very reason that when you earn the accolades you desire and deserve, the victory will be that much sweeter. You will have proven you did it the right way and 5-10 years down the road when you're doing something else you want to do or you're running the place, the lessons you've learned and the experiences you are gaining now will be invaluable.

The Vocational Viewpoint, via Vincent Scott
(Republished with permission)
"The process at my job is a disaster. What do I do?"

From today's mailbag: "The process at my job is a complete disaster. I'm surrounded by incompetence that makes it impossible to truly take care of my customers and no one really seems to care or be able to make positive change. Thoughts?"

Whether you are at a small or large company, a division or project in incubation stage or that has been around for years, you will encounter issues with process. Frankly, lots of people in leadership positions do not understand that process and people are really the main components that make things tick.

Sometimes, the people calling the shots in sales organizations have never worked in sales a day in their lives and they do not consult with the people before making process. Furthermore, there are always varying levels of excellence people have for the roles they are in. Mix these all together, and they make for an interesting cocktail.

1. Are you being a positive influencer? You may not have been consulted when the process you describe was implemented but you can certainly control your attitude and actions regarding it. Reach out to those who impact the process and ensure that they know the struggles you are having. Preface your statement with understanding of any growing pains or positive components of the process, but respectfully present issues and potential solutions you have so that you can constructively work toward fixes.

2. Consult your peers. How are others in your role dealing with the process? Surely, if you are struggling so mightily, they must be experiencing similar woes. If that is the case, they may have shortcuts, simplified ways of managing and maneuvering their way through and an answer to the specific problems you face.

3. Keep your head down; grin and bear it for now. Change is imminent. Nothing lasts forever. Yes, there are problems in the process but with your input and input from those like you, you've got to have faith that positive change will occur. It is OK to level set with your customer and ensure they know of the expected timeline of the process. It is OK to have candid conversations with your supervisor and others who can impact the process to ensure your voice is being heard - appropriately. Any company with viability will address their process problems appropriately.

Always think and operate "big picture." Yes, your customers may occasionally serve as the broken eggs that become the omelet. It is frustrating in the moment when process is a problem rather than a proponent. But you control what you can control (your attitude and actions and your input to guide the process as it evolves, because all processes are evolving) and you keep a steady hand on the wheel during this storm. Give it time, and months down the road look back and ask yourself, "Has this process improved?" If it has, great. If it hasn't, it's likely time to start asking different questions.

The Vocational Viewpoint, via Vincent Scott
(Republished with permission)
"I'm surrounded by incompetence at work. What should I do?"

From today's mailbag: "My team is incompetent. I feel like I am doing everything I can but just cannot seem to rise above the poor work ethic and lack of contribution of others. Any advice?"

There's the old adage that a team is only as strong as its weakest link. No matter how hard you try, your efforts and excellence and contribution will be leveled out and watered down by those whose pale in comparison.

1. Analyze the skill sets of the team. Does the incompetence exist because people are working well outside of their strengths? Are there ways to reorganize the work so these issues are diluted?

2. Is leadership aware of the issues? By no means am I a proponent of "tattling," but constructively presenting problems with proposed solutions is often an effective mechanism to tackle just about anything. Rather than just telling leadership that team members are not carrying their weight, present the areas that are suffering, allow leadership to draw their conclusions based on fact and seeing the issues firsthand, and present any solutions you can think of as someone on the front lines. If you do this, it builds trust and it is more likely your recommendations will be taken seriously. Those who throw their co-workers under the bus can easily be branded as disloyal, and that will be counter-productive to your cause.

3. Invest the time to help. Are you in a position to train those who are lagging behind? Are you able to take steps to improve the broken links in the process? It may be daunting and take away from the tasks at hand, but remember you are investing into future success. Wouldn't it be easier if the team worked better and the process had fewer gaps? Invest the time now to yield future successes through better trained people and improved assembly line.

It's very likely that no matter where you go, you will encounter incompetence in the workplace. However, it is not always a lack of will; it could be lack of skill that can be addressed and enhanced. It could be a lack of will that needs to be brought to the attention of leadership in a roundabout way by pointing out the obstacles you are facing and letting them draw conclusions with the help of your recommendations. Whatever the case may be, you will need to accept a certain degree of issues and obstacles and lack of effort from time to time, but take steps to minimize these issues, be a voice for positive change - and you just may find yourself in a position to impact the business even more!

The Vocational Viewpoint, via Vincent Scott
(Republished with permission)
"How do I shake the sales slump?"

From today's mailbag: "Lately, I've been in a sales slump. Nothing's working. I can't seem to get customers to say yes to my full pitch and I can't even sell the cheap plans. What do I do?"

Ahhhh, the sales slump. At times, most everyone goes through some semblance of this. Little shifts in our mechanics, a variety of intangibles like changes in the marketplace or competitor offerings and our growing desperation knock the planets out of alignment. There is a cure, and it's process. It's back to basics. And it's patience.

Something I've certainly noticed over the years of sales coaching is that no matter how rock solid the plan in the huddle, it has to be executed and has to be executed consistently for success. What I mean by this is we may devise a strategy to fix anything ailing the sales process, and a sales rep may go out and try the strategy. But if it feels a little foreign or uncomfortable, which may be common, they shy off after a few stumbles out of the gates and go back to these comfortable ways of mediocrity or failing.

In a sales slump, something has changed. It could be so slight that we ourselves don't even see it or recognize it just yet.

1. Analyze where in the sales process you are losing. Are you getting up to the presentation plate and going down swinging because you don't have the proper information typically obtained in fact finding? If you are skimping on your needs analysis questions, you'll be swinging at nothing but air when it comes to making a value presentation that fits your customers' needs and will have nothing left to overcome any objections with. Sales is a process and every step must be there.

2. Don't get desperate. Often, we will try to sell that cheaper package just to get on the sales board. However, how many of these minnows add up to the marlins or whales you could be scoring? Even if you get the puny score, is it worth it to your long-term goals to sacrifice and become a singles hitter instead of a home run hitter? Think about baseball - when in a slump, it's vital to revisit the swing mechanics that led to you hitting the ball all over and out of the park, not changing your stance or swing or approach. You've had success, so work to replicate it.

3. Be patient. Take your time. Obsess over process, not the numbers. I'm well aware this is the most difficult part. We want a sale, and we want it now! We likely have a boss who is wondering what the heck has gotten into us - hopefully, they are supportive, but sometimes they are not. In sales, you and I both know we are only as good as our last sale and last performance. Yesterday

is history, and we have to capitalize today and every day. Trust in the process and be patient that it will pay off. Don't let your frustration be reflected in any part or step of the process, because that's when you start skipping vital steps. That's what can make the slump drag on.

4. Get back to basics. Do you need to devise a script for yourself? Do you need a scratch pad to write down key things in the conversation or to remind yourself to ask certain things? There's no shame in making a strong effort in getting back to fundamentals. That's what is going to get you back in the game.

A sales slump can be caused by a variety of factors, some of which are under your control. Others can be overcome with adaptability. You must constantly reinvent yourself as a noble knight of the sales trade: if the competition's offerings have changed or the industry has changed or the economic climate has changed, you have to change with it. Modify the questions you ask and how you present your solution in the wake of how these changes impact your customer, but in the end, your steps of process will never waver.

Trust in your sales process, control what you are able to control, figure out where you are currently losing your customer and build back up that part of the chain. We'll never win every single sale, but with our best possible foot forward in every phase of the selling process, we give ourselves the best probability at success. Baseball players get on base typically anywhere from 20%-to-40% of the time, which is a pretty big "swing" - pardon the pun. Depending on your close rate, you are even less likely to see the immediate, drastic results you want. But if you are able to double or triple your close rate by making better moves in the process, your slump will be replaced with a surplus.

Good luck!

The Vocational Viewpoint, via Vincent Scott
(Republished with permission)
"Do you still believe in cold calling?"

From today's mailbag: "My leadership clings to cold calling as a large part of our outreach. Many of us think this is a dead initiative. What say you?"

I believe we should never discriminate against a potential revenue source. However, it is incumbent upon us to prioritize our lead sources. Are we cold calling when we could be pursuing other forms of outreach, marketing and targeted lead generation?

What are your absolute warmest leads? Are they being prioritized in your current setup?

There is certainly room for cold calling provided you are managing your process toward the most lucrative leads and cold calling with the time remaining when other potential opportunities are exhausted. Sometimes cold calling is the only way to truly get to those "hard to reach places." It can open doors that would otherwise remain closed.

Certainly, cold calling can come across as somewhat of an old school mentality. Often, making hundreds of dials nets us a few decent decision maker conversations and even fewer sales. It can be exhausting getting to the "yes" and our sales process suffers because our skills don't stay sharp.

On the other hand, if we are mixing in pure cold calls - whether on the phone, in person, e-mail, etc. - in with the management of our warmest leads and cultivation of seeds with a higher propensity to grow that we can build upon, it can certainly be a complement to our approach. I've known many a whale that was the result of a frigid cold call.

Does your division and leadership have a policy by which you and your team members can present feedback regarding the calling protocols? Hopefully, you are able to present any potential problems along with proposed solutions to your management. I feel any time you are able to concede to their points (i.e. that cold calling can be a worthy use of time, citing examples) all while pointing out shortcomings in the current process (citing examples) and presenting a solution that satisfies their desire for cold calling along with your mutual desire of making more money and nurturing potentially more fruitful leads, you can reach a compromise.

Maybe it's setting aside some time for this type of prospecting, but reducing the focus. Compromise is key – and can help you tap numerous potential revenue streams as opposed to one or two.

So, yes, I believe in cold calling in certain situations as a complement to your current lead sources. Explore with leadership where additional lead sources could lie! Explore with leadership different ways to make more revenue from the existing cold calling regimen! Respectfully state your case along with a well-substantiated look at what current cold dialing is yielding and present a plan that can enhance results, morale and profitability.

If you show you are after the same end results as your manager, and they are an outside the box big thinker, you have a chance to make a real difference. Sometimes that works, sometimes it doesn't, but you don't want to just be along for the ride, do you?

**The Vocational Viewpoint, via Vincent Scott
(Republished with permission)
"I'm being pressured to write up and fire my team. What do I do?"**

From today's mailbag: "I'm getting pressure from senior leadership to write up and fire people on my team with whom I still believe in, want to work with and disagree that it's the right course of action. How should I handle this?"

Your entire role exists as one of support and service to your team – enforcement of rules and holding accountable, certainly, but also making sure they have what they need to be successful. When it all comes down to it, you should know what's best for them - what course of action will result in their success, what they need to modify in their process to be more successful and ultimately if you have given them one chance too many.

Sometimes, that last one is a little tricky; at times, we give people too many chances. However, we are working with people's livelihoods so it is human nature to error on the side of caution. I've heard it said that it's business and not personal, but when you have control over someone's quality of life, their ability to put food in their families' mouths and their careers, there's nothing more personal.

From time to time, senior leadership can lose touch with the front lines. It is very important that you are at the pulse of your team. It's my philosophy that if someone earns the right to be in any position in an organization, they have the right to make many of their own choices in how they will carry out the necessary processes to fulfill their assigned tasks.

By this, I mean that until or unless you or your team is not getting the job done, there should be a degree of latitude they are allowed to do their job. If they are failing, it is up to you to make a plan with them and ensure it is executed. If they continue to choose to make the wrong decisions regarding those plans you have come up with, by all means, it is time to let them loose to be free to find their real destiny because this clearly isn't it.

That said, because sometimes senior leadership can be out of touch, they can make blanket rules and regulations and guidelines to govern all. While this may be necessary to help folks who need the guidance - the equivalent of the bumper lanes in bowling - some people do not. You cannot make all rules to govern all. It just doesn't work.

And some people in senior leadership roles in organizations never did the jobs they govern or they have forgotten when they did. We've got to have massive respect for those on the front lines, because they do the selling, the administrative work, the backbone of our business. It's why we must make decisions with their input in mind and we have to take into consideration how anything we do will impact them and our business.

If you are getting pressure to write up your team or fire your team members and you feel they are undeserving, you go to bat for them. You ask clarifying questions about the process. You make sure your team knows that you have their backs and that you are supporting them.

However, at the end of the day, the company also pays you to carry out their mission statement, their way of business and their process. It's important you don't forget that. Sometimes, it can lead you to quite the balancing act and ultimately you have to choose between your beliefs and principles or your paycheck and career.

You can certainly respectfully ask for clarification around the thought process of writing up your team or firing them; you can make a case for why someone should not warrant that type of treatment. However, when you are instructed to do something, you are being paid to carry out those orders. Don't forget that.

We are all varying degrees of important cogs in the wheel of business; while we can certainly have a high level of impact, we must also choose our battles. Everyone - people above and below us on the sales food chain - makes choices. Your defense of your team may be aesthetically appreciated and it may boost morale. But you cannot make a difference in the grand scheme if you don't play the game and you are always butting heads with those ahead of you on the corporate ladder.

Receive the message, ask for clarification of process, make any kind of case you plan to make (the problem you see with the course of action followed by a solution that will provide necessary results along with your commitment to get the team member where they need to be on an agreed-upon timeline) and accept the judgment of your superior at that point. You won't win every battle, but you'll gain the respect of your team for standing up for them and by being gracious and working with your manager and not against them, you will also likely gain their respect and trust when you successfully carry out your plan.

Sometimes, these gambles you make for your team will fail, and sometimes they will succeed. It will be just as much of a learning experience in this experiment of human behavior in the laboratory of your business.

Win, lose or draw, you did what you felt was right by your team, you supported them, you followed the direction from your manager, and you did your job. Stand proud.

The Vocational Viewpoint, via Vincent Scott
(Republished with permission)
"I'm buried in administrative sales tasks. How do I manage my time?"

From today's mailbag: "I'm literally buried in my various administrative sales tasks. How do I effectively manage my time so I can achieve the results expected of me?"

Starting out in sales, this is basically our dream, right? Seriously, it's like we oversee many different oil rigs - none of which show immediate or quick results. However, after nurturing each different pocket of our business, generating leads from various sources, developing pipeline, perfecting our pitch and growing relationships with prospects, one or multiple of these fields is going to strike oil. And, from time to time, if we're really skilled, they will gush and we face potentially drowning in the newfound success.

Time management is so important, no matter what phase of your sales process you are in. Starting out, it's all about differentiating your different prospecting methods, selectively choosing which networking methods you will employ and meeting with people in the right industries and geographies. Frankly, it's all about balance; some people just chase whales and never land anything. Others catch too many minnows and starve. There is a happy medium to each facet of managing your time.

On the other end of the spectrum, a seasoned seller has established a book of business, manages existing relationships to keep clients happy but also wants to ensure a steady stream of new business. I've seen business models that depend on 20% of their customers to deliver 80% of their business and as soon as competition undercut them, they lost those large spenders and their business was cooked. You will win with breadth of customers and well distributed influx of revenue.

So, utilize that concept and philosophy when divvying up your time.

(1) Prioritize. Do you have an existing spender needing some TLC? Do you have a current customer who has placed an order, has a problem you can provide a solution to, or can provide referrals by good word of mouth (a.k.a. the best marketing tactic)? Prioritize by real customers and real revenue - they should always come first.

(2) Looking for new ways to expound upon existing client relationships. Keep your customers happy by continuing to find new ways to provide return on investment. Check in often. Did a customer stop spending money with you? Touch base and find out what happened; often, you can right the ship and re-earn their business if you find out where something went wrong. They spent money before; they at least believed at some point, so you can rekindle the flame.

(3) Find ways to maximize quality and quantity of touches. You'll have many prospects that are just quick conversations at a networking event. You'll have some you don't talk to very often, and you may have those whom you've pitched but haven't heard from. Find ways to stay top of mind; interact with their social media posts, send out a newsletter and invite them to things of interest or send them articles that may be of interest. Marketing dictates that 5+ quality touches greatly enhance the chance of purchase - don't just send them a crappy, impersonal note, but create things of relevance or drop them a focused line which adds value. Doing this as often (without inundating) and as excellently as possible will be yet another item to increase probability of a lucrative relationship for both parties.

(4) Accept that you cannot get literally everything accomplished in a day that you want to. Complete what you know you must. Skim your e-mail and handle those of utmost importance first; then go back and continue doing the same until they are manageable. Follow the same principle with reports or other tasks; you've got to start from somewhere and you have to check items off the proverbial (or real) list.

(5) Look for support. You don't have to be Superman/Supergirl. Or Batgirl, or Iron Man, or whomever's your preference. Your supervisor, peers and subordinates - those who make up your team - can be your support structure. Often, they are very much there specifically for those purposes. If it truly becomes too much, reach out to a peer and find out how they are managing the work. Steal best practices shamelessly. Ask your supervisor for ideas, advice or the potential for having someone help out. If you have a team who works for you, pick some worthy candidates who want to move up and develop some projects with the guidance of your boss. No matter what, it's very likely you're not all alone and you can all be more productive and add more value if there is teamwork involved.

Time management really comes down to prioritization of work, customers and outreach. Find ways to integrate all of your priorities into your plan. Make a list of activities in a prioritized fashion and revisit it often! Reminding yourself how you should view and tackle your tasks can go a long way to getting you closer and closer to time optimization.

The Vocational Viewpoint, via Vincent Scott
(Republished with permission)
"I'm tired of being passed over for promotions! What do I do?"

From today's mailbag: "I'm tired of being passed over for promotions I'm more than qualified for. Should I look elsewhere? What should be my response?"

First off, don't react.

I know your initial reaction is to be angry or upset, and sometimes rightfully so. You may or may not even know the person you were "passed over" for and - in reality - your angst that is directed toward their general direction is really not about them. It's about the decision.

1. Re-focus on your priorities. You asked about leaving your current role. Well, do you have an opportunity to leave your role, not start all over, and go into a role like the one you are currently angling for? You were considered for this promotion, right? If so, wait until you have fully processed the change

and reach out to the decision maker for feedback. "Mr./Mrs. Hiring Manager, good morning! It is my hope this note finds you well. The intent of the correspondence is to reach out regarding the position we discussed of _____. As you know, I am very interested in growing in my career, and would very much like to meet or chat so I may obtain additional feedback and guidance regarding my career path and steps I may take to continue toward my goals. When would be a good time to schedule this follow-up? Thank you, and looking forward to continuing the conversation."

If NOT, and you were not considered or interviewed, why? It can still be a great move - if you haven't already - to reach out or reach out again to the decision-maker to either get on their radar or find out specifically why you are not. The response you get from the meeting request and from their feedback, the plan you agree to and your execution of said plan (along with results from your execution) determine if this is the company you will grow with or if it shall be another.

2. Perform an analysis of your strengths and areas of opportunity. Clearly, you feel you possess a large number of the attributes required to move up the corporate ladder. However, are you completely honest about any potential shortcomings you have? Remember, that often a promotion goes to just 1 person. For that role, it's likely anywhere from 50 to 100 or 1,000 people applied to the role. Fair or not, many of these hiring processes are set up as a process of elimination - to find candidates who do not possess one or more of the required elements and take them out of the running. As much as the fact you did not get the promotion stings, be honest with yourself and look at the areas where you can continue to improve. You can even highlight these along with your plan to address them while you are meeting with the hiring manager or anyone else who would be part of future decisions!

3. Be gracious. All eyes will likely be on you at this point. Your manager or the hiring manager may specifically be gauging how you react and respond to the move that was made to assess your business demeanor and how well you function as part of the team, division and company. Congratulate the candidate who earned the role, offer to help in any way you can with everything within your span of control, and control what you can; positive feedback about you at this point can greatly assist you and any negative feedback concerning your handling of the situation can and will ensure you never get a promotion. Negativity you create can and will be a reason you are eliminated from future promotion conversations before they even begin.

As painful as it feels right now, many great leaders have not been selected for a promotion while someone else was. We use this as a learning experience. We accept it as a challenge to analyze our process; we may be stronger in some areas than anyone else, however if we have a glaring area of opportunity, we must address it and become a more complete contributor.

Leaders are selected based on a variety of factors; do everything you can to determine what decision-makers are looking for, developing your process in every area that counts and constantly evolving to be a well-rounded team member. Do this, be consistent (the value of consistency is so great!) and work hard. Don't drop out of the race, don't let yourself fall back and don't show immaturity. Take it as a learning experience, ensure that you still have a viable path to your goals at your current company and move forward. Your time will come.

The Vocational Viewpoint, via Vincent Scott
(Republished with permission)
"How do I tactfully communicate with an out-of-touch boss?"

From today's mailbag: "My boss and company are behind the times and out of touch. How should I tactfully communicate with them?"

While many of us know that adaptability and response to changing times is key, these are not always common enough themes in business. It's the very reason many businesses either fail or mismanage and never reach their potential.

Any time you want to bridge a gap with your leadership, it is important to understand their priorities. These can typically be gleaned via meetings and communication; any time you hear them speak or you read their e-mail correspondence, they are likely spelling out their priorities - effectively or not. In short, you can figure out what makes them tick and what they value. You are going to have to present value if you want to get their attention.

Unfortunately, it's not uncommon for leadership to be comprised of people who have either never done the job they create policy for or have not taken the time to understand what really occurs on the front lines. Furthermore, not all managers are effective; many of them rise through the ranks due to politics or simply being the last person standing; you can be up against a variety of factors when you have a manager who does not see the true issues you and your team are grappling with and - more importantly - does not remove the roadblocks to success. That's their job - to eliminate obstacles and support you in realizing your full value you can offer the company in your career.

That said, you likely do know what matters to your manager and leadership. Find creative ways to contribute; offer to coach and counsel on areas where you have strength that align with your supervisors' priorities. Ask to meet with them to discuss suggestions you have to improve results in the areas they care about. While you have them as captive audience, not only do you broach the topics they like to talk about so you can earn their respect and buy-in, but you introduce the concepts that you know will make a difference. When they believe and trust you and know you are there to make them look good and improve results, they will be far more likely to listen when you express the issues that your group is struggling with and your proposed suggestions to fix them.

Many people are afraid of change, and managers are people. Often, they find a way of doing things and it works acceptably enough in their eyes to keep doing things the same way. If they do not spend time with their team or getting feedback on process, those processes will never be improved and optimal results will never be realized.

You can make a difference in this area by earning the respect of your leadership. The way to do this is provide them value in any way you can - coaching others, being vocal in praising the things that are going right, and in championing the causes they care about. Do those things, and you will earn your right at the table to present the things you care about. Similar to forming a political platform with which to run for office on based on the hot button issues so you can also chase your passion policies while in office, this approach will prevent you from being branded as negative or a non-team player.

The most effective way to get people to care about your issues is to genuinely show concern and attention to theirs. Doing it in a unique way will give you a better chance of standing out and getting your voice heard.

Changing managers and members of leadership who are stuck in their ways can be quite difficult, but if you do it respectfully and sequentially, you can very much make a difference!

The Vocational Viewpoint, via Vincent Scott
(Republished with permission)
"I have very demanding customers I cannot please. Help!"

From today's mailbag: "I have some customers who are extremely demanding. I do everything I can to stay on top of customer requests because I know how important communication is. However, they don't understand just how hard it is to meet every one of their requests and I'm overwhelmed. They also complain any time I cannot meet their exact demands in their timeframe. I'm afraid of losing top customers because of poor process at work. Help!"

First off, breathe.

We've been groomed in environments where the philosophy "the customer is always right" has been bandied around. The customer does come first - they are the center of our world. And they do business with us for the fact that we *are* reachable - for the fact we are able to communicate with them quickly and efficiently and be the solution to all of their problems big and small.

That said, if you do a quality job of building a customer base, creating a pipeline and managing your accounts, you will very likely eventually reach a point where you have quite a bit of work on your hands. While we strive to treat every single individual customer like they are our one and only, this can become exceptionally daunting when their demands reach a fever pitch even over the most basic of requests.

(1) Delegate where possible. Hopefully, you have support and supportive folks who can assist you in some of the tasks. Decide which ones it makes sense for you to get help on; typically, these would be administrative, non-customer facing items that may take up a chunk of time but take too much away from your other customers. These also need to be items you can train someone else to do effectively. They also need to be items that you know will be done right, so you've got to be selective.

Customers want responsiveness and results. Often, simply showing immediate or prompt responses to their questions or needs will go so far in establishing you as credible and capable. They want to be supported; put yourself in their shoes. Even if you are just bringing other folks into the project or escalating their concern, copy them in when appropriate and give them status updates. They know you cannot win every request but show them you went to the mat for them.

(2) Level set expectations. Strategically but empathetically share with your customer that their request is of the utmost importance to you and that it will be handled as quickly as possible. It is OK to put an out of office on when you are extremely busy with other activities that are taking you away from immediate response. It is OK to involve your support team and copy the customer in on some of those correspondences - often, a customer does not necessarily expect an immediate resolution but they appreciate seeing that you are working on their request. Staying in touch with and keeping tabs on their situation as often as possible even if it is not possible to deliver an immediate answer can go a long way and still maintain the relationship's smooth nature.

(3) Apologize and be forthcoming. Sometimes customers do not understand everything that goes on behind the scenes to facilitate their request. Over-communication in these situations helps, but often an explanation and apology for the time or any gaps in process can make all the difference. Ensure they know that you are providing their feedback up the chain to any applicable parties to improve process. Ensure they know you are doing the best you can to manage under the existing circumstances. Frankly, the best you can do is the best you can do.

(4) Provide feedback. If the process is not working for the customer or you need additional support or resources to fulfill your customers' needs, it is incumbent upon you to get that information into the people's hands who can help. Otherwise, you will never see positive change.

Again, make your best effort and ensure your customer sees the efforts. Prioritize the work; handle and manage the relationships you come to know need immediate responses first. Delegate where you can, communicate as much as you can, and provide feedback on how the process works and does not work for your clients. Be patient with your customers - remember, their business and the potential referrals they can bring in are always in the balance. How you handle requests after they buy that are not even tied to money are often the basis on which you are judged. Do the best you can to manage their expectations and deliver on your promises.

Sometimes, the process you are operating under will not satisfy every customer. We live and learn, and a deal we may lose today can lead to process improvement down the road that will lead to much better customer relationships. Don't lose hope, look at the big picture, and work every day to impact change for the holy sales trinity: the customer, the company, and you.

The Terry Bunche Story

It was March 2011 when I first fielded an e-mail from Vincent Scott.

In a lot of ways, it has certainly had a profound impact on my life; I was 45 at the time and my own business had not panned out. My job at the time was working in a call center for ABM's cell phone division.

Having been unemployed a few times through various ups and downs, I put on an all-out attack when looking for a job: networking and applications galore. I had a couple of decent leads, and Vincent's e-mail was responding to my application for a cell phone store manager with Cellular Horizons.

Little did I know, the management group he worked for was not the one hiring me and I was actually meeting a guy named Gabe Blankenship. Gabe was vying to buy the store needing a manager from Dustin Rollins, who went by "Bruce."

Had it just been the interview – or, rather, conversation – with Gabe, that would have been all she wrote. Gabe did not understand the business. He spent our time together just talking about how much money he made working as a rep in the store he was wanting to buy. He didn't know financials and he didn't ask me any questions. It was a disaster, and after attempting to lead the conversation toward an interview or determine next steps a couple of times, I left. I pretty quickly surmised it was a dead end.

Vincent must have known it was a disaster, because he called me a couple of days later to gauge my thoughts. It was a life-changing call, to say the least.

"Well, I'm not even really sure what to think at this point," I responded. "Gabe didn't really seem all that interested in interviewing me."

"Let me level with you," Vincent began. "Terry, I just started at this place a few weeks ago. At the time I set you up with Gabe, I was under the false impression that he would interview you like a business owner. It is true that he is in talks to buy the store itself, but he literally has no interest in managing you. I've established for certain that you'll report to me and that Gabe will simply cut the checks."

Vincent impressed me. I've worked with a lot of people in my day; I've seen managers that weren't worth a damn and I've seen blowhards his age with power that had no idea what to do with it. Vincent was different. And it was because he was different that my intuition told me to see this through.

Bruce Rollins was another setback. After I had already accepted the store manager job at the Greenfield, Minnesota, store, he came in to "train" me. I spent a day with him as he showed me how to run the till, how to process orders, how to cash out and how to process phony returns on aged inventory he couldn't sell so his balance with Moriarty Wireless – his distributor – would go to the black.

Yes, you read that right.

What I liked about Vincent was he was reachable; he'd answer my calls. He spent time in our stores and actually cared about what we thought. He never forced me to do unethical returns – he covered for me and got chewed out. He was intelligent. He was truly looking for a way we could do what we came there for: to make money and to hopefully show up on the grid for greater Cellular Horizons. We were a bright spot for them in a dark market and they loved us. At first.

These sales reps would complain about going out in the heat and putting fliers on cars. Vincent would do it himself. They'd ignore his e-mails about making outbound calls or doing promotions to lure in customers. He'd send e-mails to the whole market sharing best practices and success stories. In short, he made a difference because he cared and because he didn't let any naysayers or negative Nellies stop him from continuing to do what he knew he needed to do.

He was used to managing professionals who followed his leads, not entitled millennials who weren't moved by his motivation. But the real leaders in our band were ready to follow.

It was June when we visited the kiosk store location at the Mankato mall to breathe some life into that atrocious location. After some bad Chinese food, the plan was hatched: lead generation. Vincent already came up with the idea to buy out people's termination fees; it was his way of eliminating a viable objection to our service. We operated on a gross margin platform, so he'd gladly work directly with reps to negotiate multi-line deals, buying out termination fees, provided we made profit in the end and earned a new customer. In a system with little process, Vincent's business savvy and his trust in us to make money went farther than anyone had ever seen anyone go in this market.

Empowerment went a long way with these folks, but his verification and accountability practices ensured it was done right and responsibly. We had to do it right.

As fellow store manager Saul Portman and I got to know Vincent better, he entrusted in us his ABM backstory like Saul talked about fisticuffs with his college football coach and I divulged my nasty divorce.

Vincent looked at this disastrous debacle that was Brink Management like his penance. But he certainly didn't give the project any less than his all, despite lack of leadership from Jordan Wallace and Doug and Susie Wilson – all who were supposed to be looking at for us and supporting us.

Vincent and I created and ran with a platform that was web-based using various marketing materials – billboards, fliers, banners at events, etc. – and a toll free number that housed messages and stored tracking numbers we could tie to promotions – and it worked like a charm for our results.

Our market making 150% gains year over year, creating marketing campaigns that were used company-wide, Vincent ascending to a VP for the company and running conference calls for all stores in our bunch, and all our ambition in the world couldn't combat the disinterest and debt of Jordan Wallace and the shenanigans of unethical Bruce Rollins and the complete lack of support from Doug Wilson of Moriarty and Susie Wilson of Cellular Horizons.

Months later, we closed down the Mankato kiosk together – taking it apart and calling it a wrap. We'd have sandwiches near-daily with Saul at a deli near Eden Prairie's store and strategize about next steps – be it with or without the company. When Bruce Rollins went under and robbed both his stores blind of inventory he didn't own and Wallace made Vincent give him an envelope of thousands of dollars for it, we just sat back in disbelief. It was like the wild west. I've seen some crazy shit and worked in odd environments but this one truly topped them all in the realm of the bizarre.

We hit brick wall after brick wall, and only scaled any of them on Vincent's back – his charisma, work ethic and unwillingness to stop no matter what was happening around us was the only reason the doors were open and people were showing up only to be paid improperly if at all. I mean, this guy won the Cellular Horizons company Superstar competition pitching product against kids years younger who did it for a living. I've never seen anything like him in my lifetime.

He'd steal the show singing karaoke at a breast cancer event nailing every note of "Can't Take My Eyes Off Of You" and "Let's Get It On." He'd keep his cool leading company-wide conference calls most everyone was late for or didn't show up for despite the topic being marketing that could save our hide – it didn't matter if he was talking to 5 people or 50, he put on a show.

Didn't matter the situation or the odds – he was a bull in a china shop and just charged mercilessly into things every day. I'd follow the guy anywhere, and from a jaded, cynical old guy like me, that's saying a mouthful.

I can proudly say that at the end of Vincent's time with Cellular Horizons and Brink, I actually had an impact on him. It was the only time I saw him falter or not know what to do.

He wanted to stop trying at the very bitter end – with a week left until it was nearly inevitable he would be laid off.

Moriarty had negotiated buyout of what was left of the Brink Management Stores and those owned by Chris Jeffries (who had also bought the failed Bruce Rollins store) and Logan Tuncil. Doug and Susie Wilson were interviewing the Brink team and deciding who would be a part of the Moriarty team after they took over all of the stores. No one from Cellular Horizons or Moriarty would give Vincent the time of day, nor would they or Jordan Wallace tell Vincent if he'd have a job or even return his calls. We really saw what weasels they all were there at the end despite the fact we were still standing after everything we'd been through.

Vincent had done all he could but his destiny was not in his hands. And he didn't know what to do with that.

"I'm just going to cancel the interview blitz," Vincent announced, just a day prior to a planned interview day at our Golden Valley store where he was going to interview over 50 candidates and make changes and recommendations prior to the takeover.

"No you're not," I said firmly. "It's not your style. You're going to do every last one of those interviews. You're going to do their job until they take the keys out of your hands. You're going to do those interviews and send them a plan on everything you believe should be done. Show them that you are not going to stop doing your job no matter what happens or what they do or don't do. That's what the Vincent Scott I know would do."

Vincent was never speechless, but he was then. He stared at me almost blankly at first before that light flickered in his eyes. There was my friend.

"You're right," he surrendered, shaking his head and smiling at me. "I hate it, but you're so right. It's the only way to go out."

And he did it. He followed through with every interview and commitment until his last day, which was no small feat. During the interview blitz, he alone talked to likely 60 candidates and we all pitched in – future status be damned. He sent a plan out to the Moriarty and Cellular Horizons folks, recommending who stayed, who left and who to bring on from this new crop along with very detailed scouting reports like athletes would garner.

Never did he receive a response or a thanks or an acknowledgment, but we all saw our hero go out the only way he could go out. He lost, but was not defeated. He stood until the kingdom officially crumbled.

Vincent gave me a stellar letter of recommendation and remarkable phone reference to my new boss for my next job, a sales manager at a mechanical equipment company. I had a great run – it lasted three years. Two years in, they gutted the management team and brought in a bunch of young guys who just turned over the apple cart. I'm 50 years old – I have a lot less patience than I used to for this sort of thing.

It had been four years since I saw Vincent. He looked the same; maybe a little more beard and slightly more grey. We re-connected – I had been off the grid for a long while, just focusing on working and my relationship and my kids, but as soon as I reactivated my Facebook – there came a message from Vincent Scott.

"Because I sat in an interview with this guy five years ago, my whole career took a turn for the worse," I laughed, sitting at a table with Saul and Vincent on an April day in 2016.

"Yeah, yeah, thanks Terry. At least I gave you a glowing review at your last gig."

"Yeah, and that place went to shit, too, so thanks a lot," I laughed.

We sat around and told stories. The older I get, the less and less I will reflect or dwell on the shit. I just want to reminisce about the glory days. Thanks to Vincent Scott, I had a few with Brink and Cellular Horizons.

"They brought in Vincent's replacement, whose big thing was playing accessory hot potato," I recalled. "Imagine a 47-year old guy playing accessory hot potato with a 23 year old kid who's supposed to be his boss. There was no place for you in that mess."

We laughed and laughed. We talked about Jordan Wallace and Bruce Rollins and Logan Tuncil and Doug and Susie Wilson and the crazy shit that happened for a year in 2011. We talked about marketing and making a business team and call center on a shoestring budget and a prayer. Jordan Wallace effectively killing Aaron Hartley's cat. Rollins and Tuncil's dating website philosophies. Our psychotic B2B rep making just one sale and losing margin on it! Hiring 70+ 1099's in a matter of weeks and the company spiraling out of control and never paying the thousands of dollars it owed us.

And amidst the whole thing going to shit and the three of us being the only people trying to hold it together, Jordan Wallace wants to be a holding company, wants a clothing kiosk, wants to sell fitness and health packages, fruit smoothies and a hot dog stand. "Have you heard of Facebook? Have you heard of Amazon? Have you heard of Berkshire Hathaway?" There was a new master scheme that didn't involve our industry we committed to on a weekly basis. Now, it was just funny. It was the tie that bound us together and going through it made us friends.

"I can't imagine you ever working anywhere and not having the same issues you've always had," I leveled with Vincent. "No manager is ever going to be able to control you or even be better than you – at anything. You don't need them, and you could do their job better, which is why you're a threat. You don't need anybody, which is terrifying to a lot of weak managers."

If there's one thing I've accrued in this crazy world, it's wisdom. It may not always count for much, but there were a few days in Vincent Scott's glorious career where it made a difference – and that's good enough for me.

I made a gamble a few years back going to work for him, but my gut was right. The business went kaput and it was a long, slow death… but what a ride! That year was the most memorable of my career.

The Vocational Viewpoint, via Vincent Scott
(Republished with permission)
"Work-Life Balance: Mission impossible?"

From today's mailbag: "I'm trying to get ahead, make good money and results and survive the corporate game. That said - is work-life balance actually possible?"

It is. That said, finding that utopian balance in a frenetic working world can be one of the most challenging endeavors you will undertake.

If you are faced with this conundrum, you likely have a role which requires you to work long hours either to fulfill requirements or to achieve the results you need.

Work-life balance has a different definition for each of us: it's the contentment and peace with the place our career fits into our world; it's the belief our personal and business lives mesh well and that the former is not crushed by the prominence of the latter.

Sometimes, job requisitions, hiring managers and supervisors will be clear: "This job requires 50, 60, 70 hours." Sometimes, to make ends meet, you have to work 2, 3+ jobs and the hours pile up quickly. And then, there are roles where there is no set prescription for your commitment in the way of hours, but in order to reach the expectations from the role from quality and quantity perspectives, it's imperative you will have to put in longer hours than originally thought.

Which of these groups do you belong to?

1. Schedule. When we lack a schedule, it's quite easy for things to get out of control. While spontaneity spices up life, lack of organization in our schedule can lead to chaos. Just as you must schedule the client meetings, the debrief with your boss and your prospecting and follow up time, you've got to take that lunch break, escape and read a book or see a film or take a walk and unwind, and you've got to make time for your other passions and people in your world. If you fail to make time for the other things that matter, that part of your world will dissipate and you will be left with your career; heaven forbid something happens to jeopardize your business world at that point, but if it does - guess what you have left then?

2. Prioritize. Certainly, we work to maintain or better the life with which we have become accustomed. It's extremely important that we pay our bills and manage to get ahead so we can plan for the down side. It's important to take care of ourselves and our family. However, you are not your job. Your job is not your sole purpose. And while it is fantastic if you enjoy your job or are contributing and making a difference, you very likely have other interests and

talents in the real world outside of the office. Failure to develop those aptitudes will lead to their erosion. Yes, your job is very important for a variety of reasons - at the very heart of which is its ability to fund your fun and fundamental needs. But it is not all of you and therefore does not deserve all of you when you're off the clock.

3. Evaluate. If you're working all the time - why? Is it to get ahead - because you feel the second you let up that somebody's going to pass you up? Is it to make a ton of money that you'll never have time to spend or people to spend it on? Certainly, if in the line of duty you stop giving your best, it's very possible that others will position themselves ahead of you. However, if you.......

4. Work smarter, not harder, you'll find balance. Look for ways to delegate work by working with your supervisor and team. Look for ways to manage your day where you devote certain hours to certain components of your business. Do not get caught up in the daily minutiae - it's so easy to get lost in responding as quickly as we can to e-mail or getting bombarded by putting out fires. Each of these makes us less effective, though, because they take us away from prioritization. While we desire to complete 100% of our slated tasks in a given day, we often must accept achieving 70% of them and 100% of the absolutely necessary ones.

When work can be completed, that's when we need to shut off that aspect of our lives and throw ourselves into investing in the other ones. The people and places and activities that enrich our other persona are vital to refresh and rejuvenate us so we can be at optimum efficiency! You may feel you need to work all the time, but this will only serve to leave you run-down and less effective. If you can recharge your batteries by checking in with the best facets of your personal life, you'll return to work at your best. It's the very reason vacation makes us return with fervor and keeps us fresh and at peak performance.

Yes, work-life balance is very possible, but we often have to work just as hard to achieve that as we work to sustain a successful career and our relationships! Work issues may come up which cannot be ignored, but be sure to keep track of the time you owe yourself to invest in the other side of your life. Even when you greatly enjoy your job, it's vital you diversify your portfolio of personal preferences.

By making work-life balance a priority, scheduling for YOU and for others who enrich your life and for activities that enhance your enjoyment, you make very sure it can be a reality.

The Vocational Viewpoint, via Vincent Scott
(Republished with permission)
"Flash It or Flush It! Steps to a True and Healthy Pipeline"

Sales pipeline. If you are in sales, you'll be asked about yours on a regular basis. Whether you are on the front lines or part of management, it's rather essential not to over-value what are numbers on a spreadsheet but even more so to use this data as a tool in prioritization, following up and closing.

Far and away, salespeople indicate that following up is an ambiguous area: many struggle with how to do it, when to do it and what to say when they do. Incessant follow up can drive a prospect away and prevent time being adequately spent on other prospects and driving new business. Too little will keep you out of sight and out of mind.

It is frequent "water cooler" talk for the sales staff to stand around or chat by various mediums about their pipeline. "I'm working on a million-dollar deal/ I'm working on a thousand widget deal." While this sounds impressive, like "I'm working on becoming an astronaut," that blanket statement leaves no clues as to the stage in the game of the realized revenue. I could have bought an astronomy book or some Tang.

The point is that while a large pipeline looks grand on a spreadsheet and may get your boss off your back for this week's meeting, the time will come when you're expected to actually close some business.

Translating this into your follow up strategy, a "yes" or "no" is better than a "maybe so." I'd rather know today that there's no chance a customer will buy than to have them leave me twisting in the wind for months for fear of breaking my heart. Dump me or commit to me - don't string me along. To achieve this, it's about mutual respect; sales is about relationships and if you effectively build yours with transparency and follow through, set the right expectations and create some skin in the game on their part, it will set the stage far more masterfully for either the close or the closed door.

And a respectfully, possibly temporarily closed door at that, as you never know when their torch for your product may be reignited.

Some companies or bosses may wish to see every potential sale with even the most remote chance of success - and that's their prerogative. It's also extremely effective to keep a pipeline whether you use a proper customer relationship management tool or a spreadsheet to track your open dialogues - ensure you are not letting more than a week or two pass prior to the next *effective* outreach. Having such a mechanism will keep you on task as you monitor the intervals between contact and you move closer and closer to either flashing or flushing that opportunity.

But, for Pete's sake, don't let something sit in your pipeline for too long. Frankly, this all comes down to the effectiveness of your follow up. Don't press too hard initially, but after a couple of missed calls or unreturned e-mails, it is certainly time for, "Mr./Mrs. Customer - I certainly don't want to waste your valuable time. I've ensured that X number of widgets are set aside for you and want to ensure I'm operating on your timeline. Do you need me to continue holding these or should I open them to the waiting list?"

Direct, to the point, respectful but it also forces a response; they are more likely to respond when they know you've put forth effort and inventory or personnel are standing by to act on their behalf when they give the go-ahead. "I know we discussed your need of XYZ product by such-and-such date; as that date looms and I am in charge of lining up the proper resources for it please let me know what to inform the team that is planning the project and standing by to begin work."

So, while a pipeline report may illuminate the effectiveness by which you have reached decision makers, set appointments and pitched products, there is one number in sales that's absolute: money. If your pipeline is not coinciding with revenue, you're likely to be questioned about it at some point which is all the more reason to keep it true and tight.

What is a realistic sales cycle for the customer you are talking to? How long have they been in the pipeline? Have you given them their adequate and requested time to discuss it and provided all necessary collateral and information and demonstrations for the sale to close? Learn how to draw the line between keeping a number on a spreadsheet as a talking point and wasting time on a prospect that will never buy when you could be driving new business. You are costing yourself money while you're staring at a fake number.

Flash the sale or flush the unrealized dollar figure. Celebrate the win and go on to the next or accept the current lack of purchase, recalibrate your selling and outreach process and press forward to the multitude of other customers that are out there. Learning how to effectively manage and follow up on your pipeline will ensure a steady flow of success.

The Vocational Viewpoint, via Vincent Scott
(Republished with permission)
"Why am I always punished for being #1 on the sales report?"

From today's mailbag: "I've been very successful in every sales role I've been in, but I feel like all I attract is people picking me apart, inflated sales goals and unfair expectations while people in the middle of the pack don't experience this. Help!"

First, I'm sorry you have had this experience. Taking solace in clichés about how people like to bring you down to their level can conceivably quell this for a moment but it certainly does not eliminate the desire for recognition, the fact you have earned kudos in your role and that this is just added frustration when you've already scaled a mountain! It's like winning the World Series and being asked to play yet another game; like beating the heavyweight champ but still not being recognized as such because of this excuse or that rationale.

Let's face it: many people, especially in a very competitive environment like sales, do not like to lose! And when you are #1, everyone loses to you.

Something else you must think about is that your superiors have many more people reporting to them than just you. Often, these superiors may (unfairly) compare your results to others, hold you up as the example for them and this can cause strain between you and your peers. Furthermore, your peers may be giving all kinds of excuses as to why they cannot achieve what you do. When this happens, it can and will prompt them and others to look into every bit of what you're doing.

Is it on the level? Are you on the same playing field? Because, if you're not it lends credence to their own excuses. If you are operating on their level and doing things legitimately, it almost confounds them more - because you're just that good and they hate having no one to blame but themselves.

I know it isn't easy, but you almost have to take all of the extra and sometimes negative attention and scrutiny as a compliment. It will bother you, but it cannot deter you from the process you know is correct.

Many people are waiting for you to fall or fail so they can get a crack at the top spot, and you may even drift from the top from time to time. No bother! The key is consistently following the process that brought success. A hitter in a slump does not jettison his batting stance; he works to regain the mechanics that led to a statistical surge. So must we.

It is very rare that our time at the top will last forever; enjoy the time there, but learn from what got you there and continue to apply that process and improve on yourself so you may always be the best version of yourself.

Your success will never make everyone happy. Creation of sales goals will not be an exact science; there will be ebb and flow; you'll break the bank one month or one quarter or one year only to be given a goal impossible to hit. Trust me, it all balances out.

Focus on the process that leads to the prize rather than the prize, and everything will fall into place. Don't set out to be #1 and don't become too attached to the pole position; set out to chase the best practices of the best out there, learn from your peers and colleagues, add value wherever you go and you can minimize any animosity that others may feel toward you. Work to understand the position of your superiors and peers; offer to assist but also work to learn from them! You may be #1 but you can always be even better. Use this current feeling as the catalyst for your journey to improve even more!

And - here's to your continued success!

The Vocational Viewpoint, via Vincent Scott
(Republished with permission)
"How do I overcome having a terrible sales manager?"

From today's mailbag: "My sales manager is awful! Not helpful, not knowledgeable and not helping me get where I want to go! Help!"

True sales leadership is a real strength; one which is unfortunately a rare artifact. We must first consider, who is responsible for training and mentoring them to be a great sales manager? Is that being done? Time and time again, bad sales managers exist not out of malice but out of the fact no one is coaching them and holding them accountable and because they are not comfortable seeking out ways to improve.

We will all work for people we do not enjoy working for from time to time. Incumbent upon us in these situations is to find the strengths that the person does have and to understand how to politically position ourselves in partnership with them. For, that is what every management-employee relationship is: a partnership.

What can we do to help them? Often, it is providing results and few headaches, but when we want something from them (promotions, raises, new opportunities and challenges) we must take the initiative. Sometimes, they are caught up in the day to day minutia and unable to be effective. Sometimes, they leave us be because we are performing and they feel they have bigger fish to fry.

Whatever the reason, take the onus on yourself to reach across the aisle and schedule a meeting. Ask for their time. Introduce a plan that is respectful of their position but will give you the opportunities you seek. Seldom will a poor manager just hand you something designed to get you promoted; they may delegate and they may give you more work so they have less, but if you find that your priorities are not aligned it's certainly time to take the initiative to straighten them out.

Like anything in sales, the sales food chain (the relationship from customer to rep to manager to the individual additional layers of upper management) dictates all; we have the same relationships in each segment of the chain whereby we must understand one another's goals and work together for a solution! Just as we sell to a customer, we often "sell" to a boss; what are their needs? What benefits can we provide? How can we support them in ways they may not have previously considered? Look for a need, a problem that they may have and offer to be the solution.

Again, your "bad manager" may very well not be bad out of malice! And, even if they are, when you find ways to bring new value to them and play the political game the right way, you can still align your priorities. It can be an "I'll scratch your back if you scratch mine" mentality. Just like you are working with a customer, you find your manager's motivation and needs and you become the solution, all while working with them on a plan you both agree on that results in a mutually beneficial partnership.

You control more than you give yourself credit for in this equation! Take the initiative in the relationship and you can turn it around.

The Vocational Viewpoint, via Vincent Scott
(Republished with permission)
"How do I compete with and beat the cheaper competitor?"

From today's mailbag: "We've got a good product, but I simply cannot beat our competitors on price! I feel like I have a really good value story and can make connections but someone undercuts me every time. How can I win?"

You ask an age-old question! While this fierce competition on pricing can make the sale a challenge, it is great for the consumer. It forces us all to up the ante in bringing the best value to every customer for the money they invest. On the flip side, it can be agony for all of us who have lost deals to someone who just flat out beats us on price - specifically when there are not a lot of other value add differentiators we can introduce to the equation.

#1 - This can be remedied substantially with the quality of business relationships (of course, not entirely). You cited that you make connections. Can your customers reach you every time? Do you quickly and efficiently and correctly supply the answers to all of their needs, every time? A lot of why customers will continue to do business with you, even knowing that they may be paying more, is the reliability of the relationship. They know they pay a little more, but they are paying for you! It's why we tip more in restaurants with a great experience. I don't mind paying a premium for premium service. So many times I have had customers tell me that they stick with me because they know I'll answer their phone call, I'll respond right away to their e-mail, I'll keep them updated even if I don't really have an update - they have zero doubt I'm working for them and on their behalf at all times and that I won't forget about them, even if they have the most basic or non-revenue generating requests.

#2 - Most companies will do this, but you've got to sit down and write out your differentiating factors. What does your company do or represent or provide that stands out? Do you have free perks that go along with your product or service? Do you do something in a way that no one else does, even as a post-sales service? Why would someone choose you over any other competitor? Also, find out what the competition does - "know thy enemy" so you can adequately address the differences and be able to ask your customers what they like and dislike about the competition so you may most adequately exceed their expectations and earn their business!

#3 - Lose graciously, and with honesty! Frankly, I have to hand it to the competition sometimes! They may very well make a great product, and I'm not going to disparage it. If that is the case, sometimes, we have to own up to that and say, "Hey, we may not be the right fit this time around." Being honest with your customer will further that relationship! They will value your real feedback and the fact you weren't just trying to sell them something. This goes such a long way in any industry!

I've worked in many environments where my product wasn't the cheapest.... actually, probably all of them. But my teams win because we are passionate about people, go the extra mile, work for them even when we're not making a dime and do everything we can to make as many connections as possible. There's strength in numbers - connect as much as you can and try to support as many people as possible! You WILL win!

And when you win, ensure you nurture those relationships by being available, responsive and transparent so they see you working on their behalf.

The Vocational Viewpoint, via Vincent Scott
(Republished with permission)
"I've taken over a struggling sales team. Where do I begin?"

From today's mailbag: "I've taken over a struggling sales team. Where do I begin?"

As a sales leader, in no matter what predicament you find yourself, the key is to always re-focus and remind yourself of the two defining principles of sales/sales leadership: people and process. This is starting out, this is every day and it is certainly if and when you find yourself up against new challenges or unexpected trajectories.

Up to this point, if a sales team is struggling, the process is likely defunct and the people may be disenfranchised. However, where many managers go wrong is coming in, firing people and making changes without even knowing what they are doing. Other mistakes can include desperate actions to bail themselves out of a downward spiraling situation. Anything but righting the ship with optimal process will throw gas on the flames of the sinking ship.

Surprise them by doing the opposite of what they expect. Do nothing right out of the gates. They will be underwhelmed by any words or speeches touting clean slates and fresh starts. Actions mean everything as you build the foundation to go forward.

Get to know the people on the project. Spend time with them and see for yourself, first hand, what is working and what isn't. Get their feedback on the project - what they feel is working well, what could stand to be changed, and what their motivation is. In order to gain their buy-in, you must know your team, you must make plans with them to get them where they want to go, and you must make well thought-out decisions. Do not let anyone force your hand on making gut reactions or quick decisions.

Over a period of days and weeks, you can start to form in your mind an opinion of what the process should be. Ultimately, you will need to make changes in process and perhaps in personnel. Furthermore, you must realize that many of these people have likely seen other bosses; they may have heard the "clean slate" and "fresh start" lines before. I've learned that even letting them know - "Hey, I'm going to say clean slate and fresh start, but WE are making these changes together and WE will consistently revisit the process that WE put in place to ensure all of us - myself included - are living up to our commitments to one another." And live up to that. Revisit that commitment regularly so they can see you mean what you say and your actions will serve to gain their trust over time.

Tell them point blank that you will formulate a process together and will agree upon the process that each of you will hold each other to. "Just as I will ensure you are aligned with our process, I want you to do the same for me!"

After you have formulated the new process based on feedback from the team and from your observations of what works and what doesn't, you make changes. I wouldn't wait more than a month, frankly. Sometimes, I would make some changes within the second and third weeks. There must be a grace period, however, where you are gathering information and showing that you legitimately care about the feedback of your team. Be mindful that no matter what, they will throw former managers under the bus as they play hot potato with the blame game. Be sympathetic, but also be firm that changes must be made and you will make them with the team.

Your new team will be pleasantly surprised with the way you begin, by calling out what they expect and consciously behaving in the opposite fashion. They will see you alongside them in their roles as you learn those roles and get their feedback. People like to be heard! This is a therapy for them in a way, because failing teams often contain people who have a story to tell and some angst to shed. Take it all in; that's why you cannot make reactive decisions based on glimpses of the situation. When you've observed the sum of the parts, you can start making change.

When that change is made, it is imperative you have the buy-in of the people on your team. Certainly, there may be some folks on the team who are problems that need to be dealt with and will not buy in no matter what. However, as you identify leaders on the team who you can work with to mend fences and plan for the future, make sure their feedback and ideas are woven into the strategy you adopt and ratify as a team.

When your team sees that their input matters, that you understand their role, that you are willing to roll up your sleeves and get in the trenches with them, that your actions back up what you promised on Day 1, and they feel you have truly gotten to know them and their career aspirations and you are going to get them where they want to be, both in current results and future roles, they will follow you anywhere.

In the end, your focus on people first and on "selling" the new process and holding everyone - yourself included - to it will define the success of this project. Sales teams only falter when the right people follow the wrong process or when the wrong people follow poor process. Simplify it in this manner and you cannot lose!

The Vocational Viewpoint, via Vincent Scott
(Republished with permission)
"How do I get my sales team to care about metrics they aren't compensated for?"

From today's mailbag: "How do I get my sales team to care about metrics that they are not incented for, but I am?"

The short answer: by finding out what they do care about (often their careers and success) and showing them how that equates to all-around success.

Absolutely, we are incented based on a myriad of factors. Often, we as leaders are judged by key metrics in addition to just raw widgets and revenue. However, sometimes these metrics are not extended to our sales teams. When that happens, and they are earning commission and bonuses based on one factor or two (often based on revenue and total sales), we have to find ways to get them to perform in these areas.

The mistake many bosses make is that they think telling their team, "Sell more of this or that" will do the trick! They think that writing people up for not selling these components will work. In other words, they forget the first rules of people management: that the only things that matter are people and process!

You've got to get your people to care about the big picture. You've got to develop a process to get the metrics you desire. You've got to sell them on selling these metrics that matter to you.

The way to make the metrics matter to them can be achieved in a few different ways. When you know your team, you find out their motivation. Some people want to move up in the company; they want to be of value to the company and they wish to be successful. When you're lucky enough to have people like this, they will often want to stand out in these areas when they understand senior leadership is watching those who do. Also, when you can show these folks that overachieving pays off with promotions or you can run contests to give financial rewards of some sort behind these metrics, you can make them care about something they would not care about otherwise.

Another key way is just visibility of the metric. By showing that people are achieving in this metric and by making performance in the metric common knowledge regularly, people can see that some are achieving and some are not. This can move some to try harder....

... and this can also serve to show you with whom you must work to eliminate objections of selling the product! Take best practices and successes from your top achievers and share them with the group (the achievements here are twofold because it serves as recognition to your top players but educates the team). Spend time with the bottom achievers and find out what reasons or objections or excuses they are using to avoid selling the metric. Develop plans with them to improve their process. Hold them accountable to follow those plans!

Certainly, you cannot force someone or anyone to care about a metric they aren't compensated for or appraised on. But what you can do is formulate a process together that your employee commits to following. If they do, you will find success. If they don't, you know what to do.

Always: With people and process as your priorities, results - in ANY metric - WILL fall into place.

The Vocational Viewpoint, via Vincent Scott
(Republished with permission)
"How do I make more effective hiring decisions?"

From today's mailbag: "I keep making poor hiring decisions. I feel like I'm seeing one person on interview day and I'm seeing their evil twin show up to work. Help!"

No matter how hard we try to avoid it, we will make bad hiring decisions as leaders. That said, like our selling style and leadership style, we must evolve based on our experiences.

When we start out interviewing, often there is this benefit of the doubt which exists while we look intently at resumes and seek out those with what we deem the best or most experiences. As you hire some of these folks who either have worked in several selling jobs or who spent all of their time in another industry, you can find out relatively quickly why they didn't make it at all of those previous companies or that their different industry skills do not translate into your world.

Focus on these areas as you are looking to new candidates:

(1) Do not over-value the resume. There are countless articles out there about how often and easily these "accomplishments" are embellished. The resume is a selling tool whereby people sell themselves to us to get past that first step of screening and we know that they are obviously going to present the "first date" version of themselves. Glance it over, look for some buzz words you will want to further explore in the conversation - how did they rank in their roles? Out of how many? What did they do that made them more successful than peers? Does their resume reflect specific, number-oriented accomplishments, or is it generically written? Can you see achievements and practices that translate into your world?

(2) Look for personality! I've hired "by the numbers" with what they looked like on paper and I've hired diamond in the rough candidates with little to no experience who came across like the guy or girl who would be coachable, would come in and light the world on fire with their passion and enthusiasm and who reminded me of me when I was just starting out. The thing is: everyone, at some point, ourselves included, had zero experience at some point. Someone has to give them a chance. If we are hiring for an entry level role, what do we have to lose? Experience - as mentioned above - can be embellished or dressed up anyway. True, raw passion and enthusiasm and the attitude that they are going to do whatever it takes to be successful, why they are motivated to do so and what they plan to do once they get in there can certainly pay off.

(3) Realize that no matter how good you get at interviewing, that you will still hire duds and still pass over potential stars. It's a fact. You can get better at making these decisions by asking your candidate specific, targeted, experience-based questions. You can improve by being tougher on judging why they have had 5 jobs in 3 years or putting them on the spot with questions whose responses will address how they will react to what they will face when they work for your team. You also have to realize that this is business and just because someone is nice and has a family does not mean your job is the one for them. In fact, you would be doing them a disservice by hiring them into a role in which they will fail; in the long run, their heartbreak of working here, not cutting it and

eventually being let go would be tougher for them than you cutting ties now so they are allowed to find their real destiny.

You hold an important responsibility - you are now the gatekeeper into your organization for this candidate. No matter the outcome, your decision will impact the candidate, you, your team (their potential peers) and additional leadership. Don't over-think it, but ensure that you continue to evolve what you are looking for. Continue to be more accepting in some areas (lack of experience) and less in others (inflating the value of the resume, accepting their word for it that they were the best in their previous jobs). Somewhere in all that paper and their responses, you can ascertain if this person selling you today will still want to sell your product in two years. Somewhere you can gauge their presentation against all those presentations that have gone before and determine how they will fare in this role. And you can take their previous experiences and weigh their relevance against what they will do here. And, lastly, and most importantly, you can learn from your hiring wins and losses how to find a balanced approach to resume review, experience-based questions, and true assessment of talent potential.

The Jeff Mason Story

Summer 2001, after finishing college at Concordia in St. Paul – it was a simpler time. Most of my time back then was spent with my buddies Jason and Carl and hanging out at the bar. I got a job at ABM in their executive travel business, where I'd book the flights and travel for a lot of the bigwigs. It was easy work and I made some good contacts.

From June 11, 2001 until November 17, 2003, I was in that office; I had visions of moving into management and yet the two times spots opened up, they went to other folks. Political hires, I call them. No matter, I managed to find a role in Rockwood making more money in a sales specialist gig where I'd also get commission. I began training for my sales career in November 2003.

Our trainer was Kara Stith, an older lady who had been with ABM for 20+ years. That seemed to be the way of the world back then – there were a lot of ABM lifers who loved the company and seemingly pledged their life to it. I thought I would be one of those people.

Training was pretty brutal, but the only option was retreating back to where I came from so I stayed put. The office was doing pretty well. Shelly Cheekwood was the area manager of our office, who specialized in upselling consumer accounts. We'd field account inquiries and then be expected to follow a call flow with minimal deviations from their script.

The managers in the department were Harriet Raines, Dick Knoll, Lucy Hansen, Stacey Worth and – the office sales board leader – Vincent Scott.

The scuttlebutt in training was that you didn't want Dick Knoll – he was nicknamed "The Terminator" because he wouldn't coach or help you and if you didn't make numbers, you were fired. He infamously fired a pretty good rep on the day of his wedding and also brought on his own best friend only to eventually try to fire him, too. (Vincent wound up taking him and turned him into a rock star.)

You also didn't want Lucy Hansen, because she was terrible – no sales acumen whatsoever and all she did was monitor calls and score them brutally to the tee. She was not motivating and not friendly unless you brought her food or she could eat your leftovers. Harriet Raines was another one who really brought little to the table but gab, but if you produced, she'd leave you alone. Stacey was useless as a manager, but harmless, too – she had never written up anyone.

No, the manager to get was supposed to be Vincent Scott. And, when I came out of training effective April 1, 2004, I was on his team.

Vincent was cocky and boisterous; he was #1 every month in the office and typically pretty close out of the 121 managers doing what he did in the company. What I liked about him is that he didn't shy away from getting on the phone, taking over calls, talking about sales strategies, giving recognition and actually helping us. He also left me alone, for the most part, and he'd give me passing grades on my calls because I made money. He had been a top rep so he understood the grind and rigor and provided we were producing, he let us do our thing all while keeping us focused with direction and guidance and best practices.

It was also clear that he had his haters, as any top performer does. Dick Knoll would work consciously to undermine him, telling people in the office like me or like Danny Nance or Peter Swansea that Vincent's sales tactics were dirty and would get us into trouble. However, as I spent more time there, it was Dick who was dirty; he'd monitor people on Vincent's team trying to find things we were doing wrong and then hand us over to Shelly Cheekwood. If someone was on The Terminator's hit list, he would listen to hours and hours of their calls just to find something to fire them with.

I'll say this: Vincent's sales tactics weren't dirty. We were up against reps and teams and offices who very aggressively "bundled" calling plans into their spiel so they'd get extra revenue points toward goal. Things were weighted where we could easily manipulate the sales rankings by issuing a lot of free Internet trials... and while the customer may very well not need what we were giving them, we were following Legal-approved verbiage. It was a flawed system and we gladly manipulated it and made money. Other teams just couldn't do it as well as we could so they decided to hate on us.

What I found fascinating was how hard some people worked simply to keep us down or take us out of #1. And in the years since, I've seen a lot of things, but I've never met anyone with the tenacity and drive of workaholic Vincent Scott.

The other managers would complain that Vincent was always #1, so he would typically wind up with the worst reps out of training...only to turn them into "Top Gun" reps within a quarter or two (the top 5% of all sales reps in the company). Of course, no one would credit Vincent with that – they'd just complain further that he had all the best reps and the cycle would continue. But Vincent was able to negotiate well, and while he'd take these dog shit reps he'd also insist on keeping a core unit. Fortunately, I was always in that group.

I used to want to climb the corporate ladder, but I stopped caring about that after a while. Not long after I started working in Rockwood, I met my future wife, who already had a daughter, and when we married my top focus became providing for my family in a stable job.

Vincent, on the other hand, wanted to take over the world. Nothing was enough. He'd be #1 month after month, but insisted on some new challenge or taking more and more people on our team. It was standard for our sales managers to have 10-12 people on their team. Vincent would have 14, then 20, then 34 and then 37 while the other managers would top out around 16-20. He didn't care that it was more work – he actually thought that higher up's would see what he could do and they'd have to promote him.

But instead, they promoted Dick Knoll, who said what they wanted to hear and fired everybody that his weak leadership told him to.

I was in line to take Dick's spot; Shelly interviewed me, loved what I had to say. And then the job went to a political hire.

You know how that works, right? A buddy or an insider or somebody who fills a quota because there are too many Caucasian males on the team. I'm not saying that some good people were never picked over me, but I was sure as hell qualified and never got the nod.

Working for Vincent was great. We had fun; I sat around guys like Ted Benton, Jay Zander and Cliff Marlin and we just goofed around between calls or would stand and point or would say things on our calls just to get a rise out of our neighboring peers. When Vincent would do side-by-side monitoring with me to get my graded calls out of the way for the month, I'd pick customers who sounded like they were in a fog and just go all out: quoting Rolling Stones songs or integrating the names of Sylvester Stallone movies into my call and the customer was none the wiser.

I truly enjoyed creating sales verbiage and bouncing ideas off of Ted and Vincent. While life has taken all three of us in far different directions over the years since, we still connect on a semi-regular basis.

Realizing I wasn't going anywhere in our department, and having met Ashley – my future wife – who worked in ABM Advertising in the proofreading and publishing unit, she introduced me to the HR Manager Melissa Worthington and I was able to make a move to their customer service office in September 2004.

Even though I left, Vincent, Ted and I stayed in regular contact. We had become good friends. Whether it was just hanging out, drinking beer and watching and quoting cheesy 80's movies like *Cocktail* or going to the bar or playing games like 80's Scene-It or singing karaoke in my backyard with my father in law's equipment, we just had a good time.

I was pleased when Vincent followed suit and made the move to ABM Advertising in March 2005. He came over as a Sr. Manager in a new division that would cold call customers in markets that already had field advertising reps, trying to sell anything and everything they didn't already have. Not surprisingly, it was a success, and they grew from 10 people to 100 to eventually well over 200.

Once again, I was "earmarked" for a promotion into that division, by Vincent's then-boss Keith Dickhauser. I'll never forget the first time I met Keith – it was Vincent's first day in ABM Advertising and we were at a retirement party for a lady who had been there 30 years. Neither of us knew her, but he was invited by his new bosses and he invited me; when I met Keith, he asked me what I did, and while I was telling him, he walked away mid-sentence to go talk to someone he deemed more important.

Alas, even though I was told I was getting the final Sr. Manager role in the office, it was given to Steve Zimmerman the Third – of course, Junior was a buddy of Keith Dickhauser's. Yep, the political hire strikes again.

We didn't work together again after that. I took a "promotion" to account manager within the telephony side of ABM about a year later, but that job was a revolving door. I could see why when my manager chewed me out just a few weeks into being there for not having the forecast completed the way she wanted – even though I got no direction to begin with on how to complete the project. It wasn't worth it to stay.

Actually, over the next few years, I bounced around with Ted Benton – we worked together at BankState Financial, in IT at the military base, and brief tours in the call centers for ABM and Cellular Horizons. Then I started with the Minnesota Business Action Group where I had zero base and went around trying to sell political change.

It's funny that of all the jobs I've had, I actually enjoyed that one most but there was nothing more stressful than wondering if it was even worth it to spend the gas to visit some of these places when the success rate was so low. I did OK at it, but that wasn't the point – what difference were we really making? Was I really changing anyone's opinions? Was my company really making a difference in state and national government? I was in my 30's and having my political and personal awakening and really starting to see how politics worked.

Vincent was fired from ABM in January 2010 and he was devastated. However, I'm sure if he looked back he'd realize the good that came from the experience. He gave that company every ounce of himself for 9 years. Sure, he was a wild card and I know he pissed off some people because he always did what he wanted and took care of his teams. But the way they dumped him – while it woke him up to how corporations can work – didn't deter him from his quest to always be #1. I got laid off and I drank beer and applied to a few jobs until a buddy of mine told me about a new one. Vincent wrote a book and applied to thousands before walking in as Regional Manager for Cellular Horizons. Amazing.

We probably spent more time together than we had in years during that year he was unemployed. I was on the road with MBAG, so we'd meet up for lunch, maybe a few beers and some conversation. We'd talk about how these companies treated us. We'd talk sales strategies and verbiage. He'd help me fine tune my resume and set meetings, showing me how to use LinkedIn and how to write messages to hiring managers that actually got me a meeting… by *not* asking for the interview.

There were even two times we went on the road together – I was going to Mankato, his hometown, and he came along.

"Yeah, sure, why not – it's better than sitting around here all day feeling sorry for myself applying to 20 jobs I'll never get calls about," he said.

I picked him up, we got some jerky and sodas and I was on the road with the great Vincent Scott.

Having him there amplified my game. But it was such a crapshoot – that day, I went 5-for-5 closing down deals. My only perfect game at MBAG.

These guys would say they leaned liberal and I'd complain about Republicans I didn't like. The conservative ones ate out of my hand because I knew all the talking points and just got them complaining about the President.

"Kenny, here's the thing. Right now, who's fighting on behalf of your business?"

"Jeff, I've been here twenty years. I've done fine for myself. Neither you nor I nor anybody is going to change anything on our own. When the American people get so pissed off about politicians and their corruption and the downfall of our country, that's the only time we'll all be able to rise up together and do something about it," Ken Seabaugh, the aging farmer relayed.

"Ken, I understand where you're coming from. I'm raising two girls in this crazy world," I responded. "And, sure, you've done some things with other action groups because you care about where we're headed. But you had no proof of where your money was going. We send a newsletter monthly showing exactly the things that are happening as a direct result of your contribution. We have committee meetings monthly so you can be a part of the process. Yeah, nothing's changed because not enough has been done. We can't wait for the uprising – we've got to be the force for good and change. This is real, and it's why we've been endorsed by high ranking folks in multiple political parties. Do you want to be part of the change now, or just watch from the sidelines?"

I paused. I could actually see a hint of a smile from my sales mentor – he couldn't help himself. I knew I had this one.

"Now, Willie Lohman down the street told me you were the guy I needed to talk to when he signed up a half hour ago. He said you'd want to be in on the fight. Can we count on you?"

The whole day was like that. Vincent and I went for a fantastic feast of steak and lobster.

The next time we did the Mankato thing, I was 0-for-the-day. 0-for-19. We were pulling doors and getting turned away by gatekeepers; the pitches I gave yielded no results. Some days were like that.

It was also the same day he was interviewed by his hometown television station about *The Selling Game*, his new book.

I had never been on a television sound stage. We met the host of their business broadcast who was an evening news host: Rick Roy. He was super nice and admittedly it was pretty cool to see a friend of mine and former boss being interviewed on a book he had written.

Rick and Vincent took their seats behind the desk and after a few minutes kicked off.

"Good afternoon, and welcome to The Business Bulletin! I'm your host, Rick Roy, and with me today is local author and sales manager, Vincent Scott. How are you today, Vincent?"

"I'm great, Rick – how are you?"

"Doing well, thank you! So, you're a native of Mankato, correct?"

"Yes, that's correct – I was born and raised and spent the first 21 years of my life here. Graduated from University of Minnesota-Mankato and my parents still live here so I make it back as often as I can."

"And Vincent has authored a book – *The Selling Game*. Tell us about the book, Vincent."

"Absolutely – I had wanted to write since I was a wee lad, I just didn't know what to write. Having been in sales since college, I found I was good at it and was promoted a few times in a few industries so I had some unique perspective. I had wanted to write something about sales for a while, but didn't want to just write another sales book. I was also that young kid starting out in a career not knowing what I was doing – so I felt I could speak to that person. It gave me the chance to impart a lot of lessons I've learned while spinning in a unique sales book-inside-a-fictional business story twist."

"Definitely very unique," Rick Roy continued. "Where did you get the stories? Is it based on your life?"

Vincent chuckled. "They say you write what you know, right? I'd be remiss to say I didn't incorporate some things I've seen over the years."

"It sounds like you've walked the walk and that's a lot of what's in here."

"I'm just trying to give a little back. Hopefully, readers can learn from the mistakes I made; I made them so they don't have to."

Both of them laughed.

"How did you go about getting published?"

"The old-fashioned way, I suppose. I sent letters to over 900 publishers and agents, sifted through hundreds of rejection letters, and picked what I thought was the best distribution in the end. It was hard work, but anything worth anything is. I believe everything I've done in sales and writing can be replicated; fear and rejection inhibit far too many people from continuing down their chosen path."

"I guess this is a dream come true for you?"

"I think for anyone to hold their finished product in their hands is a dream come true, Rick."

"Did you always want to be in sales?"

Vincent laughed again. "Definitely not. I don't know that anyone growing up dreams of being in sales. It is a tough game, but pays handsomely. No, I always wanted to write – but I haven't sold enough books to retire yet."

Both of them laughed again.

"When did you start to write?" Rick inquired.

"My Mom put me in front of a typewriter at age 3. I wrote stories growing up about my friends and I going into outer space or time traveling. In college I wrote movie screenplays that never went anywhere. It's something I've just always done on the side. Lately, I've taken to writing in numerous sales publications."

"Any advice to writers?"

"Yes – just write. Even if it's bigger than you imagined, or a lot of work or you don't know where it's going. Eventually, it will take the shape it's supposed to take or serve the purpose it's supposed to serve."

"Why the book inside the book?"

"I'm not a sales guru. Sales books have been done a million times. So, I didn't set out to do something that had been done before – in fact, that's probably why it took me so long. But I was compelled to share these lessons and they could be shared in the way of stories. So I created a fictional author character who could experience these brutal lessons all while writing a book about what he's learned."

"Is this you on the cover?"

Vincent laughed again. "It could be. It could be anyone," he answered, acknowledging the silhouetted character who adorned the front flap.

"What was your inspiration to do all of this?"

"Rick, we always have impulses to do things at work that we don't follow through on because of potential consequences. The character in this book does them. He's brash, he's flawed, but redeemable. He's Superman with a briefcase."

Rick chuckled at that one, as did a couple members of the production crew.

"If I acted on everything I wanted to at work, there'd have to be a parental guideline on the book," Rick offered, prompting more laughter from all.

"I'd read that book," Vincent mused to more laughter.

"So, you live in Minneapolis now?"

"Yes, that's correct – I've been there for 10 years."

"And you've got a life-changing event in having a little girl?"

Vincent smiled. I realized in that moment how rare a real Vincent smile was, but this one was genuine.

"Yes – Elizabeth. She's my world. She'll be 3 in a few weeks. I didn't know what love was until she came along."

"She's the same age you were when you started writing – are you going to encourage her to write as well?"

"I'll encourage her to do whatever she wants. Right now, I'm just enjoying the ride. If I can be half the parent my parents were, we'll be OK. Right now, I just love that she watches cartoons I watched as a kid so I can live vicariously through her."

More laughter from all of us.

"Last question – why do you do sales?"

"Rick, I enjoy the people, the adrenaline rush from the deal, the craftsmanship. And I enjoy helping others see the light and find success. You've got to do something out of the ordinary to get people's attention. Nobody pays attention to status quo. That's why I've always done everything I can to support, to change things, to make a difference. And I pray that's my legacy."

The following year, Vincent worked at Cellular Horizons and my wife and I decided to move our family to Dallas. The cool thing was that Vincent oversaw much of the middle part of the country, so he eventually had some stores in Dallas and he'd come visit. He also dated a girl down here for a bit and came down a couple of times just for fun. Of anyone I've worked with or for, he's certainly been the only enduring friend.

We've done concerts together, spent countless hours swapping sales war stories, he's helped me out, we've been at each other's kids' birthday parties and he was even in my wedding and at my Mom's funeral.

As I've gotten older, I have cared less and less about my career versus my home life. I've got a beautiful wife and two daughters and I genuinely enjoy hanging by the pool and going to sporting events and being with family. I don't care about being #1 – it isn't worth it. Even when I work from home, I do just enough to get the job done – which is good enough for me.

And as much time as Vincent and I have spent lamenting the state of the sales world and the organizations we've toiled for, he has never made that shift. Sure, he's embraced family – he loves his daughter more than life. But while I've been a journeyman sales guy – I've moved to new roles when the previous ones grow stale and my goals have gotten jacked up so high I have no hopes of hitting them – Vincent endures everything. He somehow hits the impossible goals. He stays at a company until they kick him out or promote him – whatever happens first. They can't beat him up so bad he doesn't keep coming back.

He'd always say he wanted to let up a little bit and stop caring so much about being #1 – but he never could. Not even for a second.

I hope that somewhere in all his achievement is some genuine pride and peace, because I don't see how he finds any happiness in all that chaos.

I'm always the guy earmarked for promotion, but constantly passed over for a more political hire. Promotions they'd dangle, but never deliver. Vincent's always been the guy who somehow puts up with the joke that Corporate America often is without complaining, without quitting and without relinquishing his hold on the number 1 spot.

The Vocational Viewpoint, via Vincent Scott
(Republished with permission)
"What is a reasonable increase to an annual sales goal?"

From today's mailbag: "What is a reasonable increase to an annual sales goal? Mine went up by 50% this year, is that reasonable?"

Excellent question, and one that - if you are in sales - you will no doubt experience numerous times. Sales goals can sometimes change like the weather and, unless you work in an environment of transparency (rarer and rarer these days), often with zero rhyme or reason.

Here's the thing: goals are going to rise - it's inevitable. It is like when you get good grades and your parents start to expect it. It's like when you give your children gifts every time you come home from a trip - they expect it. Specifically if you are part of a growing sales organization and initial goals were set with mere speculation; people will start hitting the goals and they will raise them accordingly.

They shift with the rise in business and they naturally lessen bonus payouts which can cause some chagrin. They will want more and more and more; sometimes rightfully so, but there is often not enough practical process to their methods.

Let me backtrack to the goals setting process; my thought process when setting goals has always been around looking at what the second quartile of achievers was achieving and what the median was achieving; pretty much taking an average of that second quartile for each metric. I'm shooting for a lift of the average, so I plot that as the benchmark and focus on the best practices of those already hitting the mark in order to get there.

With any rule, there are exceptions, so it may not be feasible to set each goal as the 2nd quartile average if the gap between that marker and the division average are wide. Use your best judgment: it's important to make the goals high enough to surpass budget and show growth but it's equally important to make the goals attainable so your team keeps chasing them and doesn't shut down.

You don't want 50%+ of your current achievers hitting every single metric or for your initial sampling's average being better than your goal. It is also wise to set a budget goal and a stretch goal. But, that said, if 75-80% of your workforce is exceeding your revenue goal it is not out of line to expect an adjustment.

To necessitate a 50% lift in sales goals, look around. How are other performers doing relative to the goals? How many total achievers are there above and below the Mendoza line? I've literally worked in an environment where just 2 of 121 were hitting goal (thank goodness I was one of the 2) and another where 80% were; both were drastic and adjustment-worthy ends of the spectrum.

Again, the key comes to transparency. I believe a transparent leadership team will share the reason behind goals; a workforce can and should know what budgets look like to keep the lights on and the method behind the goal-setting. If your goal was hiked by 50%, relatively few people are hitting goal and no one is explaining why - there could be a serious problem. As a leader, I expect around 40% of performers to be hitting goals, but this can be much better when you have other statistical data to take into consideration. Historical data can be exceptionally helpful when charting seasonal trends and expectations. Also, what was the hike in goal from the previous year over year versus the actuals? All of these trends, coupled with changes in the industry and product offerings and pricing and competition and workforce will help clearly define how a forecast may look. But for a 50% jump, it should only occur in an environment where nearly everyone was already hitting goal and the change is being made to even things out.

If your sales goal spikes like this and you're not being given the reason why, ensure this is tactfully broached in your next meeting with your manager. But quote facts! "Mr./Mrs. Manager, last year, 80% of our workforce missed goal. Goal went up by 50%. Now, 95% of our workforce is missing goal. What is the thought process, and how do you recommend I shift my process?" Work to understand the process, and develop a strategy with your manager to get that 50% lift. Or (as is often the case), just ride it out until they come to their senses.

The Vocational Viewpoint, via Vincent Scott
(Republished with permission)
"Going the Distance in Business and Life, like Rocky Balboa"

I cannot tell you how many times I've watched the fight between Apollo Creed and Rocky Balboa from *Rocky 1* and fully embraced the metaphor between Rocky's journey and life itself.

When the fabled saga began, Rocky was a "pushing 30" underdog who took part in club fights when he could and worked for a loan shark (not breaking thumbs) to make ends meet. His biggest fear was being a bum from the neighborhood (not leaving a mark or having an impact – can we relate?). Sure, he had aspirations, but lived a simple life with his turtles and bachelor pad, making jokes with his pet shop girl.

One day, however, opportunity knocked. What happened from there was a one in a million shot, but how many times has opportunity knocked for us in life or business where we failed to answer the call? Initially, our hero was reluctant to take on the heavyweight champion of the world in a bout that made no real sense and for all practical purposes never should have landed in his lap to begin with. He didn't want to fail, which is human nature.

That said, every once in a while, we get the golden opportunity of a networking meeting, a new contact, a potential job opportunity we hear about that could better ourselves. Do we take action? Or do we decline, only to kick ourselves later? When the CEO is within earshot, do we make a move just to meet him or her? Or do we sit back and let life pass us by?

Rocky's decision to take part in the fight was one thing, but he didn't just show up. He took his training seriously - which required him accepting help from others. This is instrumental - no matter how great or talented we are, we cannot make it all alone. We need the Adrian in our corner who is there win or lose. We need the Mickey who - while he's a little angry and jaded - he's a valued mentor and friend. And, despite his flaws, we have the Paulie, who has his moments and once per film makes a heartfelt overture.

There were zero expectations of Rocky - a 20-to-1 underdog versus Apollo Creed. But what is spellbinding about the fight and film is that Rocky's goal was to go the distance - to be standing when the bell signaled the conclusion of the 15th round. When Apollo knocked Rocky out in the 14th, even Rocky's trainer told him to stay down - he felt Rocky had done enough. But Rocky didn't listen - he scrambled to his feet, came back out despite the fact he couldn't see anything, and landed body blows to Apollo then and later that almost spelled victory.

There will be times we are literally delivered knockdown punches - we don't get the promotion we're promised. We don't get the raise we deserve. We lose our job through no fault of our own. We battle through family issues or personal struggles and literally don't know what to do.

In the seventh Rocky film, *Creed*, Rocky makes perhaps the best metaphor: Take it punch by punch, step by step, round by round. When you take on the entire world, often you will fall short of goals because you are overwhelmed. The concept of being the underdog by a healthy margin, the concept of "what do I want to do for the rest of my career" or "how am I going to deal with all of this stuff" can be way too much for us to handle. Even when others doubt us, when people we thought were friends leave, we have the strength inside to take it one task, one priority, one day at a time.

Prioritize each component of what you're up against. Need a job? Put your best foot forward on each component: a rock solid resume, a unique approach at getting it in decision-makers' hands, and supreme follow-up. Hate your job? Ensure your responsibilities are taken care of, weigh the pros and cons of your role, and decide if it's something you can continue to do anew each day. Having terrible personal problems? Control what you can, eliminate negative forces and unproductive personal relationships from the fold.

Because, in the end, you must be able to live with your decisions and your legacy and your life. The people you surround yourself with must be the ones who will support, but also tell you what you need to hear. When Rocky lost his hunger for the sport in *Rocky III* it was Adrian who gave him the constructive criticism he needed to face his fear of losing face and the life he had. That said, as the Rocky story has unfolded, Balboa finds solace in a different small group of people as he loses many people close to him. That's life - it will change and force our adaptation, but it will always require we give our best to every task at hand.

The *Rocky* saga is supremely motivating because it captures the essence of the human spirit: we all want to believe that we can be champions. The beauty is that Rocky was an unlikely champion - he was an everyman. He was revered when he rose and was criticized when he fell, but he always did right by his family and those close to him and he did right by the sport, even when he did not get the recognition he deserved. Even when he was doubted, even when his talents began to fade - he always found ways to add value. We can take many cues from Rocky Balboa, and we should all always strive to get up for another round.

The Vocational Viewpoint, via Vincent Scott
(Republished with permission)
"Controlling Your Nerves: Public Speaking Mastery"

Regardless of how many times you are tasked to speak publicly about a topic, you will experience some semblance of excitement, anxiety or nerves prior to going on. While we can never fully anticipate specifically which will hit us and to what degree, we can certainly limit any potentially negative impact and also channel the emotion into a positive outcome.

1. Remember that you're the expert. If you find yourself nervous or apprehensive, reflect on the fact there is a reason you have been tapped to tackle the topic. You are speaking to a group of people about something you are likely very comfortable with. Your knowledge level on this subject is typically superior to those receiving your message. You likely spend a significant amount of time dabbling in the dialogue you will deliver; you've got this. It is your wheelhouse and you are the subject matter expert. Find solace and confidence in your unique understanding of the topic.

2. Drown out the distractions. We typically over-think in situations of this ilk. "What if I forget something?" "What if I mess up?" "What if someone asks me a question I don't have the answer to?" We can be our own worst enemy! If someone asks you something you don't know, explain - "That's a great question! In this field, things are ever-changing. I can commit to getting you the most up to date response. Let's connect afterward. Next question?"

Furthermore, think about how many times you have seen speeches delivered - you likely do not even notice the "gaffes" they themselves deem as less than their best work. You cannot control exactly how the speech will go, but you can certainly control the notes you reference during the presentation, you can control your knowledge of the subject and you can most definitely work to control what you allow to seep into your consciousness. A friend of mine once shared with me the value in literally acknowledging the presence of a negative thought or emotion and forcefully dismissing it. With practice, this process goes a long way in pushing out any unwanted anxiety.

3. Don't over-rehearse. There is something to be said for developing a comfort level with the material and your presentation. You'll hear that you can practice in the mirror or to a peer. While I firmly believe in being fully prepared to impart knowledge to your audience, it is certainly problematic when you become so prepared that you become obsessed with performing your speech precisely as rehearsed. Rather than being able to develop a rhythm and flow, you trip over trying to replicate past performances. Study and make it innate, but do not overdo it.

4. Relax. Whether nothing's at stake or whether a potentially large client or deal hangs in the balance, there are likely numerous reasons you're at the podium. We spend so much time worrying about outcomes that never become reality - and what does the worrying get us? If you're prepared, you're an expert and you are nimble and quick on your feet to answer questions and commit to finding answers on anything you don't know, you've controlled what you can control. The rest will take care of itself.

Nerves are a funny thing; they can pop up when we don't expect them and even after years of perfecting our craft. That said, funnel and channel them into an obsession with doing your subject matter justice, not an obsession over a rehearsed, canned speech. Know your audience, deliver the goods. The rest will truly fall into place, and with practice - like any other process - you will learn small tweaks you can make to enhance your performance.

And best of luck/ break a leg!

The Vocational Viewpoint, via Vincent Scott
(Republished with permission)
"Should I Stay or Should I Go?"

Besides being a quite catchy, lyrical masterpiece by the Clash, it's a very valid question we may often face when it comes to bad business, bad relationships and bad situations: should I stay, or should I go?

We've all been there (likely, and unfortunately sometimes multiple times): faced with a potentially life-changing situation whereby we have to choose between two undesirable destinies. We find ourselves in a predicament -

business or personal - that, frankly, makes us miserable; we lack the desire to get out of bed in the morning, we dread going to work, we loathe having to communicate with a person or persons and it literally consumes every fiber of our being.

On the other side, the alternative of leaving also presents challenges: while the immediate gratification of escaping said atrocious assignment is alluring, it brings with it more questions. If you are leaving a place of employment, what's to say the proverbial greener grass you pursue is going to be any better? Continuing to make lateral moves your entire career and never paying your dues to get to the position you desire will keep you just as stagnant; often the bad situation you know (that could conceivably get better or that you can withstand by taking it as it comes for as long as it takes) is just as good if not better than another potentially bad situation. Furthermore, things change; poor management has a way of not being around forever and businesses change all the time. If you can endure (and have endured), positive change could eventually be part of the mix.

The real question is this: what is the offending party bringing to the relationship? It's really that simple. Is there potential for positive change? Are your needs being met - financially and from a recognition standpoint - in a rewarding enough way? Leaving a bad situation for uncertainty is rarely advisable; happiness and being on a path that leads where you want to go is of the utmost importance, but it will never be easy anyway. You'll encounter bumps on even the smoothest of trails in business and personal relationships, so either way some hard work and hard questions will be faced.

That said, you have to evaluate what you are getting out of the relationship and the potential for future positive change. If the prospects for this are good, you can endure your present situation and keep your head down, perhaps that's the answer. If not, and you have given and given and given with relatively nothing in return, been passed over inexplicably for internal promotion while they promote or bring in their buddies from outside, or you realize that another option truly gives you more room for growth - life's too short to keep ignoring outside opportunities that can beget better benefit.

There is a reasonable amount of challenge and discomfort you will have to manage through no matter where you are. The question is can you do it, or would you rather start all over in another situation whose challenges and discomfort may be worse? Staying or going present their own unique risks.

In the end, no decision of this ilk is easy and you may make some missteps; that's what the journey is all about. Nevertheless, the answer of should you stay or should you go all boils down to which opportunity leads to bettering yourself - mentally, physically, and in your life and career.

The Vocational Viewpoint, via Vincent Scott

(Republished with permission)
"How do I compete against the sales cheaters?"

From today's mailbag: "I'm in sales. There are many 'top achievers' around me who are bending or breaking rules. How do I compete?"

FANTASTIC question, and certainly one that if you spend much time in sales you will certainly face. Also, of note, I can certainly say you can reach and maintain #1 status in your office, district or company without ever crossing any lines but it is paramount to understand and know your playing field, what your scorecard is derived from and how to master each component.

You will always be surrounded by some unscrupulous souls, for the sales population is certainly indicative of the population as a whole. People see the opportunity for a quick buck and they cheat a few times and are not caught. Unfortunately, some managers will even tell you to cheat! However, don't become someone who makes the excuse that you cannot compete because of cheaters (not that you're doing that, but I know some who hide behind this).

To compete in any realm of sales, you need to understand what are the measurements of work. Are you graded on total revenue, total transactions, several buckets of different widgets, or do you have a comprehensive scorecard with weights to different components of the business? Whatever the measurement, know it and have a defined strategy for success in each area.

Know what counts more than other facets of your role and focus on a game plan for each area. What do the current (and ethical) best do in each of these categories? Not everyone cheats, so seek out best practices or strategies of the top achievers in these areas and emulate them; make their processes and best practices your own and carry them out consistently and effectively. You'll never come right out of the batter's box hitting home runs but if you focus on the mechanics of a process that is clearly working for some, and you make it your own and make it consistent, you'll be effective.

Furthermore, ignore the cheaters! I've seen so many flash in the pan folks come out of the gates running in that sprint to get wherever they think they are going - often thinking they will have quick success and get promoted. After a few months, true colors emerge and leadership - or lack thereof - will surface. Trust me. You will look back years later and be glad you did not succumb to the cheating and you'll also find you're light years ahead of them in the pecking order. I've never seen a cheater make it very far. Honestly, nearly every one I can think of was shown the door.

Your only competition is against the best version of you! Focus on mastering each and every component of however you are graded. Learn what the best in each category does and do it better. Stay strong, stay ethical and be a noble knight of the honorable art of selling.

You'll get there! Best of luck.

The Vocational Viewpoint, via Vincent Scott
(Republished with permission)
"How do I transition to managing those who are peers and friends?"

From today's mailbag: "I'm now in a management role and leading a team of people I used to work alongside with, some of whom are my friends. Any advice?"

If you are part of an organization that hires from within, and/or if you are around long enough with one company, it is entirely possible you will find yourself superior in the hierarchy to a friend or former peer with whom you may have confided or event spent time with outside of work. They may know more about you than a typical employee or subordinate should. You may have been overly candid with them previously. All of that now has to change.

It's not to say you cannot manage a friend. In fact, if you can successfully separate business from personal, you can often have a straightforward conversation with a friend who is working for you and not doing their share. "_____, I consider us friends outside of work and I greatly value that friendship. However, your performance is reflecting poorly on me and I need your help. How can we collaborate to improve this situation?" If they are *truly* your friend, you'll find out how important that relationship is by what happens next.

You will also, fortunately and unfortunately, find out in some of these challenging situations that some of these folks were never really your friend or that they value certain things ahead of your friendship. It's a tough lesson learned.

As a rule of thumb, you should not spend time with your team outside of work engaging in non-work-sanctioned activity. Sure, you may take your team out for a meal and you may even - if your company allows it - buy a round of drinks for your team. However, when outside of the office, it is much easier to get caught up in compromising situations. It is much easier to relax your necessary guard.

You cannot get caught up in office gossip (or become any!) at such functions. You cannot show favoritism toward any member of your team, because this can come back to bite you if you need to discipline another team member. Also, if you are taking it easier on your friends, they will often try to get away with more and more. This is where these "friends" can manipulate your friendship to gain favors that other team members are not getting - and believe me, they will notice.

Be sure to have a conversation with these friends right up front to talk about how you will work through this transition. Make clear your intention to remain friends, but that the dynamic in the office has shifted. If you frequently spend time with these people in a social setting, you will need to keep from telling them anything that could compromise you or your leadership position.

Truly keep business and personal separate. And, like managing any employee, you will have a unique plan in place with them on how they work and what items you agree need to be improved by the next session.

In other words, you want to work with your former peers and friends to establish the new relationship and - if anything - utilize the friendship as a reason to work better together. They as your friend should never want to make you look bad. Never show favoritism and never allow yourself to compromise your position by slipping from the established protocol. Play it right, and former peers who respected your performance when you were peers and friends who value you can actually be the best employees you've ever had.

The Vocational Viewpoint, via Vincent Scott
(Republished with permission)
"My compensation plan makes no sense!"

From today's mailbag: "My bonus and compensation plan make no sense. I'm performing exceptionally well, but being paid less than peers who are on final warnings and I'm becoming very frustrated. What can I do?"

From the dawn of sales time, we have been paid on varying scales - sometimes high, sometimes low and sometimes we don't even know.

When imperfect people use imperfect math to predict budgets and sales numbers with less accuracy than the already tough to peg stock market, you're bound to come up with some oddities. Bonus and compensation are often created around initial expectations, but when they are eclipsed they rise.

Let's call it what it is: in sales, we are always chasing numbers. When we catch them, they are lifted higher and higher until we eventually cannot catch them. Once we fail a few times, we either lose heart or they are lowered until we hit them again and the cycle continues.

I've worked in situations where initial goals were low - we annihilated the goals and broke the bank for quite a while until that plug was pulled. I've worked in situations where my team did so well that with smaller territory than a peer I had nearly three times their objective... and my team was still hitting it and they weren't.

Too often, there is not enough rhyme or reason, but you are rarely going to encounter a supervisor or leader who is going to admit that. Even applying the most methodical of systems to set targets is still going to meet its exceptions. I've also been a top performer who was compensated less than underperforming peers for that very reason - because the compensation structure just didn't make sense and my team's prior excellence made it harder on ourselves.

The real trick of this trade is patience. I've found it almost best in some of these situations to go in with minimal expectations for bonus and be pleasantly surprised when you perform well on their scale. You will be confounded and frustrated if you try too hard to comprehend the incomprehensible. It's like a case that even Sherlock Holmes cannot crack; you're up against fuzzy math and attempts to apply rules to unequal peers.

See, that's where the real trouble lies. When different geographies and customer bases and situations come into play, the number of variables make it literally impossible to truly predict your proposed performance. Sure, it's good to have goals, but if I'm not getting the same exact lot as my peer it's instantaneously not an even playing field. Sure, the margin of error can be minimized, and odds and probability and some luck come into it, but the thing of the matter is bonus structures can be manipulated and milked and they can be made nearly impossible - seldom in the sweet spot in between.

(1) Learn the different buckets that you are accountable for. What are the items that you are paid out on? What are the ways you can perfect your process in each of these metrics? Like any facet of selling, it all comes down to your comprehensive effort in all areas - not just revenue, but attachment and any other metrics that matter.

(2) Be consistent with your process, no matter what. You are going to have months or quarters or years where everything is going your way and you crush goal. You may break the bank and make an incredible bonus. But realize that you will likely pay dearly for that with a month or quarter or year without making near the same bonus - they will level you out. Keep approaching your role the same way because only if you are doing the proper process can you maintain a good chance at some semblance of a bonus and average out in an acceptable fashion.

We may not achieve the same percent to goal month to month, but over the long haul we are compared to others who are up against similarly imperfect goal structures. We often compete quarterly and annually, so keep aiming as high as possible. In addition, it's a lot easier to explain away not achieving the same percentage to goal if you are truly following the same process and can back it up with numbers.

(3) Be patient. Often in situations where the compensation structure is tough to decipher, given additional time, more historical data can be accumulated and more accurate goals can be fleshed out. Companies and divisions realize metrics that matter and some that don't matter so much, and they will tinker with what pays out. Play the game long enough, become strong enough at what you do and you can beat the house. You'll lose your fair share of months, you'll

appear on paper and get paid less sometimes than those you dwarf in results, but - over the long haul - you do come out ahead. Don't lose heart.

Remember that the only reason your compensation structure isn't perfect is because it's compounded by imperfect processes created by imperfect humans using imperfect extrapolations and imperfect amounts of data. No planning mechanism could take into consideration all of the intangibles going on in your unique situation – but this can sometimes very much fall in your favor rather than hurt you.

Given time, given patience and given your continued striving for excellence, you'll break the bank more often than you're busted by it.

The Ted Benton Story

Very few people are made like Vincent Scott – it's why our friendship always endured. As we got older and had kids, we didn't spend near as much time together, but those carefree days of youth working together at Cooke's Grocery Store and going to bars and listening to music are days I'll never forget.

In the summer of 1997, my girlfriend Robin and I moved from Minneapolis to Mankato to attend the University of Minnesota-Mankato. We had attended junior college in St. Paul and thought it was time for a change. UMM was relatively inexpensive and it was nice to move away from the big city we had been in all our lives. I came from a family of four kids and was to be the first to graduate from college.

It was great – we got a little apartment near campus and the downtown bar area and got jobs at Cooke's as checkers. That song, "The Old Apartment" by Barenaked Ladies always reminds me of that dump. It was home. Our first child was born while we lived there – and now she's looking at colleges. It was small, but it was cheap and it was all we needed. And those were the best days of our lives.

Vincent and I weren't too sure of each other at first. Ironically, I found out later that he had a crush on Robin until he knew she was my girlfriend. I knew of Vincent as he bagged groceries and was dating another checker off and on – Janie Larkin. The "Cooke's Gang" as we called it consisted of customer service rep Stephanie and her boyfriend Justin – they were a drama-filled, off and on couple who later married – Brian Shane – also a checker, with whom I later worked in the liquor department – Heath Jurgens, Kurt Matthews, and Chet Hollis. Janie and Stephanie were best friends and Vincent would occasionally tag along with all of them.

I'm selective about who I befriend. Vincent and I didn't talk much at first, but we did find ourselves commenting to one another over 80's hair band ballads that played over the Cooke's music system. At first, he didn't really bag for me often – he certainly paid more attention to the attractive ladies who were checkers (not that I could blame him). I didn't hang out with him until one night Robin and I invited over "The Gang" for a few drinks and Janie brought him.

We wound up outside talking. As the drinks flowed, we covered more topics – we had hard-working dads and loved 80's music and had aspirations to write and loved the same movies and politics. We had old souls and didn't really fit in with some of these drama-obsessed folks at the store who had no intention to ever branch out from Mankato – God love them.

Neither Vincent or I were ever really part of "The Gang" – we did our own thing, just wanted to have a good time, have several drinks and sit outside on my porch and listen to music at 3 AM. Isn't that the American Dream?

We'd go to our favorite bar, Ronnie's, after class and we were there so often that our beers would be on the counter before we reached it. We discovered the place – I remember going when it was dead in there. Then, it became largely popular and we actually stopped going. Sadly, the place shut down a few years back, but they recently reopened it. I'd love to go back.

The reason I liked Vincent was because he was real. At least, he always was with me. Sure, I saw him put on a spectacle as a manager at ABM Telecom and later in the Advertising Bureau. But I knew the real Vincent Scott that nobody else did. And I outlasted his girlfriends. Janie and Vincent drifted apart after she slept with a guy while away at school in Milwaukee at Marquette. She came back for the summer, he found out and while he resisted her for a bit, they wound up off and on for a bit longer while he saw fit. Then there was Becky – to whom Vincent got engaged for three months in the fall of 1998 when he thought he had partied and dated too much (I'm sure his older self wished he could smack that kid upside the head).

I knew them all: Stacey, the separated co-manager who said she'd leave her husband for him, Phoebe and, of course, Abby, who certainly came in and out and into the picture numerous times.

But, let's not get ahead of ourselves. The days at Cooke's are among my favorite memories. Vincent moved to the meat department and I moved to liquor and the adventures continued. I'd call in to the customer service line asking for customer pages for Ron Jeremy or Lando Calrissian. We'd page each other in ridiculous voices. The power went out and the store had to temporarily close and we got into snowball fights with the guys from produce with the ice for the fruits and vegetables while riding around in the motorized carts chasing each other. The store expanded and the new half was closed off, and we'd sneak back there and play catch. We always got our work done, but we did it quickly enough that we had time for fun.

Somehow, back then, we'd manage to work until 10 and the night had just begun – we'd be out until 3 or 4 and somehow manage to either go to school, or, if it was summer, we'd be back at work the next day to do it all over again. Now, I can barely have a few drinks without the effects lasting for days. We aged and got responsibilities and kids. Back then, we had all the time in the world.

It's also crazy to look back and realize so many things about life and career.

Cooke's Grocery Store was rife with politics and personal drama. We worked hard but didn't get ahead. We worked around people who got jealous of Vincent and I when we started going places and just stopped talking to us when we moved to Minneapolis after college. Later we learned the fact that every workplace has issues and these same themes will always persist. The trick is finding a place you can tolerate so you can take care of your family and commitments.

Robin and I had our ups and downs, but we've been together for over two decades now. Back in those days, when I thought we might not make it, Vincent and I would talk about getting an apartment and partying all the time. We used to socialize wanting to move to Florida – Robin and me and him with whomever he would be with. We'd sit at my place and drink and eat pizza and would write songs or stories. While other people there got caught up in their drama and we occasionally showed up to their parties and get-togethers, the only real constant back then was Vincent and me.

We just got each other. We didn't need to be popular or to do anything spectacular to have a good time. We went on road trips, watched cheesy movies, played video games, listened to music, drank a lot of beer and just talked about life and love and politics – and we did that for years! In both our respective heydays, we got a lot of girls. In October 2000, I found out Robin was pregnant and that kind of changed everything.

Having a child really forced my hand on growing up. Sometimes, I wonder how Robin and I made it through everything – I was a heel sometimes in those days. But she's the best – she always understood me, too. And she was all I needed. We made plans to move back to Minneapolis in the summer of 2001 and Vincent decided to move there, too.

All my life to that point, I had wanted to be a teacher. When Vincent and I first moved back, we had to get jobs at Cooke's in Minneapolis. For a couple of years, we lived right up the street from Vincent's apartment. It would be Robin and me and Vincent and Julie. I finally got a teaching job; Vincent started working at ABM Telecom as a sales rep on the phones.

Being adults was not what either of us expected. Having wanted to be a teacher my whole life, I was rudely awakened to the politics and bullshit working with the school district and parents alike. Similarly, Vincent got his own taste of corporate politics at every level at ABM. He contemplated quitting in those early days nearly every day.

It's been well documented that teachers make a fraction financially of those in many other occupations – sales included. In fact, I think that's the only reason the sales web nabbed and retained both Vincent and me.

In April 2004, I made the move to ABM Telecom.

The experience gave me a completely altered view of Vincent. Up to that point, he had been my confidante and drinking buddy. We had made jokes and had fun being semi-slackers at the grocery store. Now, he was a sales manager for a big company; he was well-respected in the office and was the top performer in the district. I knew the guy was smart, but I also knew how introverted he truly was. I knew him as the wannabe writer who was a romantic at heart. He kept few close-knit friends, but he was lapping up the attention he got.

Look, I saw Vincent's rise and fall – and attempt to rise again. I've seen it all. And, yes, he admitted to me that if he could have done some of it over again he would have been less trusting and more humble. But I don't think there's much that can prepare you for what he tasted – we were kids used to a certain way of life who suddenly got a whiff of the money that was obtainable through sales excellence. Then he got power. And, honestly, as we worked in a department with a terrible manager who fired everybody instead of coaching them we nicknamed the Terminator, he's still the best manager I've ever had or seen. Vincent never once abused his power, but he certainly used it to get what was best for his team and he didn't care whose head he had to go over to protect the people working for him.

Working at ABM has been extremely significant in my life – I've been there for four stints covering six years. But the most noteworthy part of that was working on Vincent's crew; we were best in numbers and we made a terrible job fun.

I think that's what Vincent understood that other managers didn't: no matter how you spin it, it's no fun getting call after call after call with no break in the action of belligerent, screaming customers who are pissed off about their bill or account or their service all while having to turn around and sell them stuff.

We had division managers that told us to our face they had never even been in sales who would listen to our calls and wanted to write us up or fire us at the first sign of a bad call flow. As Vincent said, "I don't care how good you are at this job. After 50 calls of angry customers yelling about a $500 phone bill, anybody can have a bad call." He was human toward us – toward his team. He recognized our wins and genuinely worked with people to make them better and find success or get promoted or whatever they wanted to do. He protected us – hell, I remember when our area manager monitored a bad call on me and on our buddy Jeff Mason in the same day and wanted to write us up and Vincent refused.

Most of all, he cared. He worked really hard for us and did everything he could to make a lousy job better. And despite the fact it cost him lots of grief and eventually his job, he would always stand up to corrupt or incompetent powers that be. It took him a long time to figure out how to play that game.

I was really good at sales, but I hated it. I know deep down – sometimes not so deep – Vincent felt the same way. But he wasn't just good – he was the best. The best ever. No matter what unfair commission changes were made or what he had gotten chewed out for by an ungrateful flake of a boss whose job Vincent could do with his eyes shut, he'd come back every day, week, month and quarter and be best in show. He might have to find the courage to overcome his job woes or custody fight woes at the bottom of a bottle or the arms of temporary female companion, but he came back every day without fail. He didn't call in sick and he gave back weeks of vacation every year. I don't know how he did it.

And I found myself wanting Vincent to be happy I was on his team. He told me from the get-go it was very important our working relationship never interfered with our friendship. It was important for me to do well. My first month on desk, I did 200% to goal and was #1 in the department on the #1 team in the department. I met Jeff Mason and Cliff Marlin, Jay Zander, Jane Daughtry and other memorable characters on our team I still converse with to this day.

Vincent and I socialized it many times: if we could replicate what we had back then, take out the idiots who ran the office and run it ourselves, we could do it forever. But maybe that's just me; Vincent was destined for so much more. I'm happy with the money to support my family and to go to work and come home and be done with it. Vincent obsessed over the numbers and the processes all day, every day, and he was always chasing another promotion and more money. He was never happy with the current role; he'd master it and it was time to move up and onward.

Jeff Mason and I sat next to each other and would simply do ridiculous things. Toward the end, I'd find every reason imaginable to get unruly customers to another department. If they cursed me up and down swearing that they didn't recognize the call to Mexico to a person whose last name was the same as their own, I'd retort, "Absolutely – Mr. Rodriguez, since you clearly did not make that call to Eddie Rodriguez in Mexico, it's without question a repair issue. I'm going to add them to the line immediately." And I subtracted myself. I'll never forget some of the lines we used on sales calls simply to amuse each other. We made the intolerable place tolerable.

Vincent spent so much time working that his love life was a mess. It took him most of a year to get over Julie even though they were like oil and water. She was a sweet girl, but really, I just never could see Vincent in a relationship. Mostly because he was never 100% satisfied with anything and always looking for new challenges. He was in love with Stacey and that didn't work out either. And with Stacey being best friends with our office manager, Shelly, who I think also had the hots for Vincent, and Vincent brashly standing up to Shelly all the time, Shelly made things really difficult for him.

She temp-promoted "The Terminator," Dick Knoll, when she went on pregnancy leave, even though Vincent was by far the most qualified and everyone knew it. She'd make sure the absolute worst reps in every training class wound up on our team. The only reason I got to work on Vincent's team and the other talent like Jeff did was because Vincent would make deals; he'd agree to take these terrible reps in return for keeping a core of 5-to-8 people. We had almost 40 people on our team once while other managers had 15-20, but always kept our core because Vincent demanded it. And his numbers and dominance dictated that he could.

He was able to use his unique excellence for years and years to get what his team needed; he could put his reputation on the line to save our jobs and there was nothing these inept bosses could do about it – except hold him back.

When Dick Knoll got an undeserved promotion because he was an ass-kissing weasel, he would put all of his office's best reps on one team and his team of three managers would split the commission. Only our team and that one dream team of Dick's would hit goal in the entire company out of 121 teams.

Vincent needed no gimmicks or tricks; he'd just learn how to best "manipulate the playing field" – he'd call it. Like learning where to hit that bloop single to score the runners, Vincent would find that our free Internet disk trial, which no one sold with much frequency, scored quite a few points on our scorecard and he got everyone selling dozens and hundreds of them. When Dick Knoll got his friend from church a job but didn't want him on his team because he knew he'd be awful, Shelly put him on Vincent's team. His first quarter, he made Top Gun – because Vincent carefully wrote out a script for every facet of every call and just told him to read it practically verbatim.

While most managers were impersonal and just sat in their cubicles listening to calls so they could write up their team and strolled through the office a couple of times a day just to make sure their teams were working, Vincent was constantly at our desks. He would joke with us, would take calls every once in a while to show he was still the best ever, and we were really, truly a team. Every month, even when we had 40 people on our team, he would take us all out to dinner on his dime to celebrate hitting goal. And we never missed goal. I always hated to see the freeloaders who would show up just to get a meal in a to-go box and leave. Vincent would drop $1,000+ of his hard-earned commission on us some months. But he didn't care. He'd say he was rewarding excellence and making a continued investment in the best team in the company.

But he wasn't appreciated by his superiors. Hell, almost every boss I've seen him have was scared shitless of him. He could have been CEO of the company and all these lazy goofs knew it. Shelly tried to hold him back and lied to him that she would support him for lateral transfers; he found a couple of interested parties and then she blocked his move. It forced him to find a promotion into a brand new department.

The fact the place couldn't be the same without him is the very reason I went with him when he went to ABM Advertising Group.

Hilariously, eleven other reps in our center tried to transfer within weeks. It caused such a ruckus with people wanting to work for Vincent over Shelly that she had the Union get involved and force people to stay where they were instead of pursuing a better career for themselves. I pretty much had to leave because without Vincent there, Shelly started gunning for our team right away. That same Union promised me I could continue taking classes to be a tech when I transferred to the other division. They were wrong. It wasn't until years later I ended up pursuing these again.

From there, we kind of hit a fork in the road. It was an outbound, all cold-calling venture at first, and was not my cup of tea. Honestly, I had more fun just bullshitting with the customers. I made my first sale to a little record store in Ohio and had more fun just talking to those guys who were living their dream.

But this game wasn't for me; I left shortly thereafter to work in my wife Robin's office and did the mortgage business for a bit.

Vincent wasn't sure of himself at first; it was new to him as well. But he worked his process, got to know the cold-calling game and just threw himself on calls to learn how to do it. He taught himself this foreign concept – no one did it for him. He always said that if neither he nor the reps believed he was the best, his credibility would be undermined. So he made sure he was always the best.

He was obsessive about everything he wanted until he'd get it and then he'd obsess over the next thing. I remember when we saw pictures of ourselves from a Top Gun trip early on at ABM. We had both gained weight – the years of beer and pizza and no longer playing high school sports were catching up to us. And he started feverishly working out and counting calories.

Where most people do this for a brief bit, he never stopped! He dropped 25 pounds in just 8 weeks and slimmed way down before we started doing serious weight training and bulked up. I followed his lead, then surpassed him a bit, but he just kept going even when I stopped. I admit with the family life and job turmoil of the last several years, I've slipped from time to time but he never did.

So many others have only seen Vincent Scott as he wanted them to see him: uber-confident and #1 at everything he did. But I knew the real Vincent: vulnerable. One of a dying breed: a real, hard-working guy like our fathers before us. He was best man at my wedding to Robin in 2006. Ironically, I was actually out at the bar with Vincent's new advertising friends the night he took Abby Winters home for the first time later that year. Through his rise, his unemployment, Robin and I having another kid, Elizabeth Scott being born, Vincent's custody fight and frequent reconciliations with Abby, our numerous jobs trying to recapture the magic and money we had at ABM, we still managed to stay in touch and nobody could replace Vincent in my life. It's true what they say about true friends being able to just flow into the old act after months without seeing one another.

I'd say I have an extremely unique view of Vincent, knowing him at 17, through what he considered his peak and as we pushed 40. He grew more quiet and pensive, the years of unscrupulous supervisors and politics taking their toll. But he is undoubtedly the greatest man I've ever known.

The Vocational Viewpoint, via Vincent Scott
(Republished with permission)
"I lost their business. How can I win it back?"

From today's mailbag: "Due to a variety of factors, I lost a customer's business. How do I earn it back?"

You've been broken up with, or the relationship is on hiatus. How do you re-capture the old magic from someone who once believed?

1. Determine the reason for the split. If you earned the business once and if you did your due diligence of keeping your hand at the pulse of what mattered to your customer in the business relationship, you should either know why they drifted and someone caught their potentially wandering eye or you should have the rapport to be able to broach the topic.

Did they find a cheaper competitor? Did they find better options elsewhere? Were they not seeing the results from your solution? Whatever it is, you need to have the conversation and be able to take that truth. Sometimes, you have some control over a counter-solution and sometimes you do not, but your initial step here is to find out the culprit.

2. Commit to addressing their concerns. You may not be able to provide the necessary options and discounts to earn back their hearts right now; it may be imperative that you visit with leadership or crunch the numbers again or introduce some new elements to the equation to formally formulate a plan. Do not be hasty in this step; sure, there may be some quick remedies you can address during your fact-finding conversation that could quell the pain and lessen their resistance toward you, but depending on the duration and quality of your relationship the decision to move on may not have come easily. Don't hastily try to apply Band-Aid's to their wounds; show them you are serious by committing to the action of a better plan to win their hearts by putting some serious thought into it. If you offer something too hastily and drastically, they will wonder why you didn't do more to safeguard and save them.

3. Propose positive change. This is the part where you stand in their lawn with a jambox over your head blaring Peter Gabriel. While addressing their important concerns, you take ownership of past missteps, be accountable for what went wrong before and lay out the new plan for how things will be different if they give you another chance.

Literally, you have a customer who believed in you at one point. It's vital to revisit why you were the right selection then and reiterate why you are now as you also present how things will differ this time to address their concerns. In some instances, as you work with leadership or other teams and resources at your disposal you have the capability to tweak processes to their satisfaction, to find different ways of delivery that eradicate their objections and you can make a more succinct, efficient, effective program for them.

Can you make a business case to your powers that be for better discounting and more options and special treatment? Great! Your customers want to feel and know they can depend on you to answer the phone, that you care about their needs and that you will deliver, take care of them and always have their best interests at heart. Much of keeping business is being consistent in these items and making them feel like they're your only customer; much of getting them back is focusing on the strengths of your prior relationship but committing to change, really meaning it and sticking to it.

4. Respond accordingly. From here, you have said your peace; they will either accept the new deal or you will have to be patient. In some instances, you cannot meet all of their expectations right this minute; they'll likely respect the attempt, and you can continue to keep in contact as your offerings evolve to their satisfaction. If you are the one who is continually trying to woo them and make overtures for their affections, it will really come down to what love and respect they are getting from your rival. If you show how important their business is to you, your willingness to respond and go to bat and change for them, the likelihood of re-earning the business of someone who obviously once believed in you will increase by leaps and bounds.

5. Learn from the experience. If your customers are having similar issues when you communicate with them around their experiences, you can modify your approach going forward for all customers. This can teach you to preface things differently, it can teach you to approach situations differently and will certainly prepare you to handle missteps along the way - both when they happen or to avoid them altogether by proposing process changes to your leadership team that will be in the best interests of all. Sometimes, you will lose a relationship or two, but that will be the driving force in getting change to take place that will earn and retain more business in the long run!

Customers - like all of us - need and desire and deserve attention and to have us genuinely at the heart of their concerns in the solutions we present, in the ways we service them and in the ways we retain them. If you've lost their love, you'll need more than candles and wine - you'll need a real plan on how you can tend to their needs, repair any damages from situations past and truly commit to positive change that can endure and stand the test of time.

The Vocational Viewpoint, via Vincent Scott
(Republished with permission)
"Factors outside my control negatively impact my customers. What do I do?"

From today's mailbag: "Things completely outside my control are negatively impacting my customer relationships - I cannot control much beyond my sales process, like the execution of the solution. What can I do to prevent losing these customers forever?"

Many times, we on the front lines of the selling relationship can control only so much: we can sell the earth, moon and stars, we can promise and commit and spout the corporate talking points. Beyond that, we very often rely on others for administrative responsibilities, for the delivery of the solution or product or service, and we can only inspect the progress on the assembly line so far.

However, because we are on the front lines - we are the face of the company to our customers! - they will most certainly reach out to you when things go wrong, promises are broken and commitments you made go unkept on the "back end."

1. Level-set expectations. If you know that processes are ambiguous or still being ironed out, if you are in a transformational or incubational environment, or you are aware of a current issue facing potential customer satisfaction at the end result, be sure to inform your customer up front of the issue. You are often a liaison between your company and its processes and the end user: your customer. Being open about potential issues that will be faced during the process can temper the pain points down the road.

It also can cost you the business, but this does accomplish a few things: you can provide this feedback to your organization as a pain point that must be overcome, you further gain your potential customer's respect because you were honest, and once you are able to iron out these deficiencies it is more likely you can earn their repeat business down the road.

2. Be incredible at what you can control. No matter how many links there are in the chain to the solution, it's always possible hitches can present themselves. What you can control are the quantity of customers you target, the effectiveness of your pitch and message, the tenacity with which you provide efficient and consistent communication, how and how often you follow up, and the support you provide throughout all layers of the sales relationship.

You won't win everyone over, and sometimes things outside of your control will hamper your success, but no one but you can control how you react and respond to that. You choose to play the numbers' game - if 1 out of 10 customers won't do business with you solely because of process hang-up's, you can control the fact you are providing this feedback to your organization and you can control calling the necessary additional decision-makers to reach your goals.

3. Own it. There are many sales professionals who will distance themselves from the process, but your customers see only your company. Take ownership of the totality of the relationship - acknowledge that there are issues at certain stages of the game, that you take your customers' needs and feedback very seriously, that you are getting the information into the right hands, and that

you are doing everything you can to expedite the situation.

The best sales professionals and companies are willing to take risks to achieve greater reward, but also are willing to take the constructive feedback and turn it into better long-term process.

The sales food chain is very similar across all links; just like a sales team does not expect a manager to literally fix everything that ails them, they just want to see that their voice is heard, they want to see the manager communicating their issues elsewhere and they want to see the concerns addressed. We win some, we lose some, and customers can accept that. But give them a forum for process improvement! If you have the chance to get them in touch with others who impact the business and the links in the chain that are currently faltering, do just that! Your customers will be part of the solution, which gets them more involved in your operation and relationship and it strengthens that bond and enhances your chances of doing future business. They're invested. You invested in their solution and they'll be invested in the potential for a positive outcome.

4. Exercise patience and revisit the big picture. We will sometimes lose customers for one of a variety of factors. Sometimes, our organization will roll something out before it's ready because it's imperative to have something in the marketplace so they don't fall too far behind. The more plugged in you are to the overall big picture reasons why things are the way they are, the more you are taking it upon yourself to get the necessary problems with potential solutions to powers that be, the more you are positively impacting your business and the potential customer relationships to come. You've no doubt heard that to make an omelet, you have to crack a few eggs. Customer relationships can be fragile, and many times they are looking at you amongst a rather large field when making a decision.

It's possible you will not lead in every single facet when it comes to price, efficiency, productivity and capabilities, but where you can lead is in communication, honesty, building and gaining respect, and doing everything you can to provide value.

No sales product or solution is completely perfect in every way; if it was, there would be no room or need for competition! You provide a product or solution that is unique, and you are a unique additive to the solution. Be honest, be receptive to feedback, relay the feedback and needs of your customers to those who are paid to make the process enhancements and changes necessary and be effective in your outreach and support. Always remember to control what you can; don't sell yourself short on what you think you can't control, don't just accept what you view now as a failure - own the customer's experience, get them involved as you can in solutions and keep working toward an optimum experience for all. For that is the plight of all sales professionals and organizations after all.

The Vocational Viewpoint, via Vincent Scott
(Republished with permission)
"I don't want to job hop, but everywhere I go has issues!"

From today's mailbag: "I don't want to be a job-hopper, but everywhere I go I'm faced with unbelievable issues. What do I do?"

In essence, you have conducted an informal survey, albeit with a very high margin of error. Do not ignore the results of that survey: that every job has issues.

You've heard the adage that the grass is always greener on the other side, but the brighter hue could exist because of more manure (or the less appropriate word for it). It's relatively easy to be convinced that an outcome other than your current predicament is more desirable, but I can tell you from my friends who have pursued those opportunities and from someone who has been in high visibility roles in multiple big companies that your "survey results" - despite the sample size - are accurate.

In our younger days, it's far easier to be a crusader or to "follow our dream" or rely solely on our principles to guide us. We're lied to or misled, we aren't rewarded or recognized or compensated for our successes like we were promised, and our talent goes unnoticed while others of lesser caliber move up the ranks due to nepotism or favoritism or some other -ism.

It's life. It's not you, it is the system, and the quicker you realize that our dues not only never stop being collected but also are the most important thing we pay the sooner you will have a realistic approach toward your career.

You cannot go running every time something doesn't go your way. And even if you have realized this and you've had fifty or a thousand something's not go your way you've hopefully realized you still cannot run.

You've changed jobs, and when you signed on to your current post and your last post and the one before that you sold yourself, believed this was going to have a positive outcome and you approached the role like Chicago Cubs fans face every season: like a fresh start full of possibility (that eventually ends in failure). (And I have the utmost respect for Cubs fans, because unlike other teams' fan base, they remain loyal through over a century of failure to deliver a championship – though they have fielded strong teams in recent years.)

Instead of picking apart the failures of your job, present solutions for problems! Align with the people who can make a difference, or become one! You will never work in an environment that is perfect; it's not to say you will never enjoy your job, but acceptance of it and what you do and your impact will go much farther than waiting around for changes. Certainly, things may improve in your line of work - and they should over time. But you hit the nail on the head: every occupation has problems. Jobs and companies are created by people who may have one or more components of the business mastered but there remains process or people needs to complete the puzzle. Be part of the solution!

Frustration with a job is normal: many, many people face this. While these frustrations can greatly diminish your enjoyment of the business part of your world, being without a job or suffering through massive career uncertainty can trump these.

Let's face it: it's a reaction to want to look elsewhere when things are not going our way. We're in a storm. But what happens after the storm, no matter how long it lasts? The clouds part and the sun shines, and we've weathered another darkness. Stop, slow down, and think: what's better - coming out on the other end of a storm, learning from it and being more valuable to your company because of your knowledge and experience? Or jumping ship to something brand new you have less experience in where you may have to take a step back or start all over when it comes to getting ahead?

Hopefully, you will find that your current role offers you the opportunity to advance and press forward, head-on and the chance of either upward mobility or making a difference and contributing to process change to rectify the issues you currently face. Even if it does not, do you have a goal you are working toward, and is the reality of getting to that point there?

Your decision to weather the storm you're in or to jump to unknown territory that has its own unique storms is up to you, however your ability to withstand the pressures and uncertainties and process flaws in the job you currently carry will offer you experiences and value that is yet unbeknownst to you. It may very well be worth your while to explore that.

The Vocational Viewpoint, via Vincent Scott
(Republished with permission)
"My team isn't carrying their weight. How do I respond?"

From today's mailbag: "I'm part of a team where I rely on others for support and results from my peers, but most of them are not carrying their weight. How should I respond to this?"

This is similar to being assigned a school project where your group is graded based on the combined efforts of the team. Whether you do the entire project yourself to ensure it's done right or you get contribution from others, the results of the team are your results - fair or not. It is often that these scenarios do not feature a perfect balance. Hopefully, you and your peers have both the skill and will to accomplish the common task. When you do not, that is when potential conflict can arise.

Each of you has an assigned task: you may have similarities in your roles and each of you may have components unique to your job. Ideally, everyone will work together, fulfilling the fleshed out parts of their jobs and you will be a cohesive partnership when it comes to items you co-manage.

However, the reality is you can typically only control your own output. Everyone has their own motivations and work ethic and priorities and sometimes they may not all align. Furthermore, it is also quite possible your peer is just not up to snuff when it comes to managing their tasks.

1. SWOT analyze the team. Even if you are not the leader of the team, it is quite likely (and hopeful) that you have some input on how responsibilities are designated. If it is clear that someone weak on a certain component of your team output is managing that output but someone else is strong in it, either ensure that there is collaboration, training or a shift in roles. Frankly, it's great when people are challenged to develop their aptitudes in areas where they are not as strong; however, sometimes they are not up to that challenge and their mishandling of that item is of extreme detriment to the team initiative. It's important that each member of the team is accountable and aware; people should be honest with themselves and teammates about what they are comfortable with and what they could use a helping hand on. Only with this mutual respect and teamwork will the team thrive.

2. Ensure accountability. Again, you may not be the point person of this team, but each member must hold each other accountable to the tasks allotted when everyone's reputation is on the line. It's one for all and all for one, like the Musketeers (or the needs of the many outweigh the needs of the few for those *Star Trek* buffs) but whatever philosophy you're subscribing to it is critical everyone is honest about the wins and losses of the team. If someone is not carrying their weight, they need to know about it. If they can right the ship - great! If they continue to be the cause of your ship sputtering out of control, it must be addressed.

3. Be flexible. We all want to believe that all members of the team want to pitch in and do their part - it's the human nature and belief in people that exists in each of us. However, it is quite common for a team to set out on a mission under certain circumstances and parameters and processes only to see changes occur in the landscape; priorities change, goals change and the mission changes. When this happens, the adaptability of the team is paramount. This is why the relationship of the team - the mutual respect, the selflessness and the willing to help one another - will determine the success. This is why adaptability and potentially shifting roles or readjusting the game plan based on how the game is being played can have a huge impact both on the results and the relationships.

4. Communicate with the appropriate parties. If it's a skill issue, there is a lot to be gained by reaching across the aisle to help the team member who is falling behind. There may come a time when a project calls upon skills that you lack and you need someone to return the favor and reciprocate that help. The

team is as strong as its weakest link, so whomever that weak link in the chain is - swarm to help them and plug gaps in process until the machine is fine tuned. If it is a will issue, that often cannot be fixed; you cannot control the determination, motivation and effort of others. You can offer incentives, you can sell them on why they should operate at peak efficiency, but you cannot control their consistency or lack thereof.

It's likely you are not the only team member who sees it, and it's also likely that you and your fellow suffering team members have a team lead or manager you can communicate with. It's not even necessary in many instances for you to point fingers or place blame - the issues will be glaring. It is, however, vital that you communicate your perspective - that you are contributing, that you are willing to contribute in additional ways to ensure team success and focus and that you and your team are concerned about the lack of forward motion in the affected areas. Once you have done this, and followed up with further progress reports as necessary, you have done much of what you can.

Believe that your team members do want to be part of a successful team where they are carrying their weight, first and foremost. Give the benefit of the doubt, offer to help, offer to get involved in additional ways that will help the team, develop your personal aptitudes so you are even more valuable to the team and be sure to communicate successfully with everyone with a vested interest in the project. Get the best out of yourself and try to get the best out of the others in a way you can all learn.

Someone may need to be replaced on the project down the road, but always operate in the best interests of the team and the goal - even if and when that means deviating and adapting your process along the way.

The Vocational Viewpoint, via Vincent Scott
(Republished with permission)
"Nobody's hitting goal! What gives?"

From today's mailbag: "Despite growing my results year over year, I'm in an organization where next to no one is hitting goal. I have over 100 peers and only a few of us are hitting. What gives?"

Let me preface this by saying that no matter how a company derives goals, it often comes down to best guess at an equation that will benefit some and hurt others and a group of people who are not in the field and may have never been in the field coming up with goals that the feet on the street have to hit. There is necessity but occasional vexation in this method.

Every company wants to achieve a lift in results. They can take their budgets and their expenses and growing headcount costs and equipment costs associated with their internal growth and those costs will be assigned to salespeople to achieve so they can "make their number." High above us all, many equations and figures factor in to what numbers we have to hit - if a division wants to achieve 25% growth this year, guess what? Your goal is going to be 125% of what it was the year prior - across the board, no matter what's possible or feasible or changing in the environment. We can be rock stars crushing goal one year and do more the following year, miss goal, and be the goat.

The reason for these drastic swings fully illustrates the unintentional guesswork that often goes into goal-setting. No one wants to severely under-cut setting goal, because they pay out far more than they desire in bonuses. I also believe that no one wants to drastically misfire the opposite way either, because it is excruciatingly depressing to top performers to suddenly be told they are failing, to take pay cuts and be scolded despite selling more than they did when they were "great."

I've seen companies that painstakingly produce algorithms to derive goals. I've seen others that sit at a coffee shop and just guess based on literally nothing other than a lift. Both have their ups and downs.

Realize that like the House always winning, your bonuses and goals will often be offset - feast with famine. Equilibrium can be difficult to attain, specifically in newer sales channels, because no one truly knows the potential, a few huge wins can really change the curve and the dynamic dramatically, and you may break the bank one month, quarter or year only to have your goal jacked up so high that no matter how you perform you'll never get paid like that again. Or, after a period of famine, if you can survive the drought, you may get to the point where your goals are reasonably adjusted again.

It can often be an inexact science, causing the result - our performance, our recognition, our payout - to be difficult to foresee. Frustrating and perplexing, to say the least, but it's important to handle such issues similarly to other obstacles in your workplace.

1. Communicate with leadership! As always, develop a good rapport with the supervisor who is paid to protect and serve you and your peers. It's important you are tactfully and respectfully explaining the situation. The job of everyone above you on the sales food chain is to stay at the pulse of your team, so it is important you are explaining the drastic swing from everyone crushing goal to everyone missing goal is having its effect.

2. Stay the course. Be patient. As I alluded to, and let's face facts, there are times when goals are severely under-set! If this happens, you are making a ton of money during these times. Be smart, don't spend all of your bonus because a famine may follow the feast! If you spent all of the bonus money you made, this can make it increasingly difficult to keep a cool head when these swings hit. It makes those lean months really hurt; they are frustrating and can be the very catalysts to sales slumps. Make a living on your earnings and put extra earnings away if possible so you can find a consistent flow to managing the

money.

    3. See the bigger picture. Trust me - from a person who has had to set goals for brand new divisions, it is very difficult to do. Malice is not necessarily intended when goals are played with. Sure, there are companies who will make more and more profit and will find more and more ways to pay employees less - that's a completely different story and those companies certainly warrant their terrible Glassdoor reviews and low morale. But I do believe that for the most part, you have a leadership team who is making their best prognosis on what salespeople need to achieve to make the business profitable.

    If they under-cut those goals, they will attempt to right the ship. Be cognizant that sometimes that's going to result in drastic highs and lows on our bonus structures. As for how you are managed based on performance next to sometimes arbitrary goals, that's a whole other issue - that all comes down to the quality of your management.

    You're not alone in dealing with sometimes drastically moving targets on goals and bonus structures. That said, if you have a consistent way of dealing with the inconsistency, it can certainly make it easier to bear.

The Vocational Viewpoint, via Vincent Scott
(Republished with permission)
"The interviewer says 'Sell me this pen.' How do I respond?"

    From today's mailbag: "So, I'm curious as to your take on the 'sell me this pen' interview question. What do you say?"

    While I think there are better ways to gauge selling skills, you may someday face this one so be prepared.

    It's a legendary interview question for sales roles that has gained popularity in pop culture as well and exemplifies a salesperson's off-the-cuff ability to sell something tangible on a whim using only their immediately accessible skills. It's crafted to see how effectively, efficiently and confidently you can jump into your process and yield an exemplary result.

    Personally, without hesitation, I instantly jump into sales process (which is ALWAYS what you want to fall back on) - excited introduction, fact-finding to determine target customer's current process (their current pen situation, in this case), uncovering of needs and weaknesses in current process that will serve as your mechanism for selling change, and finding their potential desires. Then it's all about presenting a solution that remedies their ills while taking their process to new heights and keeping them from fearing the change. Confidence throughout, and CLOSE!

    "Hi there, how are you today? I see you have an XYZ Pen - what are your favorite features about it? That's fantastic! How often do you get it replaced? OK - if you could change anything about the features, what would you change? Is that your favorite color? How often do you use a pen? What are your employees saying about the pen and what is your current ordering process? Perfect - based on what you've told me, I'm ecstatic to say that not only can I make life easier on your writing hand, I can provide a solution that will last longer and need to be replaced less. ABC Pen comes in your favorite color, the grip is firmer and takes less of a toll on your writing hand, plus it lasts twice as long as XYZ. You will save time on having to replace it or on resting your hand after strenuous hours of writing, you'll enjoy all the features you already like but have a more comfortable pen of the color of your choice. Finally, employee satisfaction scores for ABC Pen are higher than XYZ pen and the fact you are ordering them less and your employees will be happier with the product means you have a happier team and save money. In fact, I'm going to leave this pen with you today to sample - we estimate you typically need half the ABC Pens compared to XYZ... I can check on your bundled cost right now; how many would you need to order for your office for this coming year?"

    Next up? You'll get the job.

The Eddie Haskins Story

Ten months after Vincent Scott was born, I made my grand appearance into the world. My parents were his Godparents, our mothers taught together and our fathers golfed together. We were destined to be friends. But the fact we decided to continue the friendship beyond school and outside of Mankato made us brothers.

I'm not going to deliver a puff piece on Vincent: we've annoyed the hell out of each other at times, he's been egotistical and selfish at times. We've been competitive and we've gone months without speaking But, then again, haven't we all had our moments?

What began as a mutual obsession for *Masters of the Universe* – yes, the toy line, the show, movie, everything – and *Back to the Future* and *Ghostbusters* and everything kids in the 80's loved has morphed into…well, endured, rather, and is still pretty much the same thing. Only now, we have more responsibilities.

My earliest memories of our time together include going to see a Spider-Man at the local comic book shop, living on Sherwood Lane and calling the woods down the street Sherwood Forest as we explored, putting on Wizard of Oz plays for our parents – he was always the Scarecrow and I was Tin Man, playing superheroes – he was always Superman and I was Batman, playing Atari and Coleco and eventually Nintendo, pretending to be detectives, musicians, spies, you name it, and listening to music and acting like we were radio deejays making countdowns.

I've known Vincent Scott all of my 37 years and I can say he has been my most prominent friend. I believe the reason he, Jack Johnson and I were so close-knit is that we understood one another even when we didn't agree; we had mutual interests that weren't run of the mill. We were cut from the same unique blend of cloth. We had imagination and enjoyed using it from pretending to be all of our pop culture heroes as kids to writing 26 short stories lampooning everything we loved in pop culture well after our college years. The witty banter was enjoyable and frequent. Even when it became infrequent, it was enjoyed and reminisced upon.

All three of us made some pretty dramatic metamorphoses over the years. Everyone does, but Jack went from the playful, goofy kid from Chicago to a hippie to a Navy Lieutenant Junior Grade. I was heavy into academics and straight laced but branched out considerably pledging a fraternity in college before settling down. Vincent was a brain, and then an athlete, then a salesman and a playboy and we didn't think he'd ever settle down. Eventually, we all became Dads and we all became husbands.

I've seen what the years have done to Vincent's carefree, cavalier approach to life. We don't see each other that often anymore; perhaps a couple of times per year, but he still calls me every year on my birthday and we still keep each other privy on the ups and downs in our journeys.

Our families have always been quite close; we've seen one another on holidays and birthdays. The separation began when I left for college to Bemidji State in fall 1998. Vincent and Jack stayed behind at University of Minnesota-Mankato and I'd see them when I made the 5-hour drive home for holidays and during the summer. Vincent split in 2001 and Jack in 2002; Vincent to Minneapolis and Jack to Denver. Jack came home for a while, had a stint in Minneapolis, and went into the Navy. That shocked us all. Truly, Jack has shocked us all on several occasions, but Vincent and I have always been supportive.

I was actually in sales for a brief bit in 2002-2003, which was such a departure from my anticipated career path and a far cry from my life now. The way I was sold on insurance sales after college made me believe I'd be a millionaire by 35. Now, I'm 37 and a high school teacher… but I love it, and I don't regret a second. Having been in that cold calling grind, needing connections old and new to survive, I take my hat off to this guy who has made a career out of his love-hate relationship with sales.

It was after college when we were most estranged. In fact, he let me crash at his place for three separate weeks for insurance training while I obtained various licenses and there was somewhat of a chasm. This guy who, up to now, had been pretty much just like me, had branched out and had success in his sales role. We had also discovered girls in recent years and that had a way of filling a lot of our time previously spent together.

As I embarked on a new career and we were both in relationships, I don't know either of us really related to one another at that point in time. What we agreed on most were still video game choices and our stories. Titled "Bar Wars", they started out as a *Star Wars* spoof and eventually peppered in just about every bit of popular culture from presidential elections to Vincent's passions for James Bond and *90210* to my affinity for *Star Trek* and mutual love of *He-Man*, *Cheers*, *Rocky* – you name it. We'd take turns writing chapters and funnel our creativity and witticisms into these silly stories; starting them in 1996 and even e-mailing chapters to one another when we were separated by hundreds of miles. I miss them.

Let me say that I think the wedding ceremonies of each of us were quite telling escapades in our lives.

I met my wife in late 2001 at Bemidji. Lucy Clark was a fellow English major and wannabe teacher when I met her. Fight it as we might and despite sometimes non-ideal circumstances, we both ended up in the profession.

At the time, Vincent was with Julie Lansing. He lamented that breakup for a long time and in the wake of it embraced a lot of booze and a lot of other women – including a married but separated one – while throwing himself completely into career. Whereas I found comfort being in a relationship, Vincent was rigid in the face of commitment. Knowing him as I do, it was not because he couldn't commit; he was a perfectionist. He certainly committed 100% to career, despite what it did to him over the years. But he did not commit to female relationships because he disliked confrontation and he took any sign of it as a sign that the relationship was doomed.

I get where he got it from; he grew up with this perception that his parents were perfect. Their relationship is certainly one of a kind, but like my parents and Jack's, they lasted and they seemingly never fought or even disagreed. Jack and I enjoyed being in relationships. Vincent was with Janie after high school and she cheated on him, with Becky and they always fought, with Julie and they always fought and after they split up, he was not in another relationship until the mother of his child in 2007.

Lucy and I moved to Mankato in summer 2002; my parents were stoked to have us nearby especially as my sisters were moving out of town as well for college. We were engaged in 2003 and married July 10, 2004.

Lucy was from Ely, Minnesota, about five hours north of the Twin Cities. We found an old style church and hotel for the ceremony and reception and the downstairs of the hotel was actually called "The Speakeasy." The whole shebang was fancy and full of friends and family. Vincent walked down the aisle with a bridesmaid who took quite the liking to him (and he reciprocated – for that weekend, anyway) and I recall (vaguely) a lot of partying groomsmen and $20 Johnny Walker Blue Label shots. Jack wrote a poem for the event, the reception was elegant and it was the last time I saw many of the attendees for some time. Exactly what I always imagined my wedding to be.

Jack, on the other hand, met Anita Fuentes in June 2003. She was a friend of his sister Nancy. We were a little surprised when they made the decision to marry, which they did June 4, 2005 at home in Mankato. At their wedding, Vincent walked Emily Nance down the aisle – someone who would play prominently in his future – and the reception was at a lodge on the west side of town. Lower key and just how Jack would want it.

The following years were eventful. It was summer 2005 when Lucy revealed to me she was pregnant and our son Benjamin was born March 1, 2006. I remember Vincent calling that day – it was his first day at ABM Advertising – which would also play quite notably in his future.

We would visit during the holidays or joyous occasions, but there were also the difficult times. In May 2006, Vincent's Dad, Vince, Sr., had a heart attack and nearly died. Kay, Vincent's Mom, called my Dad that afternoon and I was at the hospital when Vincent arrived. I've never seen him more serious or affected by anything, before or after.

It was February 2007 when Vincent called me to reveal he would be a father. Jack and Anita had just had their first son, Nicholas, and Vincent had been helping them move to another place in Minneapolis that day. I think him holding Nicholas made him yearn to hold his own child. I knew – from experience – that becoming a father would be a life-changing experience for my friend.

As I indicated, seeing Vincent and Jack – specifically together – has been sporadic at best for the last 15 years. Our children did meet in the summer of 2009 and have done so a few times since at my sister's wedding and on a couple of Halloweens.

Vincent and Abby lasted for part of 2007 and I know he grappled with feelings of doubt in their relationship and strong feelings for Phoebe Wells, who had been in his life previously. Vincent was with Abby in 2007, Phoebe in 2008 and his womanizing workaholic supernova experience peaked in 2009 and came to a screeching halt in 2010. Vincent went into seclusion for some time during that year; I'd check on him from time to time. I'll say this: while I know that what happened to Vincent was wrong and was tragic, and he held on to some of those grudges and axes to grind for likely too long, the person he became after was more sustainable and grounded.

While most of the times we've convened since then have been nights with Lucy out of town visiting her parents when Vincent would make the trek to Mankato for a night, Vincent and I have enjoyed the occasional evening of adult beverages, cigars and a throwback flick peppered with conversation and the occasional cameo from Jack.

When my sisters got married, I'd see Vincent with Elizabeth and how much he loves that little girl. My God, he loved her to the moon and back, would do anything for her. And I was very proud of him and who he had become.

For most people know Vincent Scott as this writer or this business sales star or as the Mankato boy who made good. I have known him my whole life and his best accomplishment is being an awesome Dad. I can see by his social media posts and pictures how proud and involved he is and when they are visiting in person she's the center of his world no matter what's going on around. No matter what he went through with Abby, he always did what was best for his daughter.

Especially after all the years of ups and downs, the many times he had sought my counsel about Janie, Becky, Julie, Stacy, Phoebe and the like, I was admittedly slightly surprised when he called me on Friday, October 16, 2015.

It was just after I had left school for the day; Vincent must have suspected he'd reach me. We often play phone tag because of our crazy schedules between work and kids, but on this day, I was able to answer.

"Hello?" I began.

"Eddie – how are you, sir?"

"I'm good, Vincent, how are you?"

"Doing well. Finished with school for the day?"

"I am. Just heading to meet Lucy and Benjamin."

"Awesome." There was a momentary pause. "Hey, I'll just cut to the chase. I'm marrying Abby next Wednesday and I want you to be there."

Of course, there was a longer pause at this point; I almost pulled off to the side of the road.

"Come again?"

"Yeah. October 21, 2015 at, say, roughly 4:29 PM."

"You're crazy," I laughed, realizing instantly that my friend had chosen the exact minute Marty McFly and Doc Brown arrived in the future in *Back to the Future Part II*. That was Vincent Scott.

"Yeah, I figured if I'm going to do this, I've got to do it on an epic date like this."

"What happened? I thought you were dating that girl from Dallas?"

"Yeah... you know, everything was great for a few weeks and we had the longest phone conversation of my life – like 6 hours. I swooped down there on a whim after not seeing her for years just to see a concert and saw her again a few weeks later... it fizzled fast and there was just too much drama."

"There's always drama."

"I know. And right after that drama, it was like I couldn't envision myself seeing her again no matter how hard I tried. The following week, Abby invited me to dinner with Elizabeth and I went. I always go when she invites me, no matter how much I try to play hard to get. It took no time at all for us to be spending time together again. We had the same old fights – about exes, about the past, about money... and about nothing. But then, we both just spent the day together this past Wednesday – the whole day. We probably drank too much. Definitely ate too much. We reminisced... even set foot together in the ABM office we met in – my first time there in 6 years.

"And we just decided to get married. I've realized – there's drama with every single one of them. But all roads, no matter what has happened, have led back to Abby. No matter what we've done to each other, no matter how much we hated each other or swore it was over or what's happened – we've done this for 9 years. I surrender. I don't want to be with anybody else; every time I have, I've grown tired of them or it hasn't clicked and I've wound up back with Abby. And, honestly, with Emily dying... I have just started taking every day at a time, enjoying life, seeking out new adventures. Forgetting and forgiving the past. And I choose to marry Abby."

Wednesday, October 21, 2015: I left right after school and managed to get to Minneapolis just in time.

I didn't know if Vincent would ever get married, but the way he did it was perfect.

Vincent's close friend from Minneapolis, Ted Benton, was there to serve as best man. Jack, Vincent and I made a pact long ago we'd never choose one of our tandem over the other for this spot. Only Vincent's parents, his Grandma, Abby's parents and grandparents and Abby's friend Tina were there.

The site of the ceremony was a slight overhang over the lake at

Powderhorn Park. I got there first; Vincent's parents were there shortly thereafter with Kay's Mom in tow.

Vincent arrived in a grey suit with blue shirt and brown tie, brown belt and shoes, and a smile on his face that I don't know if I had seen in a long time. He was genuinely happy I was able to make it. Like I told him, I wouldn't have missed it for the world.

"I wish Jack could have made it," Vincent said, and it was his only regret of the day.

We made our way with the assemblage to the spot Abby had chosen for their nuptials. Of course, she arrived separately and was out of sight until they were ready to get started. Vincent greeted the minister, who had previously worked for him in ABM Advertising. Ted arrived, Abby's family arrived.

There was a moment just minutes before starting when an absolutely beautiful girl in a skintight outfit with yoga pants was walking by with her dog. She did a double take, blatantly looking straight at Vincent and smiling.

"Your career is coming to a close in a fitting way, Vincent," Ted pointed out amusingly.

"Yeah," Vincent mused. "Been there, done that."

Vincent wore his late paternal grandfather's cufflinks and had his late maternal grandfather's prized arrowhead in his breast pocket.

Abby looked stunning. Her Dad ushered her down a long walkway to where we were standing overlooking the lake. Midway, her grandmother approached to provide a family heirloom as a broach and something borrowed.

The sun was beginning its descent, and along with it was the descent of Vincent Scott's dark times. It was a seminal moment; it wasn't like he had gone to war or lost all his money, but he had battled demons and losses from his grandfather's death through relationships and ABM and fighting to get back to what he thought he should be. It was rewarding to watch him close a chapter by beginning a new one.

Vincent entrusted Elizabeth, his Dad and me to take pictures with phones. He provided a poem by *Letters to a Young Poet* by Rainer Maria Rilke for the minister to read. They exchanged vows and a kiss. With Elizabeth, and all of us, they took pictures, then tossed flowers off into the lake together. After sunset, it was off to the 1940's retro Riverview Theater to watch *Back to the Future Part II*. Only Vincent Scott.

In a lot of ways, I think it's the best way to conclude my story on Vincent. He has put so much pressure on himself to be this larger than life character that is superhuman and invincible and he's definitely learned the realities of life and love. But to me, he's just my friend. My brother. A great Dad, reliable and trustworthy friend and now a hard-working, loving husband.

CHAPTER 3: THE SPEECH

Despite receiving the news just hours before that the promotion he had been told about a year earlier, baited with for months and promised when it finally became available a month prior while he was directly recruited for it by the hiring manager was not going to him, Vincent Scott had committed to delivering a speech to the leaders of his department and his assemblage of peers on the topic of sales excellence in the Majestech Global Business Unit.

With the responsibilities of supporting a wife and child and new home, he couldn't misstep or speak up. He knew there was no other Market Manager position that would open up within six months and even if it did, he didn't care. He would not work for Luther Petty. *Just get through this speech and this day and go home and regroup*, he told himself.

The evening event featured presentations from the training division, the marketing team, and each department head within the Global Business Unit – there were teams for each continent, Sales, Support, and the like. Vincent's speech was during the segment for the Americas and before Luther Petty would take the stage to announce his Market Managers and give out awards for the global enterprise.

CeCe Carlisle aided Luther in emceeing the event. She was the one at the podium when it came time for Vincent to take the stage.

"No matter what part of the globe you are on, this next gentleman needs no introduction," CeCe began. Eyes started to turn to Vincent. He managed a slight smirk. "We are very fortunate to have him here. It's funny, because when you find out that one of the managers you get to work with is a published author who has done countless interviews and writes articles and does videos all on the topics of sales and sales management, your first inclination is to wonder 'is he the real deal'? I think we all wondered that. But now that we have seen him at the top of our global scorecard for 6 consecutive quarters and experienced his contribution through Collaboration Station we can all certainly confirm that he is. Please welcome, from Minneapolis, Minnesota – Vincent Scott!"

The room stood and cheered vigorously.

Vincent stood. It had been 6 years since a room this size had stood and cheered for him. Rather than be a group from Minneapolis, this was a group fielded from across the world. He had – through a book made possible from his experiences, through articles, through interviews – talked with and connected with people all over the globe. Sure, he lost today, but this moment eased the pain.

Vincent made his way toward the podium, shaking hands, high-fiving, waving. He retrieved a sheet of notes from his suit jacket pocket.

"Good evening, Majestech Global Business Unit!" he boomed, raising his hand in a wave. They responded in kind. "It's been a tremendous three days.

I don't know about you, but the peaks of the time here aside from seeing the innovation ahead and accomplishments behind were certainly complemented well by the lobster from Day Two. Well done to the organizers!"

The assemblage laughed.

"It's an honor to have been asked to present on sales excellence in our channel. When I started with Majestech 2 years ago, I was overwhelmed with the multitude of new product SKU's and specs I was learning, the fast pace of our customers' needs and changes, the new processes, and the possibilities. I'm a perfectionist, like I think many of us are, and I wanted to do it right.

"Today, I'm overwhelmed by being a part of this team. I look around the room and I see about 200 people that are far more intelligent than I am, know a lot more about technology and whom I look up to and reach out to daily. There are probably far better people to have up here, but I'm happy to talk about what we've done in the North District to achieve success in numerous metrics.

"It starts with a great team. I came into the picture six months after this department started, meaning there was a bunch of the team in place. It meant listening, examining what had been done, inserting myself into relationships that already had a foundation of some kind. It meant diving into the leads that had been generated and the process that existed to find more. It meant learning the back end procedures and administrative tasks. We can't ask or expect our teams to do anything unless we know how to do these things ourselves.

"Like many of you, I've seen changes and turnover; we've been forced to adapt. When we first came in, the powers that be were looking for hunters. As time has gone by, we have needed more farmers. We've got a lot of us who are hybrids. But no matter our situation, we have learned – we've learned what works, what our customers need from our products, how to go to market, how to address our customers' concerns.

"Sales excellence is not about making excellent sales. Sure, landing a big program is great, but what did we do after the fact to nurture that relationship and grow it and uncover new needs and match them with new product as it arrives? Sales excellence is about being a student of the selling game. It's about creating and perfecting processes to address every single metric you're going after. My team has had some humongous wins but I'm most proud that we've led in unique business customers. We went about that by a number of ways.

"In the beginning of anything, you flesh out a plan and then you're tasked with carrying it out. What I found fascinating about this role was that there really wasn't a road map on how I had to do my job, so I relied on what I did know how to do. I didn't know every device personally and they came out so quickly that I never mastered each one. But what I do know is conversation. Starting and building relationships. Being responsive and reliable. Committing to the sales food chain: the customer, the company, my team and my leadership. Finding effective ways other than just calling or e-mailing about stuff I'm trying to sell to touch customers and get them interested in what we have to offer.

Following up effectively with the right words to get a response. Not clinging to hopeless pipeline. Reaching out to peers to find out what they're doing so I can make it part of my routine. Developing relationships with other businesses who sell to customers I want to sell to so I get referrals. There's no silver bullet, so you pursue process in every one of these.

"On Collaboration Station, I've talked about some of the events and webinars we did in our district. We've all done events where a few people showed up and we wind up eating the food all by ourselves, right?"

Vincent waited for the crowd to chuckle, and they did.

"And likely many of us did a couple events that were mandated by the division and stopped, right? There's no shame in it. You went on to pursue something else you thought would be more successful, and I can't fault you for that.

"But just think for a moment: we saw a legitimate possibility that an idea would work to drive leads and awareness and sales. Why jettison it so quickly? Why not tweak it? Why not ask our attending customers what more they would like to see and ask non-attending customers what would get them to future events? Why not cast a wider net with broader topics? Why not approach the very folks we are trying to build referral relationships with to co-host events so we're both sharing leads and benefiting? A good idea becomes great when it is allowed to grow.

"Our first event had five people. Another had just one. You've all got that one guy, right, who shows up for the free breakfast and coffee and talks your ear off about all of the evangelism he is doing for you and your products but yet he's never bought anything?"

The group laughed heartily.

"Yep, that's our friend Doug. God bless him.

"But even those lowly attended events didn't deter us from doing them. We analyzed why people weren't showing up. We were doing industry specific uses of products that were only attracting a few folks, so we opened it up to all industries and multiple products. We were having internal folks give all the presentations so we opened it up and collaborated with folks selling to our target audience – Internet providers, website builders, software sellers. And we played with different days of the week and times and offered options to catch people at different times of day. We also developed a newsletter to all of our leads that we allowed folks to opt in for which announced products and promotions and our events. The list kept getting bigger and bigger with every event and referral we did. When Majestech-Tablet 3000 series launched, we had the largest launch event in the world."

The audience cheered.

"And there's no reason why Minneapolis, Minnesota, should have the largest event in the world. That's the very reason it's so special. And the things we've done there can be duplicated anywhere! All we've done is take good ideas that were being used elsewhere and worked to make them great.

"We also were fully aware that just one great process – for events, for example – wasn't good enough. We needed a dozen great processes.

"Outreach and building new leads was paramount. As I mentioned, we developed a lot of referral relationships that now probably yield half our business! We found those businesses through LinkedIn and by attending local networking events – practices that a lot of us cease or never try because they take time to grow.

"Furthermore, our newsletter prompted repeat business. If a customer so much as called in or bought a charger, they were asked to opt in for our newsletter on promotions and events. They may not buy today, but we stay top of mind with a monthly newsletter and with announcements and when they need or want something, they respond. Heck, I wish I had a dollar for every time a cold lead became warm again because they got my newsletter and saw my name and realized they owed me a response.

"We also got better with our closing and follow up. Customers have a way of calling, getting the answers they want and falling off the map. They shop us against competitors. So, knowing this, why on earth do we let them off the phone without being frank? 'Mr./Mrs. Customer, what is your timeline for this need? I also want to point out that I'm aware a lot of customers shop us versus a competitor – is there a specific competitor you're looking at? I'll gladly match or beat the price and am glad to look at their website together right now to see what it will take to get our price to theirs if adjustment is needed.' Customers appreciate transparency and honesty and if you already know an objection is coming, head it off at the pass."

Many gathered in the audience cheered loudly.

"We can also get the impression sometimes after our first call or demo or answering their questions that we're not going to get a second date with these folks, am I right?"

Laughter and cheering ensued.

"We did our due diligence, we know their timeline and we quoted them multiple times, discounted generously and even special ordered product for them – and then they vanish!" More laughter from the crowd. "But we keep these folks on our pipeline report and we call them every week, spending time on them that we could be spending calling new customers. Trying to find 'the one.'

"Don't be too afraid of losing a sale you never had to begin with. E-mail, voice mail, it's time to say, 'Mr./Mrs. Customer, thank you again for the opportunity to prepare the quote for your January device need. To ensure I am operating on your timeline, I have reserved X number of units in our warehouse that are boxed and ready to ship at your direction. That said, I need to know if you wish for me to continue to hold this order or if I may release it to the waiting list. Please advise.'

"Now, there's something tangible waiting for them that they can visualize and they will feel compelled to answer one way or another – with a timeline update or a change of plans that will allow you to spend your time elsewhere. Either way, they are doing you a favor. Don't fall in love with any one of these opportunities. Every hour, every day, our primary charge is planting as many seeds in as many potential growth areas as possible, finding ways to make quality touches and then growing those relationships.

"My largest customer, which many of you know about, is a travel company in Minneapolis. They were on a list of leads when I first came on board. Just a name on a list. I started calling down the list, mostly getting voice mails. However, on this one, I did get an answer, and I got through to Murray, the IT purchaser.

"Fact is, they had actually purchased previously in a much smaller quantity but it was a one-off for 60 devices. I asked why they had stopped, and I was told they got a 2% discount elsewhere. I knew I couldn't beat it on small purchases, as they were typically buying 5-10 here or there, so I asked about the total opportunity. Murray told me if I was serious about trying to earn their business to visit them at the office and see what they do and he was open to talking to me.

"My team told me I was crazy to chase it. Someone who will remain nameless told me specifically I was wasting my time. They were serving as a reseller so it was outside of our scope – end of story. I pursued it anyway.

"Turns out, they were going to need more devices than they were getting because the Majestech-Ware 2000 series had been a hit. I presented a business case to our leadership team why we should be able to sell to them, because they were going to allow us access to all of their end users for demos and accessory sales and attachments on these devices all over the world. I supplied the forecast to our leadership team and was able to secure a 6% discount. The rest is history."

The room applauded.

"The great thing is I have a story similar to that for a number of our customers. We've got the school district who had purchased the off brand tablets for years until we were the first Majestech folks to ever visit them in North Dakota, spent a day demoing with faculty, teachers and a student focus group, and they fell in love with us. We've got the government employee who we helped with his personal tablet rather than sending him to the toll free hotline, helped his kid with his phone rather than sending him to a cell phone store, and he wound up inviting us in to bid on a 5,000 device order that we won. And we even have the eye doctor's office who buys every single month, even though it's just 20 devices we have to special order that he could get cheaper and quicker at our competitor but he buys from us because we respond within minutes to his e-mails and we take his phone calls. We're providing world class customer service and treating our smallest customer like our largest."

The room loved that, and responded with boisterous cheering.

"Sales excellence, for me, has been acknowledging from the get-go that while my previous experience got me here and in those experiences I had to be the smartest guy in the room, here I'm often the dumbest."

The crowd laughed, clapped and hollered.

"Seriously – every day is a new, unique challenge and opportunity. All you can control in a given day is how you plan, how you execute and how you respond. It's easy to get caught up in the fires that pop up, but ask yourself – does this have to be dealt with immediately, or can I see through the task I'm on? Prioritize your day. Do you have live customers or money on the table that need to be addressed? If not, do you owe anyone information or quotes? If not, do you owe your team any conversations? If not, we're not paid to sit there or take a long coffee break. Congratulations, you have time to prospect and plant seeds for new business! It never stops.

"But that's what we call job security. And it's amazing to look back after just 2 years and see all the seeds I planted when I had no idea what I was doing now fully growing and spawning new branches all on their own.

"Every single one of you has a story or ten stories that echo what I've said up here, so I hope my words were representative of these tremendous wins we've created these last few years. It is also my hope that any one of our newer business managers just starting out feeling as overwhelmed as I was when I was in your shoes is heartened by the fact that it gets better every single day. Put the mechanisms in place to create potential relationships every single day. Tend to them and continue to create new ones. Be available. Adapt. Always seek out new ways to engage and educate your customers and teams. Be innovative. Be excellent. Thank you very much."

Vincent Scott stepped back from the podium. More so than any presentation on all three days, the crowd erupted.

Vincent looked out at the crowd. The lights above him were bright, but through it all he could see faces of those he had worked with and for, people he had learned from, people he had made a difference for. And he saw Luther Petty reluctantly clapping.

The Vocational Viewpoint, via Vincent Scott
(Republished with permission)
"How do I improve my team's morale?"

From today's mailbag: "My sales team's morale is suffering, and I'm not sure what to do. I've tried catering to them, taking it easier on them, but cannot find the balance between morale and results. Any suggestions?"

Often, we attempt to cure the perceived poor morale of our sales teams by making knee jerk reactions. We may coddle them, drastically swing from one end of the accountability spectrum to the other or lend too much credence to the complaints. Remember: any time we deviate too far from proven or effective process, it can have disastrous - or non-existent, in this case – results on your intended target.

1. Isolate the real issues. Meet with your team individually and as a group. It is important to determine the problems so you can - as a team - come up with solutions. You will always make commitments and contracts with your team; as it is your role to guide them in their role and career paths and coach toward their success, it is quite important that you work with them to create solutions to the problems.

2. Create a betterment committee or allocate captain positions. Assign people that are representative of your team dynamic who are interested in being part of the solution to report and remain at the pulse of the squad. You need the real, unfiltered truth. However, you must temper and filter the results and findings; it is important you coach this committee not to just blindly buy into every complaint but to work to not let negative items simply lie.

3. Address everything. Even if you cannot change it, you must acknowledge an issue and either provide your commitment to attempt to change it or the reason why it cannot or should not be changed and the substantiation. Honestly, your team will not and does not expect you to change absolutely every beef they have. They just want someone who has their back; they want to feel supported. They want to see that you will give them the guidance they want, provide opportunities and remove barriers to their contentment and success. They want to be heard and respected.

4. Follow up, and be consistent. Remember, it's about keeping at the pulse of your team. Meet regularly with your team and with your point people for team improvement. Consistency means not making drastic changes to your approach that you cannot and should not keep up for the long haul. It means instituting permanent, positive change and monitoring the success. It means giving your team the ability to voice concerns and be part of that change and crafters and drivers of the solution. The more everyone is bought in to the

change and holding each other accountable to positivity, the more likely real change will occur.

Coddling your team or taking it easy on them can work for a day or so and yes - every once in a while, we should give our teams a break. They likely have stressful times and need to feel free to communicate that and vent. Be understanding, be respectful, praise their successes but be consistent with how you lead and how you work out solutions to any problems that plague you. Morale will have some peaks and valleys, but you can absolutely minimize the disparity on that spectrum if you manage with a steady hand on the wheel.

The Vocational Viewpoint, via Vincent Scott
(Republished with permission)
"How do I approach a bad relationship with my boss?"

From today's mailbag: "My relationship with my boss is poor. I don't feel there is any respect, I feel micro-managed and like nothing I do is right. Any suggestions are appreciated."

When a facet of your job such as the manager-employee dynamic is poor, it has a way of contaminating the entire experience. No matter how enjoyable your role, a poor relationship with your boss can destroy it all.

Remember that the manager-employee relationship is a contract. You agree to be the person you pledged to be on interview day. They agree to give you the training and support you need, to remove obstacles from your success and help you on your career path. Period. However, it's never really this easy, is it? Lots of times, managers do their part and get nothing from employees, and vice versa. Unfortunately, many managers have not gotten the training *they* need to be effective managers!

Often, all you can control is you. However, you can certainly control the steps you take to address this disconnect. This is what I call the sales food chain; your relationship with your manager is similar to your relationship with subordinates or with clients. It's about support, mutual respect, and mutually beneficial partnership.

1. Take the initiative to meet with your manager. What motivates them? Do they know what motivates you, what you need and how you like to be led? Communication is the cure to nearly all the world's problems. If they "don't trust" you or "micromanage" you, there's a reason for it. They may be getting pressure you know nothing about. They may be under a false impression about you. No matter what, you need to renew your contract like renewing your vows - revisit the agreement from when you started working for them. Express what you need from a support perspective. Make an agreement on how you will proceed.

2. Be sure to look at things from their perspective. Micromanagement is often an over-used word; the dictionary defines it as "excessive attention to minute details." Performance and process are not minute details - they are paramount. So be sure you give your manager their due; they are also under expectations and have a boss. The more you understand what your manager needs from you and the more you work together to deliver for and support each other, the better.

3. Give it time. Trust me, I know that not every frosty relationship can

thaw. You can rarely do much in the way of seeking outside help because there can very easily be repercussions for such an action no matter what any HR department will tell you. Sometimes, all you can do is persevere. If it is a completely intolerable relationship or situation, you may need to look elsewhere or seek a move to another division of your company. However, nothing lasts forever, and at some point your manager may go elsewhere and you may as well. Furthermore, if you grin and bear it and support your manager as best you can without burning the bridge, they may at some point provide some assistance.

Control what you can control. You can control taking the initiative by scheduling a meeting with your manager and communicating your perspective. You can control how you view the relationship and how you alter your process based on your manager's needs. You can control making an exit from the situation if that's what must be done. But - just like any sales opportunity - you don't move on until you've exhausted the opportunities that exist. If it's just that you feel they don't trust you and they micromanage your process, then you need to find out why this is the case before you decide that this dynamic cannot be changed.

The Vocational Viewpoint, via Vincent Scott
(Republished with permission)
"My top seller is a prima donna; how do I manage them?"

From today's mailbag: "I've got a top salesperson whose ego is over the top and regularly puts themselves ahead of the team. It's very difficult to manage the situation, but I fear living without their sales. What should I do?"

Ego in sales is very important, however no one person is more important than the team. In the end, we can all be replaced. I've had to replace numerous top producers due to promotions, job movement, attrition and because it was ultimately not a fit for the company.

1. Any time an employee's actions and behaviors are not in the best interests of the team, that very conversation must be had. "Thank you for your amazing revenue contributions. But this is a team game, it's a big picture. The company and I need you to excel in all areas of this endeavor, not just in revenue. Let's work together to make a plan to get there. What behaviors do you feel you make now that are not in the best interests of the team? How will we change them?" Get them to commit to a course of action.

2. Figure out what motivates your top seller. If it's money, and money alone, they can often keep up their detrimental behaviors unless you are able to corral them through making them fear losing what they have. "Joe/Mary Rep, I have dozens/hundreds of people applying for this role every month who will

undoubtedly pledge their devotion to the team. Sure, they may not sell like you out of the gates, but I can coach them and manage them. When your attitude continues to negatively affect our team and bring down results of others, what's stopping me from making that change?" You will learn a lot about next steps from their reaction. If they are or remain defiant, they likely have to go. If this is enough to shake them up, it's likely they will at least be willing to change.

If a promotion to a leadership position motivates them, it's another story. Some top producers feel they are ready to manage just because they can sell which is very much not the case (as you have likely witnessed examples of good salespeople who make bad managers). That is why it is important to ground their expectations and help them understand all of the components that make for a successful leader. "You sell better than most anyone else here which is absolutely an important part of sales management. What do you think are the others? How would you grade yourself in those areas?" Work with them to develop a plan to improve in areas – like their humility and team mentality – which may currently be lacking.

3. Work to get them more involved with the team. Sometimes a chasm can develop between these prima donnas and the team that seem so impossible to do away with that no one tries. Encourage your top seller to be more of a leader. If they do want to be in leadership, this is the acumen they must develop; they have the sales part down pat, but it is very unlikely they can coach someone who was once a peer if they do not even have their respect. We must work on bridging the gap between the top seller and the team; humanizing them. Sure, you can give them leadership posts and tasks and projects, but they must learn to reach out to their team members, get them involved and engaged, and work to change the perception that they are selfish and only out for themselves. A prima donna is unlikely to share his or her best practices out of selfishness; a real leader realizes that making his or her teammates better makes them more valuable to the team and company and is what ultimately will lead to recognition and promotion.

4. Work for consistency. Just like a bad relationship that can boomerang from horrible to great for a couple of weeks after making up until reverting to its true form, your top seller may try for a bit and then return to their comfortable ways of failing in the team environment. Like any sales coaching, you set clear expectations, gain their commitment, and follow up - recalling the prior conversation, discussing where you were, where you are and where you're going. Have a few of these such conversations over a period of a month or three and you'll know if this person is good or bad for the team. That will make the decision for you.

No one salesperson is more important than the team as a whole no matter what their results. They likely have a lot to offer the team in sharing best practices and helping others reach the level of success they have. If they choose not to do that, they are expendable. You can find people out there who will excel at the job and help their team members selflessly. You can replace your top seller and you likely will have to numerous times. When you identify a cancer in your organization, you cannot let it spread! You must treat it and keep it in check until the issues either subside or you decide to part ways.

The Vocational Viewpoint, via Vincent Scott
(Republished with permission)
"How do I effectively navigate office politics?"

From today's mailbag: "My department is strife with politics. I'm not a butt-kisser, and I'm tired of seeing them get praised and ahead. It just seems like if I don't, I'm never going to go anywhere. Any suggestions?"

Try as you might, you will likely never escape a scenario where you are affected by politics. Even the adage of "it's not what you know, it's who you know" governs such a large landscape in our working world. This is why we must learn how to balance our business relationships with biting our tongue and being very selective about burning our bridges. Sometimes, it's nearly impossible to emerge unscathed.

(1) Observe. Figure out who the people are that can help and hurt your career. You do need to at least know who you don't want to have as an enemy! Sometimes, you may be recruited for causes you really don't agree with or you can see groups of people who all ascend together in companies that have no business even being there - all because they look out for one another, stick together and promote each other. In business, trust - even honor among thieves - goes a long way. Be very careful about anything you ever do or say that can be construed as a statement against someone who carries a lot of influence. Figure out what these people want that falls within your ethical guidelines and deliver as best you can.

(2) Stay clean. Just as staying on the good side of those who carry influence - both good and bad - is paramount, you never want to give anyone ammunition they can use against you. Standing with a group of dissenters, speaking out either privately or publicly about things you disagree with and even standing up to superiors can severely damage your future chances.

(3) Pick your battles. I'm all for having strong principles and having lines you refuse to cross. That said, if you fight every time there's injustice or you make a large issue or grandstand about even the largest of issues, you run risk of damaging your career. Remember that perception is reality: if those who are influencers can paint you as a problem, that reputation can follow you for the rest of your days. People know people, in other departments and other companies, and a reputation like that can seriously hamper your prospects.

When directly asked by a superior how you feel about something, you can tactfully state your case. However, remember that you are paid by the company to carry out their orders. If you disagree with those orders you either have to grin and bear it, or risk your bills and family and livelihood to put it all on the line and stand up for your beliefs. That's not an easy choice sometimes.

(4) If you have to drastically change who you are, lie or do anything remotely dishonest to get something you want, it's not worth having. There will always be a variety of reasons we don't necessarily get ahead or get picked for the project or get the promotion we think we want in the moment. Politics can very well factor in. And, of course, there are the folks who are just "yes" men and women, those who always spout the company mantra and drink the Kool-Aid regardless of what is best for the people. You cannot control anyone but yourself. It's one thing to follow your marching orders, keep your head down and live an honest life and it's quite another to sell your soul for the almighty dollar.

(5) Have faith in the system. In the moment when you are passed over in favor for the butt-kisser, it is certainly difficult to see your choices and honesty and ethics paying off. But regimes change. Managers come and go and there are good ones out there who may eventually be the influencers you are trying to impress. There are many office and department and company dynamics that are less than ideal - sometimes even for long periods of time! But you cannot lose heart. These types of situations happen everywhere, so the last thing you want to do is something drastic in the moment that will have far-reaching, dramatic negative repercussions.

No matter what, I'm still a firm believer that if you apply consistent, effective process, continue to adapt in the face of your customers' and employees' needs, and always abide by the holy sales trinity on every transaction and with every decision - customer, company and you (never sacrifice any of them in your process!) that - in the long run, over the long haul, everything will turn out as it should be. Politics is a part of life and business, but just as it can hamper you in certain situations or make you lose heart, it can benefit you if you do the right things, align with the proper people and build and nurture relationships with the influencers who stand for what you do.

The Vocational Viewpoint, via Vincent Scott
(Republished with permission)
"How can I spice up my team sales meetings?"

From today's mailbag: "How can I spice up my team's sales meetings? They seem boring and redundant with the same flow and information and action items covered over and over. Any advice?"

Each and every sales meeting, like a sales call, like a salesperson, like any meeting at all, needs a unique, fresh approach. The reason people tune out at sales meetings is the same reason your cold call recipient treats you like a telemarketer - because it's just like everything else they've ever experienced. There's nothing compelling and original to grab their interest. There's not enough recognition or honesty or respect or buy-in.

(1) Grab their attention. How many times have you conducted or been to a meeting that literally just starts out with the same, boring reading of a piece of paper or "how's it going?" type of question posed to the team, followed by venting? Reading off talking points and making awkward introductions that nobody cares about is not going to energize your team. Lead off with a joke! Lead off with recognition! Lead off with passionate dialogue about things they care about! Lead off with good news! Each time out, you want a totally different attention-grabber, but use methods that will make them perk up.

(2) Stick to your program! Control the venting. Far too many team meetings get out of hand because a manager will allow the team to control the meeting. You can even say, "We're going to talk briefly about XYZ. I want to get organized, quick feedback about these items. If you have some additional feedback, we can discuss offline, one-on-one." It is up to you to control the tempo and have a solution for every problem presented. Managing a team is always about earning and maintaining respect, making the tough decisions and leading in the best interests of the team as a whole. Just like a sales call, ensure that no objection, no matter how small, goes unaddressed. If a concern or question comes up that you don't have the answer to, "With things changing, I want to get you the most up to date answer. I'll commit to finding that out today." And do it. Your team relies on you for support. You don't have to know everything and you don't have to be better at their job than they are. You have to deliver answers, support and remove obstacles to their success.

(3) Even if you've already made up your mind or are leaning in a direction on a decision that impacts them, get their feedback. It's important that the team feels like you buy in to them, value their opinion and do use it in the decision-making process. You won't always be able to allow this to be a democracy; in fact, you often cannot, however it does not mean you cannot glean their thoughts on key issues. They will buy in more to a team and team meeting where their voice is heard.

(4) Challenge them to present solutions! Remember that no problem should be introduced without a proposed solution, and you should hold your team to that as well. It's yet another way their perspectives can be ascertained, as people who are proposing solutions that will change their environment, enhance their roles and make the experience of working there better.

(5) Be a human being. Don't talk at your team, talk with your team. When you are delivering bad news, do everything you can to explain the

company stance, acknowledge the impact the change has and deliver your game plan to move forward, all while allowing their feedback and controlling any venting and offering to meet offline - see how it all ties together? Take the responsibility of supporting your team seriously! You can't always just focus on the positives (another common mistake). You also cannot celebrate empty victories - I've seen too many managers try to find too much silver lining in a day when they hit 25% to goal. It's important to point out that your team has minimum expectations and you aren't hitting them, and to examine as a team what gaps exist in process and what you're going to do about them.

Each team meeting needs an attention-grabber, organization and a plan to execute walking out of the meeting - whether you're kicking off a day, week, month or year. You spice it up by not doing exactly what's expected. You spice it up by gaining their respect buy valuing their opinion. You spice it up by making them an active part of the process - identifying where we are failing and why so you can work as a team together to eliminate those obstacles. You spice it up by empowering your team to share best practices of how they are overcoming issues so that everyone else can learn from your leaders. You spice it up by focusing on where you were, where you are now, and what you need to do as a team to move to where you all want to be.

Approach every sales meeting opportunity for what it is: a unique opportunity to celebrate wins, focus on areas of opportunity together, answer questions, provide support, keep at the pulse of your team, and take a unified approach into the future - whatever your joint goals happen to be.

The Vocational Viewpoint, via Vincent Scott
(Republished with permission)
"How do I get my sales team to stop trying to sell the cheapest plan?"

From today's mailbag: "My average buy is struggling and I'm not hitting goal. I've got reps who go for the cheapest plan right out of the gates. I'm trying to convince them to sell on value, but they just don't listen and say they are afraid of losing the sale. Help!"

It is a must that I begin by reiterating the mantra "sales is a process." For starters, you cannot be afraid of losing something you never had. Your team, often when they are slumping or worried or anxious about potential loss, will allow themselves to deviate from process. They will use the excuse that they are afraid to lose the sale or that they are slumping and just needed to get on the board. They will start pitching out of their own pocketbook, second-guessing themselves, and assuming a customer will not pay what your program is worth - solely because they have lost faith in either themselves or in their product or in their process.

When coaching, it is important to get the employee's agreement that they are not satisfied with their current results. If they have had prior success, it can also help to remind them of what their process was like when they were closing. Like a baseball hitting coach assisting a slumping player in finding his previous, successful stance and swing, like a golf instructor watching for where the mechanics of the follow-through have gotten out of whack, we as sales coaches must diagnose the destructive changes to sales process.

1. Find the reason why your team member is deviating from process. Is something on their mind, and distracting them from what they should know is the right process?

2. Re-visit the why and how of process. We make an impactful intro so we grab our customer's attention and earn the right to have a conversation. We ask insightful questions to learn the customer's motivation, gather enough of their words and passions and perspective to utilize their own philosophies in not only constructing the pitch but also overcoming their objections. We build value in our complete solution, and based on the return on investment, we make it make sense to our customer. Immediately going in and pitching the lowest common denominator does literally nothing but scoff in the face of process and if we actually do get a "sale" it will be the result with the least probability of benefiting our customer. The long-term relationship we should be striving for is destroyed before it begins.

3. Establish a commitment between your team member and you that they actually do fully understand why a change is necessary, that you will provide the help and coaching they need to implement the change, and that you will (and you actually do!) follow up to ensure it is carried out. Often, people won't change because they don't fear the potential down side worse than they fear changing. They settle for comfortable ways of failing or mediocrity. They may also buy in to the process change, but they go out in a job that's 1 for 10 or 1 for 20 or 1 for 100 as a good close rate, they fail the first few times out of the chute, and they go back to comfortable ways of failing. They don't give it enough of an opportunity to work, but they mentally tell themselves it's the process that failed, not them.

4. Finally, truly re-visit your commitment. Like renewing your vows, like re-visiting a promise or contract, you must hark back to this conversation in future ones. Always use coaching conversations to visit where you are now, look back at where you were, look at what you committed to do and if it panned out. You applaud the wins and coach the opportunities and make a plan to either continue upward trajectory or to address the fact they refused to change.

In the end, this one all boils down to ensuring your salesperson knows the process, knows why process reigns supreme and is actually following it in the field. Your part in this play is to determine any obstacles or objections they have and eradicate them... so that nothing stands in the way on the road toward successful sales that truly benefit the holy sales trinity: customer, company and you.

The Abby Winters Story

On April 11, 2006, I went to the downtown Minneapolis ABM building for a job interview. My Dad, Dan Winters, started working there in 1995 and was a 2nd level manager for the company; he got my resume in the hands of recruiting manager Melissa Worthington. Melissa called me the day before, invited me in for an interview and I was excited to get into something that wasn't retail. I was 21 years old and just got my associates degree: it was time to start my career.

I do remember it like it was yesterday; I wore a brown lace V-necked shirt with tan skirt and khaki blazer. Upon entering that 45-story building, I checked in at the front desk and waited to be fetched by the manager.

Down the escalator, wearing a lime green shirt, splashy tie and grey pants came Vincent Scott. 27 years old, short-cropped blond hair, blue eyes – I thought to myself, "I hope he's the one interviewing me, because I know I'll get the job!" I kid, but it was obviously true. I also got a lot more than I bargained for.

Much later, Vincent revealed to me that he had taken one glance at my relatively empty resume void of what he deemed real sales experience, found out I was just another corporate referral for possible nepotism and he had already decided the interview wouldn't last long and wouldn't result in a hire. Fortunately for me, he took to my looks, my voice, my attentiveness and my confidence. I was nervous, but he was easy to talk to. He was charming, confident, witty and very cute. Not only did he interview me, but he stayed talking to me for the fifteen minute gap between his interview and my interview with the department head – something he told me that he never did before or after.

Vincent was in my training class that started Monday, April 24, because, it turned out, he was new to the department, too. We had twelve in class – some like Kevin and Nate that aren't that memorable and others like Chad and Sahim and Jimmy that were a big part of my time there and beyond. What I remember of Vincent back then was that he was always first to finish every quiz, he was funny but I didn't think he really liked me or had time for anybody that wasn't on his pay scale.

Ronnie Collins sat next to me when I was assigned to a cube. He was nice, had a huge crush on me but I wasn't interested in him in that way. We did hang out every once in a while – it was fun going to hockey games and bars. But he invited me into the larger world that was the behind-the-scenes of our department. Because he, like every guy in that office, worshipped Vincent Scott.

While Vincent was in the office, he was on another planet: he would jump on calls for his sales reps, close sales, audaciously blast an air horn that I'd complain went straight to my brain stem – in an attempt to just be on his radar. He was *the* personality of that office, that department. Most of our office was young twentysomethings who were in their first structured sales job; lots of them had come from car warranty places or from door-to-door sales. As Vincent was 27 and a 2nd line manager making six figures, these kids thought he was a sales god.

We were surrounded by a lot of money-hungry kids getting their first taste of real money; back then, the commission structure was easily tackled and manipulated because the department was so new they had no idea what we were capable of. The best, most ripe time to work there!

Even for someone like me who had just moved out of my parents' house, getting that taste of meaty commission checks meant I was going out for lunch daily in downtown Minneapolis with my co-workers and going out drinking with them every night. I was also dating quite regularly; back then, I'd nickname them all after the cars they drove. Mustang didn't have a chance when Vincent entered my picture. (He was an Accord at the time – hee hee…)

It was September/October when I started accepting the invitation from Ronnie on Thursday nights to go to Finley's – a bar near where all of us lived. Vincent was the star attraction; heck, they'd even make his tab out to "The Godfather." These kids would buy him drinks and sidle up to him in hopes he'd promote them. Our office was booming and Vincent was the clear frontrunner to play more prominently as it grew. Our division leader, Derek Walters, started helping out other local telephone sales groups and when he did, Vincent would run the place in his absence. It was clear to everyone: Vincent's star was on the rise.

The funny thing is I didn't care about that at all. In fact, over the years, I have hated what him throwing himself 100% into his job has done to him.

While he clearly enjoyed telling stories to these guys and laughing with the likes of Chad, Sahim, Jimmy, Ben, Cal and Ronnie, I was one of the few girls that would show up. Kristi was a lesbian, Angie wasn't Vincent's style… but one night, he and I were the last two there from the office. Looking back, I'm not even really sure how it happened. I got there kind of late that night. Vincent and the guys were talking about selling tactics and the customers they were working. Vincent would just laugh when the guys would talk about how ineffective the other managers were compared to him. But he and I started talking toward the end of the evening and just kept going.

He asked about where I was from. We talked about our work history. I found out he was from Mankato and went to high school and college there. He was a basketball player. He told me my eyes were luminescent – I later found out it was a line from *Leaving Las Vegas*. Anyway, it worked.

We started spending many nights together and seeing each other, albeit casually, unbeknownst to everyone else. Also, I didn't sleep with him right away! But I did hang out at his place and eventually rewarded his patience. I fell hard for him but I didn't think he loved me or would love me. We stopped seeing each other for a while, and then a twist of fate on December 1 changed our lives forever.

On November 30 a snowstorm kept Vincent and a few of the sales reps downtown in a hotel. I couldn't get up the hill to the house I was sharing with my cousins, called Chad Willman assuming full well he'd know where Vincent was and found out he was at the hotel – with Vincent (even better). When I got there, Vincent, Chad, and Ben Friar were there – they had been drinking and playing pool. Vincent and I had not been seeing each other for a few weeks, but when Ben started putting the moves on me by "showing me how to play pool" with a very hands-on approach, Vincent couldn't stand it.

Vincent insisted on wooing me away to show me where I'd be sleeping. We, of course, wound up in one room watching *Superman Returns* on Pay-Per-View while the others wound up in the adjacent room. And our daughter, Elizabeth Marie Scott, was born roughly 9 months later on August 27, 2007.

There are lots of things I could say about our on-and-off relationship that ensued. Suffice it to say we were both in different places in our lives versus our ambition. I was young and just starting out and he was more experienced and obsessed with his career. Vincent was always a tremendous Daddy. I often lamented that I felt he loved our daughter far more than he would ever love anything – myself included. We both made what I believe we deemed as mistakes when we were able to look back with the perspective of thirtysomethings.

Vincent was instrumental in my evolution as a person, whether I liked him at the time or not or acknowledged it at the time or not.

I've never been able to fully understand how he remained so driven in the face of everything. I know he gave up basketball for career, lost his grandfather early on, constantly went to war with bosses he was better than whether it was career suicide or not, and he always came out unscathed until the day ABM fired him. January 22, 2010. I'll never forget it because I was a sales rep in the department and the supreme asshole clerical manager actually took pleasure in pulling me aside and telling me. I cried.

Even though we weren't together when it happened, I knew it was a crushing blow to him; Vincent practically single-handedly created our department. It started with 10 people and he grew it to 250 across three states. What was a $10 million department in year one became a $60 million department at its peak; after Vincent's demise it slumped to $29 million the first year of his absence and closed a few years later when the company sold the department. I won't say Vincent's departure was the sole reason for the demise – the outdated advertising methods and poor leadership were a big part of it – but there's no question his absence contributed to the beginning of the end. With him at the helm, it would never have collapsed. He wouldn't have let it.

Vincent was unfortunately very skilled at keeping me at arm's length. We were engaged for a few months in 2007 but it was tumultuous; I was pregnant and he was stressed out after his new promotion and the hostile work environment he had to work in. Neither of us made the situations any easier on each other and we grew apart pretty quickly… we fought over custody for years… we would link back up but the second something went wrong, one of us ran. Every time. To other people, to other situations.

I could go on and on about the differences we had then and over the years, the different guys and gals that entered the picture on both our sides, but the point is moot. I'd rather focus on the positive. That's something else Vincent inspired in me.

When I think about my favorite memories of us, I think about moving in with him in March 2007 – when we first started to get to know each other and our quirks. I remember being so cold one night that he made a couch burrito out of me with blankets and quilts his grandmother made.

I remember when he proposed to me on Easter in 2007; I was still wearing some of my Easter outfit and some of my pajamas. He was actually shaking and vulnerable and nervous – not the Vincent Scott that anyone else sees.

I remember the 4th of July that year, when I was pregnant; we sat around and watched *Die Hard* movies all day long and then drove downtown to watch fireworks at a perch on the bridge by ourselves.

I remember just before Elizabeth was born; I woke up and said, "I think it's baby time." We went to the hospital, and they wouldn't admit me yet – they told me to walk around the hospital and come back to see if I was dilated enough to be admitted. Vincent turned on the *Rocky* theme on his phone and walked around the hospital and through the parking garage with me until they would let me in a room.

I remember a day we played hooky from work, which was totally unheard of for him; we laid in bed all day and watched reality TV.

I remember January 26, 2012 when Vincent came outside one of his Cellular Horizons stores and I came out of the ABM building and we met between the two so he could make his case as to why I shouldn't get married to another man and why we should be together.

He was my shoulder to cry on when I had no one else to turn to, no matter how awful we were to each other at various points through all those years. Whether I had been mistreated by a significant other or lost a job or got bad news or had health scares, Vincent Scott was always the only one who was always there for me.

He'd write me poems, he'd send me flowers. He would never 100% leave the picture. No matter who I was with, Vincent was always on my mind.

I definitely understand the philosophy of there being a thin line between love and hate, because that line certainly gets blurred. There was such an intense feeling the whole time. It took me a long time to truly be able to put it into perspective.

The small things were what meant most to me.

But then, there was also July 4, 2014 when he took Elizabeth and me to see our favorite musical act, asked him to play "our song" which he didn't play in concert anymore and during it he proposed marriage to me. (Unfortunately, because it was us, we buckled under the pressure shortly thereafter and the engagement didn't last.)

There was October 21, 2015, when we had a low-key wedding at my favorite spot in the city park in front of our parents, surviving grandparents and our three closest friends.

Even married, Vincent still kept his career battles close to the vest. I obviously knew of his infamous court case with ABM. It took from January 22, 2010 until June 4, 2013, for Vincent to find resolution. Knowing him like I did, I know what those years did to him. Seeing everyone who revered him, everyone he promoted and did favors for and invited to our daughter's birthday parties completely abandon him destroyed much of his faith in people. Seeing him painstakingly struggle to get back into a position of the same or better caliber as quickly as possible with sometimes limited gains pushed him to his limits. But he didn't give up – he fought through each day, he provided, he improved himself and he finally got close enough to me where he didn't run.

When we married, he was a few weeks shy of 37 and we had known each other for 9 ½ years. He was a business manager with Majestech-Ware… and I know he hated it. He hated going to a job where he was once again unappreciated as #1 and buried in administrative work that was beneath him. Vincent's real passions were Elizabeth, writing, basketball, reading, and I'd like to think me. I jest a little, as I know his love for me was more than he had loved anyone and could or would love any significant other.

His attention-deficit and his obsessive compulsiveness definitely increased exponentially in his 30's. From a sales management perspective, I believe he used the ADD to his advantage – he toggled back and forth mercilessly on tasks but he did see all of them to completion somehow. I tried to watch him sometimes when he'd work from home and I couldn't make rhyme or reason out of what he was doing when he'd get involved in several corporate chat threads, answer or make unrelated calls, write different reports simultaneously and have a half dozen e-mails started sitting in draft only to be sent out hours later.

But he was very enamored with his routines – he found comfort in them. When we first got married and moved in together, it drove me crazy that he set his alarm for 3:40 AM and went to the gym down the street at 4. However, in a few months, I was doing it, too. He took solace in his writing and his reading – he had read every original and continuation James Bond and Sherlock Holmes novel he could get his hands on. He said they were his escape. We had a basketball court and tennis court in our neighborhood and he was out there every chance he got, occasionally with Elizabeth, me and the dog in tow.

When I met Vincent, he was a cocky, self-centered salesman and he became a devoted husband and father who accepted doing what he hated in an attempt to reach a plateau where his impact and influence could truly be felt to his satisfaction. That said, he was never truly satisfied.

When the six year mark of his departure from ABM came, he couldn't even remember the date; this coming from a man who was obsessed with revenge and full of hate when they wrongfully terminated him all those years ago.

And it came down to acceptance. Not just in his career, but with me. With us. Vincent didn't have to tell me, but he just reached a point when he accepted everything past and moved forward. In fact, after we married, he never even brought up any of the things or people that were wedged between us for nine years. He drew a line in the sand and made the pledge that everything going forward was approached anew.

Let me just say that our connecting the dots from engagement #2 until marriage was not a straight line. We fizzled a few weeks after getting engaged after a spat and both of us running and we both wound up dating safe old flames where the passion didn't compare – our usual routine. Vincent used the money he was going to use on our wedding and honeymoon to buy his dream car, a black Aston Martin DB7 convertible.

I do know that a great deal of Vincent's overhaul of perspective occurred when Emily Nance died in January 2015. Vincent and I weren't together, but Elizabeth was close to her and she told me when it happened. She still brought it up for years to come, and Vincent refused to talk about her or anything related to her.

I know Vincent cared deeply for her even though they were never a couple, and I know they were seeing each other when she died. After that day, he transformed. He wanted to try new things, have new adventures, really live life.

It was a week before we got married when we played hooky from work and went to breakfast together at a place called Charlie's we had never been to in St. Louis Park. Again, for him to play hooky is one thing; for him to open up something completely different.

We spent the day together. We went for a carriage ride downtown. After literally six years, he actually walked into the ABM building and strolled the lobby – just for the closure. (Turns out, one of his customers through Majestech-Ware bought the building in Greenfield he managed after they sold the company and he had recently been back in that building too; his office no longer existed.) We tried new places for both lunch and dinner. It might have been the mimosas followed by martinis for hours. It might have been the passage of time, the recent crumbling of my latest relationship, or even the maturity. But at dinner, the topic of marriage came up. Vincent, for once, didn't dismiss it; he said it would have to be on some momentous date. The following Wednesday was the date Doc Brown and Marty McFly traveled to in *Back to the Future Part II*. It was settled.

While we both had some jitters in the days between, our wedding day could not have been more perfect.

I got the dress I wanted. Vincent got me a gorgeous setting band for my ring. A previous co-worker, Paul Nichols, was an ordained minister and agreed to conduct the ceremony on short notice. We got our marriage license. We drove around and found an amazing spot at Powderhorn Park. Tina Sanders, Jimmy's wife, was able to spend the day with me and help me with my dress. I got my hair done at my favorite salon. Elizabeth was with me, my parents were there, my grandparents were there and two of Vincent's closest friends and his family were there. What was supposed to be a rainy day was sunny and bright. Vincent selected an amazing, deep, insightful poem that encompassed perfectly his feelings.

And we both said, "I do."

I've seen every side of Vincent Scott. I've seen him as sales champion with the crowds cheering loudly for him. I've seen him at his darkest, riddled with anxiety and self-doubt. I've seen him loving and attentive and giving and supportive and easygoing. I've seen him cold and distant and consciously blocking out memories of the past that brought him pain.

As a Dad, I could never complain about Vincent. He may have been beyond devoted to his career, but he dropped everything at the drop of a hat for Elizabeth. Every gymnastics practice, school function, Daddy-Daughter dance, baton, cheerleading, doctor's appointment – he'd find a way to be at all of it. Sometimes, I've been jealous of how much he loves our daughter.

I also know that we've put each other through the ringer, but it has never diminished how we truly feel about each other.

So, I guess, in closing, this chapter should probably be re-named as the Abby Scott story. ☺

The Vocational Viewpoint, via Vincent Scott
(Republished with permission)
"4th and Goal: Optimizing Fourth Quarter Sales Results"

The fourth quarter. Whether sports or sales is your arena of choice, the mere mention implies that final push for the win. Pressure, heightened sense of awareness and clutch play are commonplace during this crucial time. But what many of us lose sight of during this time is that we've been building for this all year long.

When the final quarter of the year hits, our organization and our leadership may deliver a completely different tone. We may look at our year and we fall in one of three buckets: we're having an awesome year and we've got to put an exclamation point on it, we're having a so-so year and need to get over the top or we're having a subpar season and it's time to close some serious business!

All year long, we are setting the foundation for future business. We are planting the seeds for success every day. So, in reality, the fourth quarter should absolutely not take a different tone and its arrival should absolutely not result in us drastically changing our approach. Building a pipeline means developing the relationships that will sustain you in famine and culminate in feast - and hopefully, with diligence and consistency, that feast will not end.

During this time of year, we'll hear some, "Yeah, my budget is tapped out and we're just budgeting for next year." Great - make it a point to ensure you're on their outlook for next year. However, you'll also come across your customers who have money left to spend before the year wraps - know your customers well enough to know their cycles. Find ways to stay top of mind - post industry articles on your social media so your contacts see them, send newsletters, make regular calibration calls (you should have established a regular rhythm and cadence with each customer as often as needed). Furthermore, many customers you work with operate on different fiscal cycles so don't naturally assume it's their fourth quarter too.

Prioritize your leads! Regularly visit and revisit with your top spenders. Ensure their needs are being met, ensure they are pleased with results and that you are reviewing the relationship regularly. It's kind of like your top reps, if you are a sales manager – reward and recognize and let your prized stallions lead you in the race.

That said, don't make the mistake many salespeople make and solely chase whales! Diversification of your portfolio is of the utmost importance; those who only chase whales get swallowed whole. The temptation is real; sure, these customers can make your whole year or two. But I have seen far too many people live and die by chasing their Moby Dick. Your story could have the same unhappy ending.

When you diversify, prioritization of your leads means ranking them when you are scheduling your time. Certainly sell and sell more to your top accounts; make sure they are in the know on what they need to know to make informed decisions and get the most for their money. When you have new offerings, go to them first. From there, focus on additional leads as follows:

Previous customers: Realization of who no longer does business with you and why, even if you cannot immediately solve why they left, goes a long way. Specifically, when you are trying to rekindle the flame and re-earn their business – you can't just do it with chocolates and flowers, you've got to SHOW them why things will be different this time. But, at one point they believed, so if you are able to overcome the hurdles that cost you their relationship before, you may earn them back. If they come back, often they are here to stay.

If you have company generated leads that perhaps are not yet spending money but are qualified in some way, absolutely perform outreach and get them into your pipeline. Figure out what their timelines could look like and size up potential needs. Get into a rhythm with following up and engaging them.

Finally, the cold outreach. This could be door to door, it could be utilizing social media (like LinkedIn) to meet decision makers and set appointments to qualify opportunities. As long as it is strategic and targeted based on your target audience and who needs what you've got to offer, it's got value.

There is no one dominant fountain from which your top leads will originate. If you effectively follow this process each day, week, month, quarter and year, frankly, the fourth quarter will be like any other. If you obsess over process and people, the numbers will always be there, and you will never have to worry about where your next sale comes from. Where we get off track is when we allow any outside factor, whether internal or external to our company or work group, to take us away from our process and the focus on our customers.

Have a strategy for your pipeline management, around new products and services, educating and communicating around changes in your industry, social media and each individual type of lead (from spending to pending), and simply execute on it daily. Customers will buy from you because of communication, transparency and response.

Don't solely focus on what is going to close this quarter! We must continue to plant seeds for next quarter and year so we never find ourselves in the predicament of desperately flailing to hit numbers. That's when we make mistakes. Frankly, the goal is to get to the point you really don't have to think about what quarter it is; you need only think about which customer is next to engage, why, and what your message is. Don't react, just rely on your resources and regimen.

Consistency around your process, whether you're a sales professional or leader, will ensure your fourth quarter and every quarter are as profitable as you want them to be.

The Vocational Viewpoint, via Vincent Scott
(Republished with permission)
"Why is it that in sales, nothing is ever good enough?"

From today's mailbag: "I've exceeded goals, grown year over year and done literally everything asked of me... and while it led to good early bonuses, now my goals are so high I cannot reach them. It feels like in sales, it's never enough. Any advice?"

Right or wrong, in sales, you are often only as good as your most recent win. Like being a superstar athlete, you are cheered in the moment and celebrated while you are the story of the hour, but once that moment of glory passes, everyone wants to know what you're going to do next.

From someone who has chased metrics at multiple levels of leadership my entire career, I can certainly understand your plight. While this mentality can be a mix of being a product of management that doesn't really know what it wants or how to get it along with a testament to how difficult some divisions or companies find it to make goals that are not arbitrary, when you are on the front lines there is little consolation.

Know this: what you are feeling is common. It's also why many people choose to just do enough and not seek the accolades - because often more headache and heartache come with over-achievement. There are inevitable repercussions of sales excellence - the mold isn't made for you. Typically, rules and parameters and guidelines and processes are created to manage the masses. You're the exception to the rule, but there's no exception made for you.

The status quo will not share your pain, because it isn't their goal to be the top of the heap. They may hit a goal one month, miss the next, but see a gradual, manageable increase to their expectations which makes it less complicated to achieve. If you are blasting through the stratosphere, the existing processes will buckle and be baffled and will strain to contain you. If everyone across the board is expected to have a 50% increase in productivity, the worker who had 500 widgets last year now has to do 750 while the person who did 100 only needs 150. It gets to a point where it extrapolates beyond common sense and few leaders will acknowledge fault in the logic.

My advice is persevere. Latch on with the people who are influencers in your business and get advice on how to get what you want. Sometimes, it's about accepting that you broke the bank to start and that it will take a bit of time for the compensation structure to catch back up to you. However, once you have reached the top there will always be others just waiting for you to fall, which - for some of us - makes it even more imperative we don't lest we be cast as a flash in the pan. The long and short of it is that if you are a true achiever and believer in your ability to win at all costs, you keep your head down, take one day at a time, battle through the storm of uncertainty and do the best you can. Every sales role is going to present some semblance of this challenge - it's not unique.

Ideally, you will have a manager who understands your frustration and supports you in your role. There are many managers out there who have not been trained how to lead or motivate and they are the ones fueling this "More, more, more!" mentality. Somebody barks it at them so they turn to you and repeat it.

In the end, you have to evaluate the big picture. It isn't always the best performers who get paid the most, get the most recognition or get the promotion. There are so many facets to whatever you are seeking, so perform as best you can, work to adapt your process to contain all key metrics your customer benefits from and your company endorses, and liaise with the right people on all sides of your sales food chain.

It's very likely you have peers that feel the same. It's very likely that somewhere there are leaders who understand your mission and frustration. And, if you do right by customer, company, and you on each and every transaction, you leave each transaction either closing the business or knowing the specific reason why you didn't, and you support everyone subordinate to you on the sales food chain - employees, customers, etc. - you've done your job. Sometimes, it's just about celebrating a job well done, even if right now you're the only one celebrating. Everything comes back around.

Even if your effort and contribution doesn't feel like it's enough for others, make sure it's enough for you. That's all you can control and that's all that matters.

The Vocational Viewpoint, via Vincent Scott
(Republished with permission)
"Selling Well Despite the Economy"

I have never been an "excuses" kind of guy, nor have I accepted them in my years of sales leadership. Excuses are like objections; you must acknowledge them, respectfully analyze and put them in their proper place with reason and logic, and move forward in your agenda.

The economy takes a lot of flak these days for being the reason sales can be a difficult occupation. Difficult, maybe, but never impossible.

The trick to selling in any condition (in this case, the economy) is first discerning how your product or service, tangible or intangible, transcends that condition. First, the condition will not last forever; nothing does. Whether the country is on the road to economic recovery or not (depending on what political pundits you are tuning into these days) your product, service or offering must have value that speaks to a potential buyer regardless of circumstance.

Case in point: people will always need vehicles, vacuum cleaners, advertising, utensils, pharmaceuticals and medical equipment. "The economy has hit us hard" is simply another translation of "we can't afford it" when it comes to customer objections – be sure you are fluent in this language.

Remember, it all comes down to LACK OF BELIEF. A potential customer will tell you the economy has impacted them, times are tight and that their wallets are closed for bidders like you because of outside forces. However, if you convince them the potential benefits of your product or service outweigh the prospect of sitting idly by and hoping for a change in circumstances without changing approach, you can still win despite the "tough economy."

Needs and weaknesses; these are what makes the sales world go 'round. People always need something and where there's a need, there's a way.

Focus on learning your customer's needs and weaknesses; because this is a lost art, many will succumb to the "economic factors" objection as a reason they walked away from a potential sale with little pushback. Some customers know this and it's the very reason they say it to end the conversation. If you don't let it be a conversation-stopper, you keep your chances alive

Find the ways that your bag of goodies is necessary despite whatever conditions you are selling against. And ALWAYS challenge the customer: "Mr./Mrs. Customer, I 100% understand that your gut reaction is to look at the tough economy we are facing. However, on the same token, sitting pat and not taking advantage of opportunities is not going to aid you in any way. You still have to be cutting edge. Your customers still look to you and you have to create need within them. Let's face it – if you believed this would work for you, money and economic issues notwithstanding, you'd jump at this chance. For what specific reason do you not believe this will work for you?"

Make it not about the economy, or any other factor they bring to the table. The economy is just another potential way the customer can shut down your pitch. Don't let them.

Sales is a service; the better of a job you do in learning what your customer's needs and weaknesses are and showing them that you've got the cure for what ails them, the better shot you have of taking care of THE CUSTOMER, YOUR COMPANY, AND YOU. And that, my friends, is the holy trinity of sales. Make it a great selling day (no matter what the economy is up to)!

The Vocational Viewpoint, via Vincent Scott
(Republished with permission)
"How can I make trade shows and events profitable?"

From today's mailbag: "My company sends me to a lot of networking events and trade shows, but I rarely see results from them in the way of sales. Any recommendation?"

There are varying level of warmth of leads. It is very important that we manage our leads and prioritize them based on warmth because the ones that are the warmest will be the ones that keep us warm during those chilly selling periods where we resort on cold calling and networking events. That said, each and every day we are planting seeds that will grow into future sales harvest. We are beginning relationships that will bear fruit at some unforeseeable point down the road.

While some of these networking event contacts may have an immediate need you can fill, remember why they are likely at the event or trade show to begin with - to sell. Your best way in with any potential new customer or contact is to focus on giving rather than receiving - to add value and to earn their respect and trust and partnership by offering to aid them first.

1. What do you have to offer of value to those you interact with at these events? Treat it just like any other selling opportunity - ask questions, learn about them and what they do, find out their target customer and their hot-button priorities and figure out how you can potentially help them. Can you connect them with someone who would benefit them? Can you recommend someone who could benefit from them? They will have a vested interest in working with you and continuing the conversation if you provide them ample reason to.

2. Don't rule anyone out. You literally never know who you will come into contact with at these events. You may come into direct contact with decision makers, with people who can introduce you to decision makers or to people who will refer you to contacts of theirs it would behoove you to meet. Always keep an open mind as to where these conversations can go. Don't

stress. Not every lead will lead to a sale, but you literally never know when a new contact can pop up again or who they can put you in touch with.

3. Remember the law of averages. Marketing dictates that your sale will typically occur after fifth contact; these contacts can be from seeing an ad for your brand, meeting you, getting your follow up call, and having a colleague of theirs speak highly of you or your product. Make each contact a quality one, including the first impression, and every step of the sales cycle will enhance your probability of successfully realizing revenue from the relationship.

4. Look at the types of shows or events you are going to. Are they the most applicable to what you have to offer? Is there a better audience you should be in front of? If you have any say or control over which you partake in, be willing to try anything - don't discriminate against any potential revenue streams. Be a resource to as many groups as you can so that word of your value can spread!

5. Follow up. Most sales seedlings die relatively quickly because they are not given the opportunity to grow. Did you collect business cards? Do you have a roster of event attendees? Have you reached back out to those you met, whether connecting on LinkedIn, sending an e-mail, calling, or all of the above? You can't give out a business card and expect someone to just magically call you. It's possible, but you don't stand out as the unique, best option unless you are following up on your proposal to add value. Continue to find ways to stay in touch with your target audience, be it from initial follow up, newsletters, and relevant content you post on social media that your new contacts can see.

Every method of obtaining leads has its place and validity. While you want to put your warmest leads first, you can certainly find the start of new business relationships anywhere at any time. Be ready! And be ready to provide value up front and as time goes on.

The Vocational Viewpoint, via Vincent Scott
(Republished with permission)
"How do I market an event effectively?"

From today's mailbag: "I have been charged with marketing for an event we are putting on. How should I go about it?"

Marketing fundamentals, while they vary in scale of execution, typically remain revolved around target audience, geography and message content.

The marketing process for an event starts long before the event takes place, as you must ensure there is a mechanism in place to capture leads and allow your customers to opt-in to a lead capturing device. For some, this happens on the website you maintain; a visitor has the opportunity to opt-in to newsletters and notifications and stay abreast of the goings-on of your business. For others, you may utilize a CRM tool to store customer information and export data for such a task. No matter what you are using to secure leads, this segment will be imperative when it comes time to market for an event.

1. Consider your target audience. Who do you want to attract for this event? What topics will be the most well-attended or be of most value to the target audience? In essence, you are forming a commercial - a call-to-action - for this target demographic you seek. Put yourself in their shoes and contemplate what wording and event content would prompt you to make this a must-see! Current methodology of lead storage and social media will give you the capability to geo-target, find groups and meet-up organizations whose interests are closely aligned with yours and will also give you a platform with which to submit your information. Furthermore, everything you need to know as you market this event is centered around adding value to your target audience.

2. Examine your methods of outreach. Sending a newsletter that can be personalized, utilizing or even forming your own social media groups, using meet-up organizations that are available in your location, liaising with local networking groups like Chambers or BNI or affiliations that are in line with you or your company's goals - there are a litany of different ways to get your branding and message in front of the right eyes. Success can certainly be found a number of different ways by not discriminating against any of the potential portals of participants.

Think about where your target audience is viewing information and where your desired customers are looking for events and plant yourself there. You have also accumulated a number of leads and will continue to do so; having a newsletter that goes out to them can spread the word, but many of these will also provide analytics so you can see what topics are highly regarded and where your customers are engaging the newsletter - this assists you in the future as you continue to market more events and solutions.

3. Invest in your message. You want to make your message really speak to your audience. Is it something very specific and niche to a select group of people, an industry or an area of specialization? Then your messaging will reflect that - spelling out and fine-tuning the verbiage specific to that group. Are you trying to cast a wide net to attract a larger audience? Utilize appropriate wording to entice large groups to take interest; be relatively broad about the topic - feel free to spell out any specific items that will be covered, but give a more general message so that the curiosity of your recipients will be piqued.

Continue to evolve this process as well. Often, it takes time to build a following - just like building a sales funnel. In reality, you are building a community around your brand. Depending on where the recognition level currently lies of you, your brand and your events, you can be at a starting point that will require consistent application of the aforementioned principles in order to thrive. As word spreads of your events, you continue to add leads who are on the receiving end of your newsletter, and you figure out what really works and what doesn't in these events and your outreach, the momentum will grow and you can reach optimum levels in effectiveness and productivity - and value for all!

The Vocational Viewpoint, via Vincent Scott
(Republished with permission)
"Rumor has it, I'm cheating on my sales. How do I prove otherwise?"

From today's mailbag: "I'm doing very well at my job. Rumor has it, I'm cheating to achieve my sales. These rumors drive me nuts! How do I prove that I'm not? Thank you!"

Lots of people in history have been falsely accused of worse, but this never seems to quell the pain we feel when our hard-earned recognition and results come into question.

1) Do the claims have any basis in reality? If not, first off, be very proud of your accomplishments. Whether your fan club is limited to one (you) or the masses, the most important things are to stick to your principles and processes. Don't change your approach and don't be ashamed of any facet of what you're doing.

2) Talk to your boss. Don't feel the need to respond or reach out to the haters. Trust me when I tell you that they will always be there. No matter what you do, if you're good at it, you'll attract the negative attention from people who are jealous and would love to see you not set the example of what they could do if they didn't make excuses. Make sure the people who matter know that there is no validity to these statements, that you do care about public perception and that you are affected. Your boss exists to support you; they should be able to ensure these vicious attacks never hurt you in any attempts at getting ahead.

3) Offer to let others be along for the ride. You have nothing to hide, so let anyone who doubts you come along for your sales calls, listen in and observe. The best way to show anyone anything is to do just that: show there is literally no reason to doubt your abilities and results. Just as negative rumors can spread, so can positive ones and you can fight falsehoods with fantastic displays of your process.

4) Move forward! So many detractors will try to debilitate you on your journey - in your life and career. As you no doubt have realized, you cannot let any of them deter you from doing what you know is right, what is best and what is your responsibility. You're paid to execute on your job exceptionally. You're doing it. Others want to convince themselves or others why you are achieving results that they either don't have the talent or are making excuses why they

won't put forth the effort to achieve. That's their problem. They are trying to drag you down. Don't let them have the satisfaction. This too will pass. Let the people that matter sing your praises. Let anyone who doubts see the truth. And remember that you cannot control the thoughts and actions of others: you can only control how you react and respond. Respond with class.

And kudos to you for your job performance - I hope many people tell you that!

The Vocational Viewpoint, via Vincent Scott
(Republished with permission)
"My diverse sales team is bilingual and I'm not - how do I effectively coach them?"

From today's mailbag: "My sales team is bilingual and I'm not. How do I successfully coach them on transactions and best utilize their talents?"

It's quite a unique situation when a fair amount of your employees' transactions cannot be adequately monitored and critiqued. Furthermore, your employees can carry on full conversations that you are not privy to (yet, if you think about it, they can do this while you're not there as well). Finally, your team possesses skills that make them even more valuable because they have the ability to communicate with more customers thanks to their knowledge of different tongues. It's a three-pronged possibility.

1. Coaching transactions: In the early going of the aforementioned environment, your primary challenges in coaching will be when your team members are speaking with customers in the language you do not know. As they are bilingual, you will be privy to the conversations in your native tongue, which will likely be the basis of your early deductions of their sales and service process. While your sampling of their transactions may be smaller and margin of error on your conclusions higher, you will still have some metrics to go on.

Much of sales leadership is the ability to drive metrics through coaching your team's understanding of why they are important and how to achieve them. The fundamentals are the same: you must discern what makes your team tick, what their goals are and your role in guiding them and helping them achieve these accolades. As you continue to work with your team, it's also hopeful and likely that leaders will emerge - leaders you can trust. As a bilingual leader emerges that you can delegate to and whom you can entrust the responsibility of coaching and critiquing the transactions in other languages, you not only strengthen your team through appointing additional leaders but you can plug any gaps that exist in your coaching process because of your lack of understanding of a language they speak.

2. Trust. It's my philosophy that if your employee earned the right to be in the position they are in, which you decided upon hire or promotion, that it falls upon them to utilize the training and coaching they receive to perform the job the way they see fit. It's rare, and not even preferable, that our sales personnel will conduct themselves precisely as we do. It requires trust on our part. When your employees can also carry on whole conversations literally while you are in the room that you cannot understand, it could require even more trust. That said, like parenting or being in a relationship of any kind, we control what we can: the interactions with our team, the coaching and training we disseminate and the effort we put in to eliminating obstacles to their success and helping them develop the tools and talents that will further their career.

The language barrier cannot deter your willingness and desire to work on behalf of your team. Allow your team to grow and flourish - you have a diverse team whose abilities to transcend language barriers and help a larger group of customers will actually yield far more positives in the face of the challenges. Your team will actually respect you even more as you show your trust of them on their transactions, and you will have measurable data to show that they either are or are not conducting their transactions as effectively as they should be. Finally, you can still ask them to give you a rundown of the sales conversations you cannot understand - what did they glean from their fact-finding, what was the customer response and why did they decline the product or any attachments? It won't be a perfect science, but nothing in sales ever is.

3. Promotion of your team. Just like the ability to drive sales better than others, the ability to speak multiple languages is a marketable skill that can open additional doors for your team members. It's up to us as leaders to know our team - what motivates them and where they want to go - and to diagnose their strengths and areas of opportunity. There are often job requisitions that call exclusively for associates who are bilingual. This gives you an added item to assess when you are working with your team on a career path: they have skills which lend to certain roles that you will want to put on their radar.

Do you have some of your team members emerging as leaders as we discussed before? Could they benefit your team or division in a larger capacity? Is the bilingual ability something that is prominent in your larger work group, market or division? If so, perhaps your peers are facing similar opportunities and you can work with your peers on solutions that benefit all of you - do you have bilingual peers? Would it benefit you to do so? Make your leaders aware of this potential opportunity in your region and perhaps they can devise a solution that is in everyone's best interests: the furthering and promotion of your team, the added coaching from a bilingual manager, and you can work together with that manager so you are each adding value to one another's work.

Your situation of having an entirely or nearly entirely bilingual team is certainly unique, and just as when you have anyone who is uniquely great at their role you harness their strengths and find ways to help them, trust them, promote them and make them more effective. This scenario can certainly be a new one for many, but once you explore and discover new ways of coaching them and you get their feedback on what they need from you to aid in their current role and in getting to their next one, it can be harmonious for all.

You need each other; they need your knowledge and support and you need their buy-in to the right way of conducting business. In the end, you can find these things by ensuring you're speaking the same language: that of teamwork.

The Vocational Viewpoint, via Vincent Scott
(Republished with permission)
"What has been your greatest sales achievement?"

From today's mailbag: "I was recently asked what my greatest sales accomplishment has been, and I had trouble answering. There are a lot of cool things I've been privileged to be a part of, so pinpointing one is tough. What would you say is yours?"

Wow! What a thought-provoking question. Thanks for asking it.

My greatest accomplishment in my sales/sales management career has been the people I've had the pleasure of working with. Seriously - I've met so many amazing people from around the world that I've collaborated with or that have worked for me. I've learned so much of what to do (and what not to do, sometimes) from the people I've met along this journey.

When I first started out in sales and in management, my goals were really just around being the best I could be. As I have matured in life and my career, my goal has been around adding the most value possible - and I have to say, once that changed, the relationships got so much better. When you are genuinely attempting to provide additional worth to your teams, you make a difference in someone's career by helping them put more food on the table or you find ways to share your talents and impact your organization, nothing compares. People will gravitate toward you because they want to be associated with you... and it's awesome. I still have great relationships with so many people that I have met along my career journey for this very reason.

Sure, we may contribute hundreds of millions of dollars to the bottom lines of the companies we work for, we may land some deals that come along with a fun story that you could write a novel about ☺ .... and we will undoubtedly have some achievements and awards and recognition and contributions we really hold dear, but - in the end - it's all about the lives we've touched and that have touched us along the path.

CHAPTER 4: CONCLUSION

After an introduction from CeCe, Luther Petty took the microphone at the presentation and began transition to the awards banquet. He announced all of the assumed Market Managers save one. The promotion to Market Manager of the Americas went to Melton Stein.

It made sense. From the first awkward conversation between Luther and Vincent, Luther had led off by talking way too much about Vincent's past and other accomplishments. Luther was a fish out of water – he had literally no business being in this role. The Peter Principle at its finest.

Luther was intimidated by Vincent Scott and rather than let him rise and flourish and coach and develop the team, which would have resulted in hundreds of millions of dollars in additional hardware sales, he promoted someone who would regurgitate his talking points. In the months to come, Melton Stein would go on to send out a total of zero sales reports, zero communication about best practices and zero recognition e-mails. His visit to Minneapolis featured him asking Vincent what he needed, which Vincent informed him, "With all due respect, I've been asked that a number of times, have made recommendations on process changes our division needs and have seen none of it in two years. What will be different this time?"

The response? "Me," Melton said arrogantly. "I'm the difference-maker. You haven't seen me in action yet." Melton committed to fighting to support Vincent and his team, a spiel Vincent had heard numerous times before. Immediately upon Melton's departure and return to his home office, he worked with Luther Petty to take Vincent's top customer away and give it to the inside device team for "better, more consistent" customer experience. That team still rolled up to Luther and Melton, but not to Vincent. Vincent sat on calls going through why Luther had agreed this was Vincent's customer the last three times this debate had come up. Eventually, he let it go. One thing he never relinquished: he was still the top Regional Business Manager in the company even without that customer.

At the awards banquet, leaders from all over the world were recognized for numerous metrics. Vincent did not have the largest sale nor the most devices or the most warranty or attachment or accessory results, but he was pound for pound the undisputed champ in everyone's eyes.

When the time came for Luther to recognize Vincent's incredible year, leading the entire world out of Minneapolis, Minnesota, he gave the award for Business Manager of the Year to Christopher Talisman out of Ontario.

Vincent quietly accepted the state of affairs that was his role in the Global Business Unit of Majestech-Ware. Attempts to be promoted into other parts of the business had gone unrequited. The role he had been promised was given to someone else. The sales he had toiled so tirelessly for were taken away from him. The recognition he richly deserved was not received.

The treadmill and weight bench by morning and a restorative scotch by night and the times with family in between kept Vincent afloat and enriched.

Perhaps Vincent was not meant to peak twice? Perhaps these setbacks and losses were supposed to be teaching him some cosmic lesson he still had not learned. He had exhausted his mind and body on his current role, his seeking of a better one and his quest of making a difference on a grander scale.

The business events continued to flourish – and far more than just Doug Lambert were in attendance. Referrals came in so furiously that Vincent really did not need to lift a finger. The first two quarters of 2016, Vincent was still #1 in his position. And he had resigned himself to his fate.

The beauty was that he could ease up a little. Rather than toil a 10-to-15 hour workday, he would cut short and take Elizabeth to the park or Abby to the movies. He would go in later and leave earlier while still being available if something came up. He would delegate more to his team. They were on auto-pilot thanks to 2+ years of him leading the charge in prospecting and pitching and following up and closing.

One day, the receptionist at Vincent's office instant messaged him to let him know Doug Lambert was in the building. *How odd?* Vincent thought, as Vincent had never seen him anywhere but the events they did at the nearby conference center.

Vincent left his office and made his way to the front desk. Doug was there with another gentlemen; both of them were in their fifties.

"Doug, how are you today? Great to see you!" Vincent exclaimed, shaking his hand.

"You, too, Vincent!" Doug responded. He turned to the gentleman next to him. "I'd like you to meet Dr. Stan Wells. He is the head of numerous medical boards across the country."

Vincent shook Stan's hand as well. "Great to meet you, Dr. Wells."

"Well, Vincent, we did it!" Doug reported.

"What do you mean?" Vincent asked, somewhat warily. The last time he had seen Doug, Lambert was returning a device he had purchased for a refund. The guy never bought anything despite attending every event Vincent's team threw.

"Well, the device I returned was one I wanted to present to the medical board. You see, they love the Majestech-Ware 3000. Stan is actually based here, and is signing the paperwork today for a purchasing vehicle out of Minnesota that will outfit hospitals all over the world. The purchasing body will acquire the devices, load a medical application that we've worked with a partner to develop and ship them out ready to use. They currently serve roughly 1,000 hospitals who will need a couple hundred devices apiece. Can you get me a quote?"

The total sale Doug Lambert delivered after eating 62 breakfasts and returning one tablet totaled $57 million. Majestech-Ware did not have a commission structure constructed to cap sales that large.

Two days later, after the deal was inked with Dr. Stan Wells and the production and rollout plan was confirmed with the Majestech-Ware 3000 hardware team, Vincent fielded a phone call from a 202 area code. He knew it was Washington, D.C., and took the call.

"Hello, this is Vincent."

"Vincent Scott? This is Miranda Bond."

Vincent had heard some shocking words in his life that had stopped him dead in his tracks. Learning he was going to be a Dad was one of them. Learning he was terminated from a division he built was one of them. Learning that he wasn't being picked up by Moriarty Wireless or Cellular Horizons, being promoted by Tel-Cell and being promoted by Luther Petty all loomed large. But having the CEO of Majestech-Ware on the other end of the line ranked high on the list.

"Um…hello! Yes. What can I do for you, Miranda?"

"You've done it, Vincent. You single-handedly hit our hardware division's budget for the quarter. From what I understand, you've built a pretty amazing team there and have a lot of fans. I just watched a couple of your videos – one on sales and one on you singing 'Can't Take My Eyes Off Of You' at a breast cancer awareness event – and was impressed by both!"

"Ah, thank you," Vincent responded, blushing for a moment. "I'm flattered."

"I'm sure you've done the math on the commission check you're due at the end of this month."

"Yes, ma'am," Vincent responded coolly. He had talked to CEO's before – *act like you've done this before, Vincent!*

"I admit I had heard of you only briefly before this week," Miranda stated. "I had heard of your book and I saw your name on reports but for some reason was hearing more about some of your peers. I think I've figured out why."

"Oh?" Vincent replied.

"Vincent, I won't mince words. You – your attitude, your approach, your results – all outstanding. These videos – you've been making them for years and they are all so relevant and energetic and powerful. I've seen your resume and I've seen your video resume! I can't believe someone so young has done so much. I even read your books straight through last night. Not only do you have the philosophies and the words but you've had the actions to back them up in every role you've ever been in. And I don't want to lose you."

"I'm not sure what you mean?"

"Vincent, I'm creating a position on my direct staff for a Sales Optimization VP and I'm offering it to you and only you. It will involve whatever you want it to involve. We'll work together to craft plans to optimize sales and metrics for our entire portfolio. What do you say?"

"Miranda, I'm beyond flattered. Right now, I have on my mind getting the bonus and taking some time to be with my family. I don't know what that means just yet. Can I think about it?"

"Of course. Take some time. This is my direct number. At best, you'll call and we'll take Majestech-Ware to the top of the Fortune 500. At worst, I want an autographed copy of your next book."

Vincent chuckled. "I don't know if I have another in me."

"Thank you for taking my call, Vincent."

"Miranda – thank you for the call, for the offer, for everything. I'll be in touch."

The Biographer's Story

Vincent and I were great friends growing up. I met him in third grade when he skipped second. I remember our teacher told us he was coming and asked us to be as welcoming as possible. He and I were the only redheads in the class and we both were drawn to very creative elements that perhaps did not interest others as much – mostly in the vein of creative writing. Go figure: I grew up to become a film director and he writes books.

He had so much passion for the movies and pop culture of our youth in the 80's. Most of our time back then was playing video games, riding bikes around our neighborhoods, pretending. He was a smart guy which I could absolutely respect; we just kind of clicked and connected. He played basketball, baseball, soccer, golf, piano, guitar, and trumpet, could do multi-number math problems in his head, had a photographic memory, was a spelling bee champion who could tell you everything about every President who ever lived…and is apparently the greatest salesman to ever play the game.

I have zero interest in sales. Literally zero. And I often wondered how this guy I knew to be so creative and non-conformist could get so caught up in that world and then become so successful in it. His struggle to conform to its confines likely well illustrates that predicament.

Most profoundly, the differences he could make gave him fulfillment. Sure, he loved the money, many of the people he encountered and there were enriching, thrilling experiences (worthy of a future movie by yours truly, I hope!) but the reason he did it was because he could have an impact and leave a legacy. He just wanted his parents and his family to be proud of him.

There was no short supply of people willing to talk to me to fill in the pieces of my friend's story. There were also a handful who declined comment – I'm sure you can guess on some of them.

There were some stories that didn't make the cut, but are worth including. Vincent's Majestech-Ware team was going to lose a pretty large sale to a school simply because they did not carry the cases the school wanted; they had plenty of alternatives, as, of course, the tablets were first party, but the school IT folks were eccentric and wanted this special case from China that could probably protect it from a bomb. But Vincent found a way – he talked leadership into letting him expense the cases, hold them in an inventory warehouse locally for a month until the deal signed, and re-sell them to the school. It was a risk, but Vincent found a way.

Vincent always found a way. When his ABM team was near landing its largest profile client but in danger of losing them to competition, he got creative with zoning and geographies and headings to ensure the best available pricing and discounting and keywords and spent hours on the proposal draft after draft.

He would stay late and jump on to close sales for his teams so they could all go home. He took time on his own vacation to step in to what could have been a termination meeting to coach and vouch for someone to save their job. He gave a second chance to a sales rep with a drug problem who was MIA for days when his boss directed Vincent to fire him and the guy went on to stay clean, be a top rep, start a family and become a college professor.

He forced himself to learn every job so he could best coach it. He was not above rolling up his sleeves and getting in the trenches when reps called in or someone quit or when he needed to lead by example and teach a lesson or skill. He got to the root of why customers didn't want to do business and he made it right or went down swinging. He'd do anything for the relationship and the sale because it meant success for the customer and his team.

"He believed in me," I heard on numerous occasions, from people who thought their career was going nowhere that he got to know and promised to work with and eventually promoted to people who had no penchant for sales who other managers tried to fire but he turned into rock stars.

People remembered so many epic speeches the guy would give, whether the audience was 2 or 200. "Don't over-complicate! Keep your pitch simple until the conversation necessitates more complexity." "Don't bludgeon your customer with too much information or too strong a close! Get to know them and show them why what you propose is better than what they do or don't do now. It's that simple!"

A sales rep told me the delight he had one day when he put their dialer into Elizabeth City, North Dakota, because it was his kid's namesake.

Everyone I talked to that knew him well told me how much he had done for his daughter and to be with his daughter. And that she saved his life.

Even the people who didn't always like him admitted that he was a great leader, made good and tough decisions and made a positive impact on a lot of people. Sure, there were some who pointed out his arrogance and bad decisions when it came to ladies and liquor in his twenties but his weaknesses could have been worse.

There were people who didn't want to like him, but he won them over.

Sure, the guy had detractors, and he absolutely did some stupid things in his youth. Don't we all? He's not applying for sainthood any time soon, but the sacrifices he made for his daughter, his family, his teams and his company time and time again in spite of being let down time and time again speak volumes. I'm proud to know him.

I filmed the infamous sales videos for him pro bono. It was right after ABM and he was at a low place and I like to think that just getting in front of a potential audience (that eventually numbered hundreds of thousands on the Internet) and talking about things he was passionate about like sales and leadership and having fun with it helped get him through that rough patch.

Most amazing of all has been watching the transformation: the brash, 25 year old sales manager with zero filter became a Dad and a husband and a survivor. He peaked twice.

Losing his grandfather, losing friends, losing his first career, and being in therapy had profound impacts on Vincent. He wouldn't bring these things up or comment, but they taught him to optimize every day, to slow things down rather than let them spiral out of control and to realize what is yielding results versus the ridiculousness of some of his own fears or thoughts. He took solace in routines. He became patient and he learned – finally – how to play the game for the sake of those he was responsible for.

He told me that a great salesperson is defined by their intricate knowledge of how to ethically and effectively utilize every facet and variable of their playing field to better the situation of everyone the sale touches and their ability to still convince you they are on top of the mountain long after the politics of business have eroded their passion, always mindful of what's next while mastering what's now.

Vincent Scott is approaching life focused on the now, optimizing it as best he can and come what may… not looking back anymore and not looking too far ahead.

His career has been characterized by hard (over-)work, perfectionism, competiveness and sheer dominance at every level in any field. His personal life features a good close family, some bumps and bruises from a few that mattered and letting fewer get close but in the end being close with who he needs and who he needs things to work with.

The glory wasn't always real. The next moment after the summit – no matter how you slice it – was also a step down the mountain, however slightly. Vincent realized he couldn't take the awards with him, but he could imprint everything that followed. That was when the real difference and real learning began.

You land on your feet enough times and people come to expect it from you. Vincent Scott picked up the best and worst practices from everyone he encountered. The trick was deciphering which was which and executing best.

I'd say he's done all right and, knowing him, the best is yet to come.

The Vincent Scott Story

It's fitting that I should get the final say on my own story, right? Insert smiley face emoticon here.

Yes, this is the part where typically everything gets wrapped up nicely and neatly with a sense of closure and promise of a bright future. I'm not going to do that, which should come as no surprise to you.

I've found it interesting – the thoughts of those who have played such prominent roles in my life. In some relationships, little has changed in the dynamic since their take on our interactions. In others, more significant changes have transpired. Either way, every story is a snapshot at that moment in time. I will do nothing to unravel or unweave what has been told.

Every part of the journey – even the debilitating losses – were essential. The losses make us appreciate the wins we have to work so hard for. The inevitable descent and painstaking effort to peak again after losing it aid in putting everything into perspective. It was all worth it.

I left sales once. I left sales to pursue what I felt in my heart I truly wanted to do and was passionate about only to find out very quickly that the financial tradeoff necessitated that I return to what I was sometimes reluctantly good at doing.

Certainly, the highs of my life in sales have been quite captivating but the far more frequent lows or lulls have undermined that euphoria.

I won't pretend I've "had it bad." I know how fortunate I've been overall. But as most of us have charted a course or had a course charted for us only to see it uncontrollably derailed, it's a tough pill to swallow. There's a feeling that won't go away, nagging at you: where would I be now had I just done that one thing differently?

Of course, it's pointless to dwell on what was or could have been; all that matters is what is and can be and how you will respond to future recurrences of the situations you learned from in the past.

It was a big decision for me to leave sales behind. Sure, everything requires us to flex sales muscles at times but I gravitated toward the concept of coaching people and businesses on how to improve their management. It seemed too good to be true – and it was – and I found myself in my mid-30's wondering what the hell I was supposed to do with my life all over again.

Fortunately, I was promised a sales manager role with a good company shortly thereafter and I decided to bide my time until my start date. The start date came and went and I could not get ahold of anyone to figure out what was going on. Finally, they told me the opening they anticipated didn't exist and there was no timetable.

Specifically when experiencing these setbacks, it's natural to do two things: miss your "prime" and become frustrated with the fact your progress has not been what you have wanted it to be. You romanticize the past that cannot be restored, and in many cases if you really think about it you would not want it to be – because it was far from perfect.

Uncertainty in any moment is a tough hurdle to scale because you have far less success at that instant working to subside the doubt and questions in your mind. When will things look up? When will I feel like myself again? What could I or should I have done differently to have avoided this? We make the mistake of looking back rather than assessing the current status and options and plotting a new path to the goal – or realizing the goal post moved on us.

A connection had reached out to me a few months prior and gauged my interest in a role that was a bit of a step back. However, the money was good and it was better for my career than binge watching Netflix and sipping vodka. Whereas I had turned it down then, I reconsidered now. Somehow, while the position had been predictably filled in the interim, the candidate backed out literally one day prior to my call and they were desperate to fill the role. I stepped in.

Opportunity knocks, sometimes in mysterious ways, and we have to answer without waiting around for the knock we think we want.

I had the option of starting work the following week and flying to headquarters in Washington, D.C., or spending spring break week with my daughter. I chose the latter without hesitation. It was the difference that being a Daddy made; the old me would have jumped at the networking chance and prospect of getting a leg up. This version knew the value of something more important than my work.

At 36 years old, I came into a role similar in many ways to something I had done at 22. It was more of a player-coach type role which was brand new and part of a division in its infancy (also enticing, because I could mold it into my own). The pros were I was used to managing, knew sales, was not intimidated by meeting with CEO's, CIO's, business owners and the like. The cons were it was hardware and software – specs and hundreds of SKU's and RAM and processing power and monitor resolutions and managing sales reps that were predominantly 18 to 24 who knew far more about the stuff than I did and cared about selling far less than I.

Sure, I was sought for this role because of success in previous ones. I brought kind of an X-factor as a sales manager who had excelled in a few different verticals that had managed in ambiguous, relatively new divisions like this one was.

The majority of my global peers in this position were younger, strictly business to business types who had sold hardware and software in their previous roles. My first two weeks solid were spent isolated in a room performing online training courses that felt way over my head, all while feeling the pressure to start producing and earning my keep as soon as possible.

My role contained more sales functions than I had been responsible for in over a decade. Much of the prospecting and outreach fell on my shoulders; if I wanted it done right, I had to build this book of business and fill the funnel and take the lead on ensuring the deals were flowing and closing.

I felt old and out of place. Worse than when I was overseeing retail cell phone stores because at least then I could fall back on my comfort zone: management. I didn't have to be in the trenches all the time. Here, I had to learn how to sell all over again.

Here, I had to get millennials who were tech geniuses to follow my lead, help me get leads, support my efforts and produce results. It was not at all something that happened quickly. I also had to dust off sales techniques: prospecting, cold calling and talking to gatekeepers all on my own. I had coached it for years; now I had to see if the stuff I did 15 years prior held up in today's selling world.

After being the #1 company producer in each role I'd held previously, I knew that run had to end eventually and I accepted that it would end here. I was ready to be a bit player, a contributor, a sixth-man. It was all I could do to get through these training courses and meddle my way through conversations with business owners understanding a fraction of what was said. I closed my first sale in a role where it was my responsibility again for the first time in 12 years… and it was $2,500. In my 20's I drove hundreds of millions of dollars and now I was nickel and diming my way back to relevance.

Generating millions of dollars per month, giving *Wolf of Wall Street* type sales speeches every day to hundreds of hungry sales reps, shifting our teams through carefully planned out dialer schedules, diving into the statistics and coaching managers and reps making six-figures had transformed into me being tired, overwhelmed and unsure of myself in a sales role – again. Only this time I was 36 instead of 22.

The approach was the same, though; I dusted off the classic "You're the Best" by Joe "Bean" Esposito from *The Karate Kid* and listened to it every morning on the way to work to convince myself I could do it another day. I worked out in the mornings and got my kid ready for school instead of waking up from a bourbon and pizza-induced stupor. Overloading on caffeine was still a constant. The primary parallel was construction of a process for outreach, pitch, closing, overcoming and following up. The results also had quite a few similarities.

It didn't take long at all. I came in to be a contributor. I was #1 of 71 the first quarter I was there. As the team expanded, I was still #1 out of 89, 106, 116. The challenge then became one of endurance and staying at the top and hearing from cynics and critics all the excuses why I was #1 and they weren't.

Similar to my previous experiences, it did not take long for senior leadership to bandy around the prospect of a promotion for me. Alas, it was nowhere near in the immediate cards, forcing me to continue to create new challenges and grow our business beyond what anyone could ever have imagined possible. So we did.

I spent 8 quarters in that role and was #1 on the planet an unprecedented, unbelievable even to me 8 times.

Any time your life undergoes a substantial change, it is common to reflect; to look back and realize what mattered most and what you thought mattered but really didn't. There's also something to be said for letting go of old baggage whose influence on the future is inconsequential. If it cannot be changed, deal with it – relegate it to its proper place and move forward, taking each day at a time controlling what you can and focusing on optimizing just that day…until you're fortunate enough to get another.

Much of the past is a blip. Memories stored deep in the archives of the mind and soul are quickly conjured up by pictures or stories or conversations but they mostly lie dormant with the primary focus on the here and now. That said, they are all part of the foundation.

My childhood dog, the scar I got on my hand in preschool, playing in my old house (hiding under the staircase, playing in our green room with He-Man figures, old friends long gone), my Grandparents' farm they sold off twenty years ago, my Grandpa and the last time we talked, my basketball career (scoring 32 one game and draining a last-second game-winner in another), Janie (the Bob Seger song "Against the Wind" always reminds me of her and of the journey since), Julie and the few ladies that mattered along the way, the speeches and the cheering and the ridiculous sales numbers… and the joy of being a Daddy. Playing hide and seek with my daughter, watching her do gymnastics or cheerleading or baton and being the center of attention with her friends, her waking me up with kisses, and telling me, "Daddy, I'm so proud of you for getting a new job" when I finally started mounting my comeback.

I've always felt the film *The Natural* an appropriate analogy for my sales career. Roy Hobbs was a young and brash phenom, cut down in his prime only to return years later wiser and still effective but having lost a step and carrying substantial emotional baggage he worked hard to hide.

Late in the film, Hobbs says, "Things sure turned out different. For years, I've lived with the idea that I could be the best in the game."

Iris responds, "You're so good *now*."

"I could've been better. I could've broke every record in the book."

"And then?"

"And *then*? When I walked down the street, people would've said, 'There goes Roy Hobbs, the best there ever was in this game.'"

"You know, I believe we have two lives. The life we learn with and the life we live with after that."

Life has a way of answering your questions for you, albeit not when you want the answers. God is a better writer and director and cinematographer than any of us could aspire to be.

Nick Hornby's *High Fidelity* and the John Cusack film hilariously follow its protagonist through revisiting previous relationships and surprisingly getting nice, neat closure. We should all be so lucky, right?

In my final years before marrying, I somehow got closure with every open end, every former crush, the ones I wondered if they got away and ones I had been curious about. You reach a point when you realize you're a certain brand of crazy, everyone's their own brand of crazy, and the objective is to find someone with whom you mutually agree to accept each other's crazy because you don't want anyone else's.

But each of these people fill their special role; there were times when these figures were there for me during critical losses or moments of doubt. There are things they have said to me or done to me that stuck with me or made me stronger. In hindsight, it all makes sense and wrapped up as it needed to.

I've also run into many former co-workers at multiple employers – some with whom the bridge had been burned by one of us or the other, some who abandoned me in the dark times only to want to latch on again, others whom I used to partner with or banter with daily only to now be met with a chilly reception.

There is also the realization many people will continue to attempt to latch on for their benefit, which replaced the naivety that everyone wants to legitimately be a friend. As Ronald Reagan said, "Trust, but verify."

It surprised me that when I learned the person who had intentionally caused me the most pain and loss was finally terminated from his job, the obsession with revenge that once dominated my thoughts was completely gone. I felt nothing. He had slipped up one too many times; one of his many verbal slip-up's wound up giving me the very closure I had previously sought for three years.

Every relationship changes; some end, and the ones that are supposed to endure do so.

At age 17 I called a psychic late at night because the infomercial was hosted by Billy Dee Williams. If it was good enough for Lando Calrissian to endorse, it was precisely what I wanted.

The psychic correctly predicted my next girlfriend whom I had yet to meet, details about our dates, information about my future career that was years away, and told me the numbers 27 and 38 had something to do with my future wife and that I'd go through three more relationships before finding the one. I didn't realize what they meant until recently... I met her at 27 and our second child will be born when I'm 38.

There have been moments when I asked myself, "Is there any of the old

Vincent Scott left?" and was unsure of the answer until faced with decisions or situations that yielded victories and accolades. Sometimes I had to get creative, scramble to outside-the-box solutions and conclusions with zero support or structure around me, against all odds with the processes I was supposed to be able to count on caving in from all sides and the clock winding down – but I always emerged victorious…sometimes with a little left in the tank.

    Just as personal relationships tied themselves up nicely and neatly, each career step along the journey makes more sense in retrospection as well. At the consulting firm that duped me, I met a guy who told me I was too closed up and the front I was putting on hid all my real feelings – that I had to let someone in or I'd be alone forever. I also met a lady who was so talented and driven and undeterred by setbacks that I partnered with in a future role as well. She unfortunately died from cancer just two years later at age 42.

    I strolled back into business buildings I once reigned king over only to see my old offices eradicated and faces different.

    Driving by offices or stores I once oversaw only to see them now lie vacant or having been turned into a tax preparation building or vape cigarette store or eye-care office signified the passing of time and the clear indication these once significant fixtures had played their parts. It also reinforces that no matter how you've romanticized what you love about the past, there is no going back and no way of recreating it.

    I had to realize that even if I revisited my "peak" it would not be, nor could ever be, the same. The innocence was gone, the people and products and predicaments changed. I'd be trying to recreate something that was once flawed but great like rebooting an 80's television show that should stay cemented as it was. There are new stories to come and the things we love from the past often exist as fond memories.

    Ironically, my departure had resulted in a reverse golden touch; my old offices and regions would close down or be sold off or drop off to the tune of 30%-to-70% of revenue and results within weeks or months. It was sad to watch, but made me even more proud of what my teams had accomplished and built during those magical times.

    Even at the roles beneath what I had once done while I was fighting my way back up, I heard concepts or picked up approaches which would become part of my permanent process.

    When filling these roles, I wondered *how long will this seemingly never-ending penance last?* A friend I made along the way told me, "Be patient, and follow the zeroes: go where what you're selling is going to be a big part of the future… and is extremely expensive. That way you have job security and you get paid."

    At a CIO summit, I had an epiphany: don't chase a position or a promotion or money. Apply the same principles to life as you now do to career – put a process in place, follow it, evolve and the results will follow. Be the solution to the problems you see. Contribute something every day and you'll look back and the contribution will be significant.

The result? Once again, I did not get the promotion I thought I wanted that I had been promised. I was offered a better one.

Being interviewed about sales and leadership and innovation and motivation by people all over the world has been an unexpected but welcome byproduct of writing my thoughts and musings in books and articles. Talking motivation and management and selling with people globally and learning from their experiences has been exceptionally rewarding. The topics are near and dear to my heart and they light and reignite my inner fire every time. Even during times when I was uncertain about my next job or suffering through months of unemployment these engagements or public speaking gigs would reinforce that I was alive… still Vincent Scott.

Hosting a radio show, being interviewed by television stations and radio stations and for podcasts: none of it would have happened had the previous tribulations not been endured.

Making the march in the cold to the unemployment office every few weeks to re-register for benefits and constructing or updating a resume can be arduous and being rejected to countless jobs quite numbing, but making a video resume and realizing just how much I had actually done – putting it into words and perspective in that moment and speaking them – was comforting. It also made me even more ready for whatever was to happen next.

Toiling away at entrepreneurial roles for months wondering where my next actual paycheck was coming from made me more thankful and rational when holding substantial gainful employment and more practical in the face of the types of circumstances I once ardently crusaded against.

There is one very fortunate side effect of sales excellence: you'll always be able to find something to do somewhere.

I've worked with thousands of customers in my career. Once, there was a gentleman who called in to ABM while I was an inbound sales rep. It was the only time I allowed myself to talk to a customer without caring remotely about my average call length. This was a guy I knew would resonate: he talked about how he gave his career to the system for a considerable amount of time as a professor. When I spoke to him, he was simply calling for phone service in the cabin he retired to in Oklahoma. I'll never forget him.

He was now a writer and just wanted to be away from everything and everyone: I understand all too well his perspective.

Admitting defeat and acknowledging the immense hurt I had endured and once consumed me was freeing. I learned to dismiss the absurd absolutes in my head, to target what I really did need and want, and to just fall back and relax on the fact that my daughter was OK… I was OK. In the grand scheme of things, my action and reaction was not always required.

In the last few years, I've lost a close friend and multiple close co-workers, past and present. It certainly forces you to put a lot of things into perspective and value what matters most.

When I finally moved out of my bachelor pad apartment and neighborhood I had lived in the entirety of my time in Minneapolis to date, I scrapped all my posters that had once prominently dominated my walls (well, except *Goldfinger*) and various other things I had collected over the years whose significance was not important to the road ahead.

Part of that process necessitated me revisiting the files and awards and court documentation from years past. They would jar memories – some good, some better left behind – before much of it ended up discarded. It felt like a lifetime ago. But it all contributed to the sum of the parts.

Without all of those sometimes gnarly experiences and mistakes scattered with wins and losses, I don't know what I'd be. I made plenty of mistakes in my career so hopefully someone else doesn't have to!

I'd also like to believe there are bigger victories in store, anyway.

And as I key these final words from my laptop at the Cruise Bar in Jamaica where they filmed 80's classic, *Cocktail* and my family swims nearby, I have what I need.

The obvious question is whether I'll ever return to my prior life... to the selling game. Yet, the obvious answer is I never left. I'm a salesman forever.

AUTHOR BIOGRAPHY

Carson V. Heady, 37, was born in Cape Girardeau, MO, where his parents still reside.

He entered sales at age 22 and has found success at every level, from award-winning sales representative and account manager to multi-region director and Sales VP at multiple companies and a management and marketing consultant.

Once Carson realized his aptitude in the game of sales, he decided to write his first novel – *Birth of a Salesman* – which told the story of a young man who came into prominence in sales and sales leadership and doubled as a self-help selling and management manual to guide others to the level of success he achieved. The story continued in 2014's *The Salesman Against the World*.

Carson is a profound public speaker, successful corporate leader and his articles have appeared in several noteworthy publications such as LinkedIn Pulse, SalesGravy, Smash! Sales, Salesopedia and the Baylor Sports Department S3 Report. He has co-hosted the Smart Biz Show on EG Radio and has been interviewed on that show and the shows of "Coach" Ron Tunick, Andre' Harrell, Jean Oursler, Bill Crespo, Marlene Chism, Matt Tanguay's "B2B Sales Geniuses" and Chad Bostick's "Hello Tech Pros."

Carson lives in St. Louis, MO, with his wife and daughter.

www.ingramcontent.com/pod-product-compliance
Lightning Source LLC
Chambersburg PA
CBHW070224190526
45169CB00001B/68